Freelancing For Dummies®

W9-CUO-142

Cheat Sheet

Ten Traits You Need to Make It as a Freelancer

Before you make the break, consider the traits that contribute to freelancer success.

- ✔ Sense of humor
- ✔ Attention to detail
- ✔ Ability to negotiate
- ✔ Ability to *multitask* (juggle lots of tasks)
- ✔ Willingness to compromise
- ✔ Flexibility
- ✔ Self-starting personality
- ✔ Stick-to-itiveness (as your fourth grade teacher described)
- ✔ Desire to succeed against all odds
- ✔ Sense of humor

Eight Freelance Mistakes to Avoid

Why do freelancers fail? Perhaps because they break one of the cardinal rules of working for themselves. If an official association certified freelancers, the following would surely be among the requirements for freelance success.

- ✔ Don't burn bridges. You never know where people will end up.
- ✔ Don't miss deadlines without warning the client (flip to Chapter 13).
- ✔ Don't go over budget without warning the client (see Chapter 13).
- ✔ Don't worry too much.
- ✔ Don't underestimate how much cash reserve you need (see Chapter 4).
- ✔ Don't refuse help when friends offer.
- ✔ Don't work all the time (check out Chapter 21).
- ✔ Don't stop believing that you can succeed.

Twelve Steps to Starting Your Freelance Business

- ✔ Have your head examined. Assuming that you're found to be of sound mind, proceed with the rest of this list.
- ✔ Decide what business you want to be in (see Chapter 3).
- ✔ Write a business plan (discussed in Chapter 4).
- ✔ Start developing contacts (detailed in Chapter 4).
- ✔ Try moonlighting on a few projects (check out Chapter 4).
- ✔ Save enough money to live on for six months (see Chapter 4).
- ✔ Assess whether you're still having fun (discussed in every chapter in this book!).
- ✔ Determine what type of business organization you should operate under (outlined in Chapter 5).
- ✔ Choose a business name (see Chapter 5).
- ✔ Form your company (flip to Chapter 5).
- ✔ Set up your office (visit Chapter 6).
- ✔ Quit your job.

Hungry Minds™

For Dummies: Bestselling Book Series for Beginners

Freelancing For Dummies®

Cheat Sheet

Start-up Checklist

When you start working for yourself, how will you get done the million things you need to do? This checklist helps you make sure you have your bases covered before you open your doors for business.

Equipment: See Chapter 6 for information on all the office furnishings and electronic equipment you'll need to do your job.

- Computer (notebook/laptop or desktop)
- Software packages: word processing, spread-sheet, accounting, project management
- Cell phone and regular
- Copier/fax
- Desk
- File cabinet
- Comfortable desk chair
- Personal data system (an electronic, pocket-sized device that's easy to carry around and holds contact phone numbers, addresses, and other important business data)
- Calculator
- Rolodex-style address keeper or electronic program

Supplies: See Chapter 6 to quickly create a shopping list of supplies that are the backbone of every office. You can't work without these!

- Copy paper
- Legal pads
- Letterhead stationery and envelopes
- Calendar or organizer
- Sticky-backed notes
- Pens and pencils
- Highlighter pens

- Correction fluid to paint out printed mistakes
- Computer disks or CDs
- Paper clips
- Hole punch
- Stapler and staples
- File folders and hanging files
- Dictionary, thesaurus, and word speller (an abbreviated listing of words for quick spelling reference — a handy tool when you don't have your computer along)

Accounts: Chapter 8 helps you decide what kind of services you can affordably buy as a supplement to your office. Without hiring a staff, you can make your job easier and quickly satisfy clients' requests.

- Overnight delivery service
- In-town courier service
- Office supply
- Quick print shop

Professional services: Chapter 8 suggests building a relationship with experts who can advise you in how to run your business legally, efficiently, and with professionalism.

- Accountant
- Attorney
- Graphic designer
- Bookkeeper
- Temporary help

For Dummies: Bestselling Book Series for Beginners

 ™

References for the Rest of Us!®

BESTSELLING BOOK SERIES

Do you find that traditional reference books are overloaded with technical details and advice you'll never use? Do you postpone important life decisions because you just don't want to deal with them? Then our *For Dummies*® business and general reference book series is for you.

For Dummies business and general reference books are written for those frustrated and hard-working souls who know they aren't dumb, but find that the myriad of personal and business issues and the accompanying horror stories make them feel helpless. *For Dummies* books use a lighthearted approach, a down-to-earth style, and even cartoons and humorous icons to dispel fears and build confidence. Lighthearted but not lightweight, these books are perfect survival guides to solve your everyday personal and business problems.

> *"More than a publishing phenomenon, 'Dummies' is a sign of the times."*
> — *The New York Times*

> *"A world of detailed and authoritative information is packed into them..."*
> — *U.S. News and World Report*

> *"...you won't go wrong buying them."*
> — *Walter Mossberg, Wall Street Journal, on For Dummies books*

Already, millions of satisfied readers agree. They have made For Dummies the #1 introductory level computer book series and a best-selling business book series. They have written asking for more. So, if you're looking for the best and easiest way to learn about business and other general reference topics, look to For Dummies to give you a helping hand.

Hungry Minds™

1/01

Freelancing
FOR
DUMMIES®

Freelancing
FOR
DUMMIES®

by Susan M. Drake

Hungry Minds™

HUNGRY MINDS, INC.

New York, NY ◆ Cleveland, OH ◆ Indianapolis, IN

Freelancing For Dummies®

Published by:
Hungry Minds, Inc.
909 Third Avenue
New York, NY 10022
www.hungryminds.com
www.dummies.com

Library of Congress Control Number: 2001089292

ISBN: 0-7645-5369-0

10 9 8 7 6 5 4 3 2 1

1O/TR/QV/QR/IN

Distributed by CDG Books Canada Inc. for Canada; by Transworld Publishers Limited in the United Kingdom; by IDG Norge Books for Norway; by IDG Sweden Books for Sweden; by IDG Books Australia Publishing Corporation Pty. Ltd. for Australia and New Zealand; by TransQuest Publishers Pte Ltd. for Singapore, Malaysia, Thailand, Indonesia, and Hong Kong; by Gotop Information Inc. for Taiwan; by ICG Muse, Inc. for Japan; by Intersoft for South Africa; by Eyrolles for France; by International Thomson Publishing for Germany, Austria and Switzerland; by Distribuidora Cuspide for Argentina; by LR International for Brazil; by Galileo Libros for Chile; by Ediciones ZETA S.C.R. Ltda. for Peru; by WS Computer Publishing Corporation, Inc., for the Philippines; by Contemporanea de Ediciones for Venezuela; by Express Computer Distributors for the Caribbean and West Indies; by Micronesia Media Distributor, Inc. for Micronesia; by Chips Computadoras S.A. de C.V. for Mexico; by Editorial Norma de Panama S.A. for Panama; by American Bookshops for Finland.

For general information on Hungry Minds' products and services please contact our Customer Care department; within the U.S. at 800-762-2974, outside the U.S. at 317-572-3993 or fax 317-572-4002.

For sales inquiries and resellers information, including discounts, premium and bulk quantity sales and foreign language translations please contact our Customer Care department at 800-434-3422, fax 317-572-4002 or write to Hungry Minds, Inc., Attn: Customer Care department, 10475 Crosspoint Boulevard, Indianapolis, IN 46256.

For information on licensing foreign or domestic rights, please contact our Sub-Rights Customer Care department at 212-884-5000

For information on using Hungry Minds' products and services in the classroom or for ordering examination copies, please contact our Educational Sales department at 800-434-2086 or fax 317-572-4005.

Please contact our Public Relations department at 212-884-5163 for press review copies or 212-884-5000 for author interviews and other publicity information or fax 212-884-5400.

For authorization to photocopy items for corporate, personal, or educational use, please contact Copyright Clearance Center, 222 Rosewood Drive, Danvers, MA 01923, or fax 978-750-4470.

HungryMinds⁻ is a trademark of Hungry Minds, Inc.

About the Author

Susan M. Drake, who lives and works in Memphis, TN, is the founder and president of Spellbinders, Inc., a marketing and corporate-communications company. She and her associates are dedicated to the proposition that you can have fun while making clients' lives easier and their businesses more profitable. Susan has been a communications professional for 20 years, and she enjoys the freedom and diverse assignments that self-employment allow. Her clients hire her to provide communications counsel, plan corporate meetings, write speeches, design marketing plans, and generally assist them to do anything from difficult to all-but-impossible jobs. Spellbinders' hallmark is nonconformist solutions that absolutely work. Susan has received multiple awards from both the International Association of Business Communicators and the Public Relations Society of America.

She also enjoys writing books, going to the theater, ballroom dancing, and most of all, attending Rolling Stones' concerts.

For more information about Spellbinders, Inc. services, call 901-762-8012 or e-mail sdrake@midsouth.rr.com.

Dedication

When I was a young, unemployed person with nothing but a journalism degree, a woman named Mike Ballard gave me a job. I was a divorced mother with no experience (except for six months I spent cutting fabric part-time at Cloth World), and I applied for a public relations job at Holiday Inns, Incorporated. I had no concept of what I would be expected to do, nor how I would do it, but I was sure I could do the job. I asked Mike to trust me, and she did. Because of her, I have a career. I don't know where Mike is today, but I send my fondest wishes to her for what she gave me.

I also dedicate this book to Paula Kovarik, the consummate freelancer. I aspire to her level of integrity and talent.

And finally, to my friends Denise Temofeew, Laura Derrington, and Don Morgan, who have taught me a lot about the most important things in life.

Acknowledgments

Thank you to Tere Drenth, a smart, helpful, understanding, and fun editor.

Thanks to Karen Doran, who hired me for this project and who was always so gracious and kind.

Thank you to Renee Dingler, technical editor and outstanding friend.

Thanks to the Hungry Minds production staff, who make books look grand.

Thank you to Sheree Bykofsky, my wonderful agent.

Thank you to Susan Gross. I don't believe I can ever write a book without her.

And thank you to all the business people and freelancers who exist in this book either in name or in spirit: Colleen Wells, Scott Drake, Lauralee Dobbins, Laura Koss-Feder, Elise Mitchell, Helen Halladay, Jackie Nerren, Mr. Anonymous, Willy Taylor, Robin Thomas, David Rawlinson, Chris Crouch, Linda Delaney, John Snyder, Jody Pendergrast, J. D. Estes, Dusky Norsworthy, Bob Palmer, Ann Davis, Ed Iannarella, Norman Adcox, Sherry Henson, and Phil Schaefgen. We are family.

Publisher's Acknowledgments

We're proud of this book; please send us your comments through our Online Registration Form located at www.hungryminds.com

Some of the people who helped bring this book to market include the following:

Acquisitions, Editorial, and Media Development

Project Editor: Tere Drenth

Acquisitions Editor: Karen Doran

General Reviewer: Renee Dingler

Editorial Manager: Pamela Mourouzis

Editorial Administrator: Michelle Hacher

Editorial Assistant: Carol Strickland

Production

Project Coordinator: Nancee Reeves

Layout and Graphics: Jackie Nicholas, Barry Offrings, Brian Torwelle, Julie Trippetti, Jeremey Unger

Proofreaders: Laura Albert, Laura L. Bowman, Nancy Price, Charles Spencer, TECHBOOKS Production Services

Indexer: TECHBOOKS Production Services

Special Help

Mark Butler, Senior Acquisitions Editor

General and Administrative

Hungry Minds, Inc.: John Kilcullen, CEO; Bill Barry, President and COO; John Ball, Executive VP, Operations & Administration; John Harris, CFO

Hungry Minds Consumer Reference Group

Business: Kathleen Nebenhaus, Vice President and Publisher; Kevin Thornton, Acquisitions Manager

Cooking/Gardening: Jennifer Feldman, Associate Vice President and Publisher; Anne Ficklen, Executive Editor

Education/Reference: Diane Graves Steele, Vice President and Publisher

Lifestyles: Kathleen Nebenhaus, Vice President and Publisher; Tracy Boggier, Managing Editor

Pets: Dominique De Vito, Associate Vice President and Publisher; Tracy Boggier, Managing Editor

Travel: Michael Spring, Vice President and Publisher; Brice Gosnell, Publishing Director; Suzanne Jannetta, Editorial Director

Hungry Minds Consumer Editorial Services: Kathleen Nebenhaus, Vice President and Publisher; Kristin A. Cocks, Editorial Director; Cindy Kitchel, Editorial Director

Hungry Minds Consumer Production: Debbie Stailey, Production Director

◆

The publisher would like to give special thanks to Patrick J. McGovern, without whom this book would not have been possible.

◆

Contents at a Glance

Cartoons at a Glance

By Rich Tennant

The 5th Wave By Rich Tennant

WORKING DECKSIDE, FREELANCER JANINE WALKER MISTAKENLY COATS HERSELF WITH WRITER'S BLOCK INSTEAD OF SUN BLOCK

page 5

The 5th Wave By Rich Tennant

FREELANCER NED WILLIS CONSULTS WITH A MEMBER OF HIS TECHNICAL STAFF

"...and that's pretty much all there is to converting a document to an HTML file."

page 61

The 5th Wave By Rich Tennant

"You know, I don't mind hiring freelancers, but I do resent it when their work comes in smelling like suntan lotion and guacamole."

page 305

The 5th Wave By Rich Tennant

AS A CONSCIENTIOUS FREELANCER, MONA ALWAYS HAD HER CONTRACTS CHECKED BY AN ATTORNEY, COPIED IN DUPLICATE, AND ROLLED FOR CAT HAIRS BEFORE SENDING THEM OUT

page 219

The 5th Wave By Rich Tennant

FREELANCE PEPPERIER

I just got tired of the 9-to-5 grind. Say when...

SOUP 'N SALAD

page 125

Cartoon Information:
Fax: 978-546-7747
E-Mail: richtennant@the5thwave.com
World Wide Web: www.the5thwave.com

Table of Contents

Introduction

*I*f you're thinking of going out on your own, chances are you're the type of person who likes to forge a new path. You have a lot of energy, and I suspect you put your all into the work you feel passionate about. You have places to go people to see, and things to do, which means you have to find the most efficient and effective way to do everything — and that includes your freelance practice.

This book is a good place to start. It combines the knowledge of a host of freelancers: an accountant, computer trainer, graphic designer, writer, desktop publisher, market researcher and personal services planner, medical transcriber, event planner, and more. Some of the freelancers who contributed to this book have been around a long time; others are more recent additions to the club. But all have tips to share.

About This Book

When I embarked on the freelance trail, every day I felt as if I were making it up as I went along. Fortunately for you, you don't have to do that. You have this book! Read it, and you'll get a head start, avoid some drastic mistakes, and have a lot of fun.

This book helps you understand how to get your business started, jumpstart a business you've had for years, find new clients, establish your rates, set up your office, keep your books, pay taxes, buy insurance, advertise your business, and more! Use it as a ready reference or as moral support.

Foolish Assumptions

Because you've picked this book off the shelf, I assume you're a freelancer or thinking of becoming one. You may already have an area of specialty or you may have great skills and want to figure out how to market them. This book can help you focus your search for a freelance niche. In any case, I think you'll enjoy *Freelancing For Dummies*. By using this book, you can unearth new opportunities, set up your business, or just get support when times are lean. And if you're wavering in your resolve to jump into the freelance fray, this book reminds you why you thought this path was a good idea in the first place.

How This Book Is Organized

When you're going into business for yourself, you need to become an expert at a lot of things in a very short time. This book tells you what you need to know about any and every facet of freelancing quickly and easily in six easy parts that cover every major area of starting and running your own freelancing business. The following is a summary of each part.

Part I: Getting Ready to Go It Alone

Will you thrive in the freelance world? No crystal ball can predict your future, but you can look for signs to help you avoid unpleasant surprises. Before you redefine your life, start with the chapters in this part to see if you and freelancing are a good fit. This part helps you evaluate your strengths and weaknesses, identify viable freelance opportunities, and get ready to make your break from the corporate world.

Part II: Opening Your Doors for Business

This part shares information on whether to incorporate, how to get business licenses, and how to find supportive experts who can help you with aspects of your business. It also describes what you'll need in the way of office equipment and suggests smart ways of organizing your time.

Part III: Bringing Your Work to Life

This part helps you prepare to serve your clients' needs in the most efficient and effective way. It describes and offers tips on creating a professional image, creating demand for your services, finding and managing clients, evaluating jobs and projects, and staying current in your field.

Part IV: Managing Your Money

Sure, the work is fulfilling, but you also want some financial rewards from your hard day's work. This part gives you tips for planning, budgeting, and accounting; tells you how to get paid; gives you guidelines for filing tax forms and buying insurance; and shares how to invest for the future.

Part V: The Part of Tens

Like Mr. Blackwell's list of best and worst dressed, this part advises you how to look like the star that you are. The lists of ten in this part include ways to enjoy your new life, avoid stress, and satisfy clients.

Icons Used in This Book

Throughout this book, you can find little pictures in the margins. These pictures, called *icons,* alert you to quick snippets of information or stories that are particularly important or enlightening. The four following icons appear in this book:

This icon helps you find shortcuts that save you time, money, energy, and gray hair.

Tie a string around your finger to remind you of these very important points. If you don't take away anything else from this book, at least take these tips and tricks.

This icon introduces true-life adventures of people who have lived the freelance life. Read all about how successful freelancers handle touchy situations, build their businesses, and even decide that this life isn't for them.

The freeway of freelancing can be a perilous road. Heed these icons to avoid collisions.

Where to Go from Here

Whether you're embarking on your freelance journey or you're an old hand looking for straighter paths to follow, you can get there from here. Whether you start at the beginning and let *Freelancing For Dummies* give you a methodical process that guides you every step of the way, or pick and choose a few subjects from the Index or the Table of Contents, every chapter stands on its own and can answer your questions or soothe your fears.

Part I

Getting Ready to Go It Alone

In this part . . .

*B*efore you ride off into the sunset on your gallant steed, consider whether you're cut out for the freelance life and then take some steps to ensure your success.

This part describes the characteristics of a freelancer and gives pointers on how to ease your transition to the freelance life.

Chapter 1

Are You a Born Freelancer?

In This Chapter

▶ Defining yourself as a free agent

▶ Making sure your personality fits

▶ Creating your own job description

▶ Assessing your skills

*I*n times of old, knights traveled the countryside, hiring themselves out to fight battles on behalf of various kings and countries. These brave warriors carried weapons called *lances*. Because they were free of an ongoing commitment to any one employer, they were called *freelancers*.

If you think you want to work for yourself, you'll probably discover that you're one of a growing number of brave hearts roaming the business world looking for Camelot. This chapter explores what makes a freelancer tick and helps you decide whether you want to join this merry band.

Describing the Footloose and Fancy Freelancer

The wonderful world of freelancing can be described as any work situation that lets you define the following:

✔ What service you provide

✔ How you accomplish your work

✔ How and how much you will be paid

Seafood, mascara, and gold forks

When I talked with freelance public relations professional Lauralee Dobbins, she was preparing to spray paint some forks gold. It may not sound like a typical freelance assignment, but Lauralee has built a successful business on getting things done, no matter how unusual they are. Like so many self-employed people, Lauralee was "downsized" from her corporate position. She'd been considering freelancing for awhile and considered this a great time to leap from the nest. "It's a good time to be at this sort of work," she says. "It's more socially and financially acceptable to not have a corporate title now. In the past, you could hardly get a loan or establish any credibility, but today, it's perfectly okay."

After indulging in a three-day vacation in between real work and her new life, Lauralee came back to discover her first project awaited her: planning a fresh seafood festival. Her next project, writing a beauty book, required her to repeatedly test different mascaras on each eye. On any give day, you may find her one day running a PR campaign for an upcoming tax referendum, participating in a bean bag toss to raise money for the blind, or writing and selling corporate profiles for a specialty book.

Being prepared to take advantage of opportunities seems to be a common trait among successful freelancers. "I tell people I have a small PR firm, but my real job is that I'm a get-stuff-done person." It's no surprise that Lauralee says work "falls in her lap;" her willing attitude gives it a sizable push.

Given the perks of working in a corporate environment, why do people break loose from that world and take up freelancing? The following are just a few reasons:

- To make more money
- To work fewer hours
- To have more fun
- To escape from stress
- To have greater freedom

Whatever your reason, if you're cut out for it, working for yourself can be a real joyride: fun, exciting, and, as a side benefit, profitable. Of course, you may or may not realize the benefits you set out to gain, but you may enjoy others you never expected.

Reviewing the Various Types of Freelance Work Arrangements

Freelancers go by several names, and they work in a variety of ways.

✔ **Free agents/self-employed people:** Free agents/self-employed people may work on an hourly or project basis, taking projects or pieces of projects for several clients. The length of projects varies from an hour to months at a time. These freelancers may charge an hourly rate or agree to a certain amount for the entire job. Writing a brochure, planning a meeting, and setting up accounting records are examples of work that a free agent may do.

✔ **Contract employee:** Contract employees accept project work under contract and usually work on-site in a company's offices, sometimes even commuting to an out-of-town location each week or month. Jobs are generally limited in their duration. For example, a computer programmer may accept a project working full time for a corporation for three months until a special project is complete. Fees may be hourly or for an entire project. Examples of contract work include developing a software program, developing a training program, or designing a building addition.

✔ **Consultants:** Consultants work for a variety of organizations, spending time assisting with a particular area, such as human resources or operations. Consultants may be specialists or management generalists. In some cases, they work on a retainer, meaning that they are guaranteed a minimum payment each month for a certain length of time and are paid additional fees if they work more than that minimum. Under these arrangements, the employer may choose to use the consultant's services for a variety of purposes. Examples of consulting work include evaluating a division's profitability, developing a new process for employee orientation, and examining a departmental organizational problem.

Textbook definitions like the ones in the previous bullet list may help you imagine potential arrangements, but in the world of self-employment, you do the defining. Because you can decide what works best for you and your clients, you may be defined as a free agent, contract employee, or consultant, or you may have some other arrangement, depending on the job and the people involved. In freelancing, you won't find many rules, so your work style can be as creative as you are.

Whether you call yourself a freelancer or Supreme Commander, the joy of freelancing lies in the freedom to be yourself! That's what freelancers do. As a freelancer, you can let your true talents shine through. You determine exactly what you want to be and how you want to be it. Like a piece of clay, you can mold your work world to your liking, as long as you can figure out how to get someone to pay you for your creation.

Living without a Boss

I asked one of my freelance buddies what her favorite thing about her job is, and she said, "Great boss!"

At times, you will revel in having complete control over how you structure your work life. At other times, you'll long for someone else to be responsible for a decision or two. Like the proverbial double-edged sword, the letters "free" in the word "freelancing" cut both ways. It's the ultimate freedom and, at the same time, the ultimate responsibility.

Bosses, bosses everywhere

In the corporate world, you have only one boss; in your own company, every client is your boss. If you have a lot of clients, as you probably hope you will, you'll have a lot of people telling you what to do. So, while freelancing initially brings a sense of being on your own, to be successful, you have to develop rapport with many different bosses.

Each client has distinctive needs: Some want you to do a lot of hand-holding; others will be grateful for you to take the initiative and leave them alone. Freelance finesse lies in figuring out which style works best with each client. As you develop your reputation, you may have the luxury of picking and choosing the clients with whom you are most compatible. That's what every freelancer strives for!

If you're considering freelancing because you want to avoid dealing with people you don't enjoy, keep this in mind: To be a successful freelancer, you need the good will of every vendor, every client, and every competitor in your sphere. You're going to have to be nice to a lot more people, bite your tongue more often, and compromise much more frequently than you ever did in a corporation.

Managing yourself

In the television show *Malcolm in the Middle,* the theme music repeats, "You're not the boss of me now." But if you're a freelancer, yes you are! While you have to answer to a lot of client bosses, ultimately you're the big Kahuna. As you envision your company, think about what kind of boss you want to be. What are the things you would do for other employees? Strangely, you may have more difficulty being a good boss to yourself than to others. Make the decision upfront to treat yourself with the same dignity and respect you would show another employee. That means the following:

- ✔ Giving yourself time to learn the job
- ✔ Recognizing your accomplishments
- ✔ Rewarding yourself for a job well done
- ✔ Giving yourself downtime to relax and re-energize

One of the dangers of freelancing is that you can become the toughest taskmaster and the worst boss you ever had. But if you find yourself working long hours and not enjoying your job, you can simply walk into the bathroom, look in the mirror, and have a heart-to-heart chat with yourself.

Freelance Position Available: Deciding Whether You're a Good Match

Almost everyone I meet tells me how much they would love to have my job; that is, to be independent and run their own businesses. They think they would like it, but could they actually work for themselves? Not everyone can. You have to figure out the following:

- ✔ Are you naturally suited to freelancing?
- ✔ Can you adapt to the tasks that aren't a natural fit?
- ✔ Can you find a creative way to accomplish tasks that doesn't require you to do them yourself?

Consider how well your personality is suited to the demands of self-employment. I once accepted a position as a media relations specialist for a company that required me to talk guardedly about sensitive corporate issues, to dance around topics, and to generally tell the truth only when it made the company look good. Having always been a bad poker player and a worse liar, I was miserable in that job, and I was a miserable failure at it, too. Although I may have had the technical skills for it, I didn't have the personality.

Although freelancers come in all shapes and sizes, you can find some basic qualities that are do-or-die in the freelance world. The following sections share the key personality traits that contribute to or detract from a freelancer's success.

Will you love it?

People who thrive as freelancers aren't necessarily the devil-may-care, defiant types you may think. To succeed as an independent worker, you actually need a great deal of discipline and finesse. The ideal freelancer combines the creative and risk-taking qualities of an entrepreneur with the planning and organizational traits of a professional manager. The closer you are to a balance of those two, the easier you will find it to be on your own.

Three other characteristics are absolutely essential:

- ✔ **Leadership:** You guide clients and potentially direct the activities of members of their staff or of subcontractors. You should feel comfortable in a leadership role.

- ✔ **Decision-making ability:** This comes into play many times every day, not only in determining how you run your own business, but also in deciding how to execute projects for your clients. You'll probably be happier in freelancing if you have a high comfort level with calling the shots.

- ✔ **Self-motivation:** Who decides when you should make sales calls? You do. Who assigns your next project? You do. Who takes you to task if you don't? No one. It's up to you to create your own schedule, decide what needs to be done, and get up off the couch to do it. One of my former employees used to come to me and say, "I need a stern lecture." You may have to occasionally give yourself one of these.

By accepting control over your own daily schedule, you have to accept the responsibility for what happens — or what doesn't. Ultimately, the happiest freelancers are people who enjoy the fact that only they make or break their own business.

Will you leave it?

Joe: "I can't wait to get out on my own."

(Ten months later)

Joe (sheepishly): "Well, I've decided to take a full-time job with . . . ."

Within a year or so of starting to freelance, many people give it up and return to the corporate fold. Their dream of freedom has turned into a nightmare of insecurity and dread. Why? Well, some people simply don't fare well in a freelance situation. The following are some of the most common areas that cause discomfort:

- ✔ **Lack of security:** For people who need security, freelancing may be a bit too nerve-racking. You may have steady work, but without a long-term contract you don't have a guarantee of a paycheck beyond the jobs currently in your shop. And if you're on a long-term contract, aren't you sort of . . . well, the same as an employee?

- ✔ **Need to constantly sell:** Technical skill without sales savvy is worthless in the freelance world. Freelancers who want to be left alone to do their work find that the cycle of selling, doing the work, and selling again is drudgery.

✔ **Unstructured environment:** Without structure, freelancing can become a free-for-all. Many people leave the confines of corporate America seeking flexibility and no boundaries. Yet it takes structure and organization to get any job done. When you work for someone else, they provide the structure. When you work for yourself, you have to create it for yourself. People who have difficulty creating their own structure frequently flounder in the freedom of freelancing.

✔ **Unrealistic client expectations:** Clients want what they want when they want it. They don't always give you the time you need, the creative freedom, or the support that will allow you to do your best work. Tough. Your job as a freelancer is to find a way to do it. Period. If you need things set in stone, you may find that freelancing is a constant frustration.

✔ **The need to settle:** Because clients may not share your view of the ideal solution, they may ask you to produce a product that doesn't exactly meet your standards. As you build a relationship and trust with clients, you may be able to educate them and move them toward more effective solutions. In the meantime, however, you have to give them what they want or find another way to eat. If you can't ever settle for less than perfection, life will be difficult.

Predicting Your Success

People say that after you get married, the same things that attracted you to a person become the things that ultimately drive you crazy. That's also probably true of freelancing. Whether you "stay married" to your freelance career depends entirely on your ability to recognize the good — and the humor — in the mixture of both happy and not-so-happy things that happen.

Can you always tell at the beginning whether freelancing will suit your fancy? Not necessarily. You may have to jump in and try it to discover whether it makes you happy. The good news is that freelancing, even for a limited time, teaches you a lot. If you do decide to re-enter the traditional workplace, you'll be a more valuable employee. You may even be more content working for someone else after you've seen the other side. If you don't at least try working for yourself, you may always have that nagging feeling of "what if?"

Table 1-1 shows you the qualities that either help you succeed or hold you back as a freelancer.

Table 1-1	Does the Freelance Armor Fit?
Personality Traits That Help	*Personality Traits That Hinder*
Resiliency	Rigidity
Flexibility	Perfectionism; one-track mind
Ability to live with uncertainty	Need for someone else to provide structure
Assertiveness	Aggressiveness
Dedication	Procrastination
Desire to grow and learn	Confrontational attitude
Optimistic outlook	Negative outlook
Ability to bounce back from mistakes	Tendency to beat yourself up and blame yourself when you make a mistake or things don't go as planned
Belief in your own ability to succeed	Need for constant positive feedback on your work

Uncovering the Skills That Freelancers Require

Aside from your substantial skill in your specialty, you need to be blessed with (or cultivate) a talent for managing yourself, your clients, and your work, and the ability to move mountains at will.

When I look at successful freelancers, I see some similar skills. Here are the ones I think are essential:

 ✔ **Organization:** Where's that memo? When is that desk being delivered? Who's going to pick up the copies? Your time may be all you have to sell, and you probably won't have an assistant on hand to answer the phone, make copies, remind you of appointments, or take the dog to the vet. Getting organized is the only way you'll manage to know where everything is and be able to get everything done on time. Because freelancing is, by definition, undefined, you have to create your own structure.

 ✔ **Discipline:** Spring fever can affect you just as much when you work for yourself as it did when you worked within the four padded walls of a cubicle. Just because you make your own schedule doesn't mean you can sit outside and listen to the birds all the time. You have to be able to tell yourself it's time to work and to follow through on actually sitting at your desk. There's time enough to commune with nature . . . as long as you also commune with *billable hours* (time for which you can send a client a bill).

✔ **Multitasking:** If you expect to make any money, you'll probably have to balance a lot of spinning plates at one time. You simply can't complete one project and then look for another one. You have to work a continuous cycle of selling, doing the work, and selling while you do the work. I frequently find myself writing a book, trying to pitch a proposal, meeting with a client, and signing checks all at once (in between communing with nature).

✔ **Communication:** How do you tell a client that his taste is awful or ask someone to pay an overdue bill? Very carefully. A lot of people want to freelance so they can say exactly what they think, but you may be surprised at how tactful you have to be when your paycheck is riding on it. Your honest opinion, without tact, can be an expensive luxury in the freelance world.

✔ **Flexibility:** In 15 years, I've discovered that hardly any projects start or finish on schedule. Clients cancel projects or have emergency needs, managers get fired or their priorities change — the list is endless. Part of the fun of freelancing is the variety of projects and schedules. It's also part of the challenge.

✔ **Ability to compromise:** Most people start freelancing so that they can live up to the high standards they place on themselves. But guess what: Compromise is always a part of making clients happy. I've never been able to complete a project without compromising on at least one point.

✔ **Ability to withstand rejection and to not take it personally:** Salespeople say that they make ten sales calls to make one sale. I know one persistent freelancer who expects to make three to five contacts with the same prospect before they sign on the dotted line. Learn to accept rejection happily. After all, if you think about it, each rejection you rack up puts you one step closer to a sale.

If you want to freelance so you won't have to be bothered with all the red tape, paperwork, and extraneous junk inside a company, you may be in for a bit of a surprise. Being self-employed requires that you handle not only all of the paperwork but also every other job function. A freelancer must be a Jack or Jill of all trades, with a list of job duties that looks remarkably like a corporate department index. You'll be the vice president of the following:

✔ **Marketing, advertising, and sales:** Word-of-mouth is the most effective way to get new business, and if you're good at what you do, you'll eventually have lots of that. But at least in the beginning, you also have to develop a plan to make people want what you have to sell. That means pricing your services or product, positioning it in the market, building a consistent image, and so on.

✔ **Public relations (PR):** Some call this "free advertising," but there's nothing free about public relations. It requires a lot of time and energy, as well as proactive thinking and creativity.

✔ **Accounting and finance:** Unless you take the letters f-r-e-e in freelance literally, your business is all about making money. But whether you make money or not, the IRS and assorted state and local agencies require that you keep detailed records and file reports about your income, expenses, sales tax (if required), and other bits of financial information.

✔ **Purchasing:** Even if you don't have an elaborate office, you still require some equipment and supplies, so you're the procurement officer of your corporate headquarters. If your business requires you to purchase services or products on your clients' behalf, you'll also put on your purchasing hat to know where and how to make the most of their dollars.

✔ **Quality assurance:** Quality is your most important success factor. In addition to living up to the highest standards, you have to follow up to make certain your clients feel they've received a good value for their money. You can't rely on them to tell you how you're doing; you must ask them point blank.

✔ **Janitorial services:** As a freelance writer/consultant/project manager, I've had to do the following. In You, Inc., you're the clean up crew in more ways than one.

   • Clean meeting rooms that weren't ready for workshops.

   • Find out where to rent portable toilets for a corporate family day.

   • Shred documents and dispose of them appropriately.

You can spend a great deal of time doing things over and above the creative, wonderful work you were born to do. You may want to take the time, then, to brush up on some of those "useless" courses you took in high school or college or to develop some additional skills. You undoubtedly enjoy some of these roles more than others. The fun and the challenge are in learning about all aspects of what makes a company tick and making your profit-and-loss statement sing. Very simply stated, a *profit-and-loss statement,* commonly called *P&L* by most business folks, is a report of all the money you've taken in, all the money you've paid out, and what's left over.

Vice presidents have the prerogative of delegation. If you can afford it, hire people to help with some of your duties. (I talk more about this in Chapter 8.) But no matter how uninvolved you may choose to be in certain areas, you still need a basic knowledge of all the territory.

Two words you may never hear a freelancer say: I'm bored. If variety appeals to you, freelancing is the ticket because, for most freelancers, every day is different. Each client has unique eccentricities. Each industry has its own challenges. Each job function has its upside and its downside. Variety is truly the spice of the freelancer's life.

Lagniappe

In New Orleans they use the word *lagniappe* to mean "a little something extra." One of the perks of freelancing is that in finding out how to run your own business, you also hone skills that apply to your work. You may be amazed at how this broader knowledge increases your value to your clients and makes you more effective in every aspect of service you deliver. Having an owner's perspective helps you make more practical recommendations and helps you be empathetic to your clients' problems.

Understanding the Joy of Freelancing

Perhaps the best way I can wrap up this chapter is to draw your attention to the fact that, as the writer of this book, I'm clearly still freelancing. Sometimes I wonder if my life wouldn't be easier if I just got "a real job," but after one and a half decades, I'm still on my own.

I admit that on occasion, after a particularly frustrating job, I seriously consider looking for a full-time position. I even call a contact or two. But when I really think about what that would mean and what I would give up, I resist, procrastinate, repeatedly weigh the pros and cons, and finally admit that I just can't go back to working in a structured environment that someone else created.

There is something thrilling about winning a job; something rewarding about knowing that 90 percent of your work is repeat business; something fun about getting the lowdown on different industries, different companies, different work styles and practices; something special about developing relationships with a wide variety of wonderful people who value your talent and actually seek you out to do very important things for them.

Yes, there are frustrations. Sure, there are some clients I wouldn't want to work for again. Yes, there are projects that make me tear my hair out and swear I'm going to work at a fast-food restaurant. But, all in all, would I do it over again? You bet I would.

Chapter 2

Understanding the Realities of Working for Yourself

*E*ver heard of something called the *geographic cure?* That's when you move to another city thinking you'll leave all your problems behind. It never seems to work.

In the same way, moving out on your own isn't guaranteed to wipeout your work frustrations, increase your I. Q., fatten your wallet, or remove your insecurities. Whether you work in a corporation or for yourself, work is still work. No situation is perfect, and you will have to make trade-offs. They're not necessarily bad trade-offs; they're just things that work differently than you may expect.

I find that in most situations, when I have idealized expectations, I risk disappointment; when I have realistic expectations, I generally have not only satisfying results, but also delightful surprises. This chapter helps you increase your chances of getting pleasant surprises by shedding light on some of the realities of working for yourself.

Going It Alone

Very cool things happen when you go out on your own. First and foremost, as long as you have a home office, you can work in your pajamas. I can't overstate the importance of this. Not only does it save money in wardrobe costs, it also makes getting dressed for work a breeze.

Other cool things about being on your own include gaining the following:

- ✔ Power
- ✔ Freedom
- ✔ Flexibility

These may not be exactly unexpected benefits; in fact, they're probably the reasons you chose to go solo. What is surprising is how addictive these attributes become. After a short while, you probably won't know how you ever lived within the confines of a "real job."

Losing Your Identity

Not only do great things happen when you go out on your own, very strange things also take place. The first weird surprise I experienced was that I felt naked without my corporate title. I had worked for one of the largest, most respected companies in town, where I was Director of Communications. Impressive, huh? When I left that company, I was just "Susan Drake, Freelancer." No power, no prestige, no business card with a fancy logo and big shot title. I worried that people would think I was an amateur working out of a corner of my bedroom. For two years I introduced myself like this: "Hi, I'm Susan Drake, a freelance writer, but I used to be director of communications for Holiday Inn." I said it as one long sentence, without taking a breath. That way, before my audience could react to my untitle, I'd slap them with my former really important title to prove my worth. It took me a long time to realize that I was perfectly okay as "just a freelancer."

Be kind to yourself: Start your new life with confidence and respect for your own talent and value. As long as you demonstrate professionalism, you will command the respect you deserve. And remember, just about everyone you deal with envies the fact that you have the guts and talent to go out on your own. When you've had a chance to establish a reputation, it will be your identity and yours alone.

Uncovering the Illusion of Insecurity

People always wonder how a freelancer can deal with the loss of job security. I wondered the same thing! Here I was, voluntarily leaving the safety of a multi-billion-dollar corporation, complete with automatic payroll deposit and hospitalization, all for the uncertainty of sporadic paychecks. Interestingly, shortly after I left, the company was sold, headquarters moved to Atlanta, and half my friends were living on severance pay. So much for job security.

"Hello, this is the White House calling . . . "

Laura Koss-Feder is a business writer who is regularly published in *Time, Investor's Business Daily, Business Week, Newsday, The New York Times,* and MSNBC . com. She lost her job as a managing editor when a publication downsized, and she decided to try working on her own for six months. Soon after she started freelancing, the disastrous crash of TWA flight 800 occurred near her home. News agencies from around the world were covering the tragedy 'round the clock, trying to deliver information about how and why it happened. *U. S. News & World Report* didn't have a reporter in that area, so they called Laura, who had to react quickly to the horrifying situation and keep a level head. She says, "I borrowed a cell phone, took a sandwich, and drove to the scene, where hundreds of reporters were camped out on the beach."

That was certainly a harsh introduction to freelancing; most of her current work involves business writing. The advantages of freelancing hit home for her one winter day when she was writing a story that required a comment from the White House. "I was on the phone talking to someone from the White House — they clearly didn't realize that I was sitting there bundled up in my pajamas, wearing no makeup. At that point, my dog came up and offered me his chew toy. I said to myself, 'This is pretty cool.'"

Laura's work style is certainly not business casual. She has set hours and approaches her workday methodically. "I get up, get dressed, and open the blinds. I take an hour for lunch, and then I'm back at my desk." Her caveat to anyone working on their own is, "You're always proving yourself, because you're only as good as your last assignment."

What you may consider to be a predictable paycheck can stop at any time. Downsizing, mergers, reengineering, and all the other recent corporate maneuverings have all played a role in wiping out whatever security employees used to feel. About all you can hope for today is that if you do get outplaced, you'll at least have a decent warning.

Surviving when you're pushed from the nest

Quite a few of my freelance friends became self-employed by default. They lost their jobs and said, "Well, what the heck? I may as well try this." Not everyone has the nerve to take the freelance plunge without some not-so-gentle encouragement. They find, though, that after they've been pushed from the nest, they seldom feel the need to go back. They're happy after all, finding fortune in misfortune.

Holding the purse strings

How does working in a corporation, with the threat of outplacement hanging over your head, compare with being self-employed? You actually have more security being self-employed because of the following:

- ✔ You're in charge of sales.
- ✔ You're in charge of marketing.
- ✔ You're in charge of quality.
- ✔ You're in charge of customer satisfaction.
- ✔ You're in charge of spending.

In other words, you're in charge of all the factors that contribute to whether you make money or not. You're in charge of your own paycheck.

Who could you possibly trust more with your well-being than yourself? As long as you're willing to put in the time and energy to do each of your jobs effectively, you can have more security as a freelancer than as an employee of a corporation.

At least a third of the freelancers I talked with say the biggest surprise and challenge they experienced was in the amount of taxes they owed and in the timing of the tax payments. Self-employment taxes are steep and, in certain circumstances, you have to make tax payments quarterly or monthly. Be sure to read Chapter 17 before you assume you will make a killing. Taxes could kill your enthusiasm.

Balancing Your Work and Your Personal Life

An old joke says that when you work for yourself you only work half days . . . whichever 12 hours you prefer. Freelancers are known for working hard, but that's by choice. You actually do have flexibility in scheduling your work. The decision is yours to increase your income (by increasing your work hours) or to decrease your work hours (thereby decreasing your income). The thing to remember is that you make a tradeoff: When you're not working, you're not making money. If you take Wednesdays off to play golf, you may have to substitute some other work time to meet your clients' deadlines: That other work time may very well be at night or on a weekend.

Your first project: Positive thinking

I heard a story recently about a golfer who focused so much mental energy on a water hazard that he hit his ball right into it. It's a human shortcoming: We seem to always project the worst and, by thinking so hard about it, we create a self-fulfilling prophecy.

When I was considering freelancing, I asked myself what the worst thing was that could happen. I speculated that I may make about half as much money as I did working for the corporation. I tried to envision what sacrifices I would

have to make. I was shocked when, the first year, I made twice as much. I had always been successful at my job, so why had I expected the worst?

Positive thinking, affirmations, projecting abundance — call it what you will, but do it. Instead of thinking, "What if I don't make enough money?" tell yourself, "I think I'll become rich." If I had projected wealth, I may have made five times as much money. Start focusing on fabulous outcomes and they'll certainly come true.

Figure 2-1 shows you the cycle of self-employment. It tends to go like this:

- ✔ You work lots of hours to get your business started.
- ✔ Your investment pays off; you have plenty of clients.
- ✔ You work lots of hours to keep up.
- ✔ You do good work, and your clients refer their friends to you.
- ✔ You have more work.
- ✔ You work lots of hours to keep up with your success.

How do you cope with this cycle? Master the art of selecting the most advantageous jobs and turning down the ones that don't move you toward your goal of a financially comfortable and balanced life. You can also choose to delay a project if it fits your client's needs. You may be amazed at how often a client will wait for you.

The only person who controls your work flow is you; you do have options!

When you work for yourself, the line between work and life can become blurred, especially if you have a home office. People who don't physically leave work have a difficult time mentally leaving it. And if you're all work and no play — well, you're at risk for burnout.

For many freelancers, early mornings, late nights, and weekends are the time to concentrate and get the real work done. That's when there are no interruptions. But here's the rub: During "normal" work hours, you have to meet with clients, make sales calls, return calls, deliver projects, and do all the things that regular people do from 9 to 5. This means that you could be working early morning, all day, at night, and on weekends. At first, you may feel great about all the work you're getting and how rich you will undoubtedly be. But one day you may awaken and say, "Hey, where's my life?"

Self-Employment Work Cycle

Figure 2-1:
A never-ending cycle.

Take the following steps to set the stage for balance:

- As the Supreme Commander, set not only work hours, but also play hours. Include a specified amount of time off each day.

- Close the door. Walk out of your work area and, if possible, literally close the door to the office. A physical barrier helps keep you from too readily dropping in to jot a quick note or make a call.

- When you leave the office, leave the office. Do something that helps you make the mental break from work. Read the paper, watch TV, or take a walk.

- Don't interrupt your off time by dropping in the office just to answer an e-mail or two or to return a few calls. After you're in the office, time keeps on slippin', slippin', slippin', into the future.

Only you can decide how to maintain your balance. Make the deliberate decision to do it, and force yourself to practice the self-discipline to carry it out.

Enjoying Solitude and Avoiding Loneliness

I have a framed cartoon showing a guy sitting by himself under a tree with a party hat on his head and a noisemaker in his hand. The caption reads: "Self-Employed Person's Annual Employee Picnic." Ha, ha, very funny. Yes, very funny, until I was sitting in my home office surrounded by dead silence and missing all those people who used to drive me crazy.

When I first started freelancing, I was shocked to discover how lonely I felt and how much I missed the camaraderie of the group. Oh, sure, when you're by yourself you get lots done. You have no extended coffee breaks, no birthday celebrations, no staff meetings or impromptu discussions of "How 'bout those Mets?" But you may also feel lonely or need a mental break that involves other human beings.

Expect to be a little unnerved by your sudden aloneness. Use the suggestions in the following sections to make sure that even when you're alone, you're not lonely.

Developing necessary interruptions

I've developed what I call "necessary interruptions." Here are a few suggestions for coping with a lack of officemates:

✔ **Develop a network of freelance friends.** Call them for advice, for lunch, or to commiserate. Be considerate of their time, however. You're all working to make a buck, but a quick hello won't cut too drastically into their paychecks or yours.

✔ **Participate in associations to meet other freelancers in your profession.** Meetings provide great visibility, enlightenment, and enjoyment.

✔ **Join groups in professions that are related to yours.** For example, if you're a writer who wants to write about human resources topics, join the Society for Human Resource Managers (SHRM). If you're a market researcher who does communications surveys, join the International Association of Business Communicators (IABC). At regular lunch meetings you can learn more about these other areas, which will make you a more valuable freelancer. Best of all, you can also meet potential clients.

✔ **Start your own informal freelance group just to chat.** I know one group that holds a regular poker night just for the creative camaraderie. You'll probably find that other freelancers are eager for contact, too.

> ✓ **Use e-mail to stay in touch with your buddies without disrupting their think time or yours.** Everyone has the option of checking e-mail at convenient times. One friend and I touch base each Monday just to remind each other that there's intelligent life in the universe.

Even if you tend to be social, you can derive some unexpected benefits from solitude. Instead of trying to fill up your hours with activity, use your time for reflection. Sit quietly, close your eyes, and let your mind wander. You may discover that some of your goals become clearer and your concerns disappear when you spend some concerted time alone.

Friends and neighbors who don't work at home may not realize that you don't have time to be interrupted for chitchat. Getting caught off guard can result in some awkward moments or can mean that you sacrifice critical work time for idle talk. To avoid either, prepare what you will say to friends who arrive unexpectedly and expect you to drop everything.

Avoiding interruptions

To keep your day within your control, have a plan for avoiding interruptions. The following tools and techniques can help:

✓ **Use caller ID.** Oh, the miracles of modern technology. This wonderful feature available from your phone company allows you to see who's calling before you answer. If you have call waiting, you can also sign up for a deluxe caller ID service that even reveals who's on the line while you're on another call.

✓ **Disconnect your phone.** When you're engaged in something that requires concentration, turn off the ringer on your phone. If you hear it ringing, you may be tempted to pick it up.

✓ **Hang out a sign.** Put a sign on your door asking delivery people to leave packages without ringing the bell.

✓ **Ask for a family "vacation."** Family members can be unaware of your need for solitude. Put a sign on your office door that says, "Genius at work" or use another notice that you're in a work trance and need

to be left alone. Train them that this message means business . . . really.

✓ **Change your message.** If you have a message service, change your message to let clients know you'll be out of the office for a certain time. That way, they won't expect a return call until the time you specify you'll be back. Of course, prepare for the onslaught when your time is up.

✓ **Hire a stand-in.** Ask a freelance associate to back you up while you're "out of the office." Brief the person on anything that needs to be taken care of right away and trust them to handle things. Let the person know what kinds of things you must be interrupted for.

✓ **Take a meeting — with yourself.** Pretend that you are your own client. You've hired yourself to do some work, and you must set aside time to "meet" with yourself to get it done. Take your project time seriously and treat it just as you would any other meeting time with a client.

An even easier option is to have both a home and a business phone. During your work hours, don't answer your home phone. You wouldn't be answering it if you were gone to an office away from home, so what's the difference?

Dealing with reasonable people is easy. Say lightheartedly, "I'd love to talk, but my boss has me on the clock." For those who aren't as likely to take a hint, be more straightforward: "Jack, I'm in the middle of an important project and I need to stay on this. How about lunch tomorrow?"

Fido and Fluffy make excellent officemates, although they sometimes beg you to play at inopportune moments. Regardless, pets are comforting and fun, and when you have a bad day, they offer much-needed consolation. Best of all, unlike coworkers, they don't take the last cup of coffee in the pot.

Steering clear of dangerous liaisons

The flip side of being alone is that if you're already quite comfortable being a solitary soul, you may find you love the silence a little too much. Enjoy it, but don't slip too far into recluse-land. That can be counterproductive for the following reasons:

- ✔ **It doesn't contribute to your marketing efforts.** Without putting forth a little extra oomph, you could not only be alone, you could also be without work. Make sure you keep in touch with the people who write your paychecks.

- ✔ **You may focus too much on you.** You could become a bit too introspective or self-involved.

- ✔ **You may be out of touch.** When you cut yourself off from the mainstream, you tend to lose touch with the latest trends.

Balance in your worklife is a must, but moderation doesn't seem to come naturally or easily to freelancers. Only planning and discipline gets you there.

My friend Renee Dingler, a management consultant, says that you open yourself up to discouragement and depression if you cut yourself off from human contact and stare at a computer screen all day. She says: "It's so easy to stay locked up in your office and forget there's a world out there. Don't do it!"

Remembering That Money Matters

Freelancers are like pregnant women who say, "I'll *never* let *my* child eat sugar . . . " and end up eating their words after the baby arrives. Don't set yourself up by swearing you'll never settle or sell out. After you're relying on yourself for a paycheck, you may discover you have to compromise more than you'd like, for one simple reason: Money talks.

Ten signs you're spending too much time alone

When you're working on a project with a looming deadline, you may lose track of time and space. Here are ten signs that you may need to get out of the office:

✔ Your eyes can't adjust to sunlight.

✔ Tuna cans are piling up outside your door.

✔ Your dog is bored with your company.

✔ You realize you've been wearing the same sweatshirt for six days.

✔ Your spouse suggests you take a vacation to Hawaii . . . alone.

✔ The batteries in your TV remote have gone dead.

✔ You no longer use a fork to eat pasta.

✔ You consider talking to yourself a stimulating conversation.

✔ You're leading the charge on deodorant conservation.

✔ Your eyes light up at the signal that "you've got mail."

No matter how committed you are to doing things perfectly, in some cases, you'll find you have to deliver something that's less than perfect in order to meet your deadline or to get paid. The cold, hard fact of freelance life is this: Talk all you want about high-minded ideals. When the mortgage payment is due, you have to pay it with something more tangible than high standards.

Don't worry. Selling out doesn't mean sacrificing your principles. It doesn't mean you're a bad person or a less-than-perfect worker. It just means you're a realist. And when you're in business, you must be a realist.

Enduring your transition period

I can give you all the warnings in the world, but you can't possibly know what surprises await you. What surprised my friends and me may not be what surprises you. The best way to go into the freelance life is to realize that you will experience a transition period. Any time things change, you tend to experience discomfort, even if the changes are for the good. To get used to freelancing as painlessly as possible, follow these rules:

✔ Accept that change is unsettling.

✔ Realize that nothing lasts forever.

✔ Be patient with yourself as you learn the ropes.

> ✔ Don't be too rigid about anything until you've had a chance to try on a variety of rules and techniques.
>
> ✔ Never say never.

Flexibility takes you a long way in a freelance career. You may as well start practicing!

Hoping and planning

The independence of working for yourself can be heady stuff. As the boss of You, Inc., you can create work that's up to your highest standards, make decisions to your heart's content, and — best of all — get paid for it. Aside from working in your pajamas, these are big advantages to people who like to take charge.

Launching a new life is an exciting and hope-filled adventure. You're taking this uncharted path because you anticipate that it will offer you a different, better way of life. What a wonderful place to be!

Make your plans. Dream your dreams. Temper your expectations. Do the right stuff and the right stuff will come your way . . . really.

Chapter 3

Making the Decision to Freelance

*D*ream up your ideal freelance job and, chances are, it can become a reality. The question is, will it be what you want it to be?

My father was self-employed, and when I told him I was abandoning the corporate world to work for myself, his reaction was surprising. He said: "Susan, I sent you to college so you could get somebody to hire you and you wouldn't have to work for yourself!" I was shocked. He didn't see freelancing as a choice, but I did.

You, too, have a choice to make. I decided it was right for me, but I did that with practically no forethought to whether I was cut out for freelancing. In fact, I had little idea of what freelancing entailed. You have the opportunity to think about a few important factors before you assume the life of a freelancer is for you. This chapter helps you do that.

Considering a Variety of Jobs

Tons of jobs can be done from a home or independent office. Which one will you choose? You may have a particular career, such as writing or accounting, that you can do on your own, and you're clear about what you want to do. Or you may have skills that you believe are useful and could be developed as a business, without a clear idea of what job you can apply those skills to. Last, but not least, you may have a career you've decided to ditch in favor of something more fun. There's a good chance you can do any or all of those as a freelancer, as discussed in the following sections.

Creative work

Creative people are surely the ones for whom the word *freelance* was invented. Of course, remember that the term "starving artist" was also invented for creative types!

- ✔ **Writer and editor:** Both large companies and small need people who can write and edit brochures, advertising copy, speeches, corporate video scripts, package information, technical manuals, books, and more. In addition, the Internet has created a whole new venue for writers — Web writing is a new specialty that's wide open for a writer getting started. Have computer? Will write.

- ✔ **Author:** If I can do it, so can you. Writers who long for the fulfillment of publishing a book can break into the field through traditional publishing or by self-publishing. Do your research to find out where and how.

- ✔ **Artist or graphic designer:** Do you draw cartoons, create illustrations, design brochures, or layout newsletters? There's a market for people who can bring ideas to life visually.

- ✔ **Fine artist:** If your creative slant leads you to paint pictures, do etchings, sculpt nudes, or pursue any of the fine arts, you can probably survive as a freelancer. Have a musical bent? Long to try out your talents on stage? Live performers can find work at corporate meetings and events, performing in videos, entertaining at parties, or teaching classes for kids.

- ✔ **Video producer:** One of my most important suppliers is a woman who handles video production from her home. We determine what kind of production the client needs, and she assembles all the resources we need: the equipment, script writer, director, videographer, actors, makeup artist, location, editing facility, and more.

- ✔ **Photographer:** Virtually all of the photographers I work with are freelancers. They hire out for a particular photo shoot, which means they generally come to the location and provide the camera, lighting, and whatever other equipment is necessary. The photographer is also in charge of processing the film and delivering the product, which may be 35mm negatives, color prints, or color transparencies. Good photographers are extremely patient and can lug equipment with ease. They must also invest quite a lot of money in photographic equipment.

Financial positions

Financial positions generally require schooling, credentials, and licenses, depending upon the state requirements.

- ✔ **Certified public accountant (CPA):** These professionals perform accounting functions for small businesses, such as doing taxes, auditing records, preparing financial statements that help in managing the business, and giving advice about how to handle certain aspects of the business.

- ✔ **Tax practitioner:** A tax practitioner prepares tax returns and gives advice on tax matters. While they aren't required to be certified public accountants, they must meet certain IRS requirements.

- ✔ **Bookkeeper:** Small businesses need bookkeepers to set up a system of record keeping, maintain their accounts, send out invoices to customers, take care of payroll, and make sure businesses are following tax laws and guidelines. A bookkeeper can also prepare information for tax purposes.

High-tech jobs

In this high-speed world, freelance high-tech jobs are some of the easiest to land. Firms that specialize in computer assistance often hire part-time freelance staff members to serve their clients. Small- and medium-sized businesses that can't afford to hire full-time computer staff certainly appreciate personal service from specialists. And people (like me) who aren't technically inclined are more than happy to pay an hourly consulting fee to get guidance through the computer world.

- ✔ **Computer technician:** Few people are as important to me as my computer guru, who helps me install new software, repairs my computer when it goes down, recommends new equipment and resources, and generally holds my hand through the confusing technological world.

- ✔ **Computer programmer:** Writing computer programs is something you can easily do at home, or you can work on-site as a contract employee. Pick what you like: a time-limited project that offers flexibility, or a long-term project that can offer steady income.

- ✔ **Web site designer:** This field is hot, hot, hot. Everyone wants their own site on the Internet, and it takes a certain knowledge to create them. Do this from your home armed with your trusty computer.

- ✔ **Computer trainer:** As technology becomes a more important part of our business and personal lives, computer training is a potentially lucrative business.

Be wary of quick-fix business opportunities, ads offering "high paying self-employment," and companies that promise to turn you into an expert overnight (for a fee). Many can be nothing more than expensive — and empty — promises. As a college student, my daughter once came home overjoyed at the high potential job she had landed . . . selling knives. The only catch? We had to buy the knives upfront.

Such schemes can come in sophisticated packages, too. A close friend invested $12,000 in a business-consulting system that she never earned a penny from. She wasn't the only one to lose a lot of money. Just ask the FBI: They investigated the whole business.

Personal services

People have less time to do both the fun and the fundamental things in their lives and, as a result, you can find numerous opportunities to perform personal services.

- ✔ **Personal shopper:** If spending other people's money appeals to you, try being a personal shopper. You can spend your time finding the perfect gift for a boss or spouse, locating the ideal business suit for your customer's interview, or hiring a florist to deliver and decorate the world's most beautiful Christmas tree.

- ✔ **Garden and yard designer and caretaker:** When I decided to put in a perennial garden, I had no idea where to start. I first contacted a nursery, and they were happy to provide me with a landscape architect who drew a sample plan that would cost only $12,000. Because that was a bit out of my budget, I called a local artist who happened to be doing gardens on the side. For $300, she created a garden plan and helped me select the plants and set them out. It was the perfect service for my needs.

- ✔ **Interior designer:** Take your flair for color, form, and function and put it to work helping others design their work or home spaces. It won't all be a piece of cake, though, because you have to design to their tastes, not yours. You also have to be good at contracting with painters, plumbers, flooring experts, and the like, to make everything come together harmoniously.

- ✔ **Tutor:** Do you have a special skill that people would like to learn? For example, if you know a second language, what about teaching it? As global travel increases, and the world becomes more culturally diverse, learning a second (or third or fourth) language is becoming a more important part of many people's lives. Tutoring can extend to any skill or hobby, such as sewing or woodworking, that you know well.

- ✔ **Personal chef:** If you love to cook, you may find this to be your recipe for success. Lots of harried business people are willing to pay someone to create their menus, do the shopping, and prepare meals. And with so many people watching what they eat, you can give your sales pitch a boost by offering services such as food that's low in fat or meant for diabetics.

- ✔ **Housecleaner:** Housecleaners may be among the first professionals to take their shows on the road. Keeping other people's abodes spic 'n' span is a natural freelance position.

Business opportunities

One extremely lucrative opportunity is being in business to serve business. The practice of *outsourcing* has become popular as companies hire independent workers to do things traditionally done by employees. Outsourcing saves the cost of paying employee benefits and providing office space, not to mention the headache of laying people off when a merger or downsize takes place. What has become a source of unemployment for some people can be a big opportunity for you. If you have a skill that you can sell to businesses, go for it!

- **Public speaker and trainer:** Develop a workshop on a hot business topic, and you can sell it to corporations as a developmental tool. If you're a dynamite public speaker, you may also be able to make money doing speaking engagements. This is a highly competitive field, however, and not one you can get started in quickly. You need credentials associated with your topic, as well as a speaking track record. An agent is a real plus. Coaching executives to do presentations is another area where a good public speaker can do training.

- **Mystery shopper (quality auditor):** Companies are more concerned with quality than ever. It's tough to check on quality internally, so they sometimes hire outsiders to play the role of customers and rate how well employees serve.

- **Medical transcriber:** Doctors dictate notes about their patients' visits and treatments, and a specially trained transcriber types those notes and delivers them back to the doctor to be put in the patients' charts. You can work directly for a doctor's office or through a transcribing agency.

- **Management consultant:** Just about anyone who has worked in a management role in a corporation can find a way to "consult" in that field. People who are "down-sized" often go freelance as an interim way to earn money until they find a position, and then discover they can make a good living without finding another corporate job. It's not unusual for the people who are down-sized to end up selling their services back to the same company they used to work for . . . sometimes for a higher price!

- **Events planner:** Corporate meetings, community events, and parties are all special events that require planning and implementation by someone with a fine eye for detail and the ability to juggle multiple tasks.

- **Market researcher:** Researchers may conduct focus groups, design surveys, conduct telemarketing research, and otherwise find out how people feel about everything from their local grocery stores to the state of world politics.

- **Career counselor:** Helping people answer the question, "What do I want to be when I grow up?" is a job with built-in security. I've certainly asked myself this repeatedly in my life. You'll need special training to conduct testing and evaluate a person's skills and aptitudes.

Stirring things up

Helen Halladay was working as a hair stylist, renting a booth at a salon. She was essentially in business for herself, but it just didn't pay as much as she wanted. One day she saw an ad in *Eating Well* magazine advertising a plan for becoming a personal chef. The ad described a business in which a person would plan menus, shop, and cook for others in their homes. It was just the ticket for Helen, an amateur chef who saw an opportunity to combine her desire for more income with her knack for cooking.

"Every single member of my family and all of my friends said, 'No one will pay for this.' I didn't believe it. I bought the plan and I implemented every single step. I started cooking for people part time and word spread. For a year, I cooked part time while I worked at the salon. A newspaper reporter wanted to do a story on me, but I turned it down because I wasn't ready to handle additional business. Several months later, they did the story. I got 60 calls the next day!"

Helen has been operating Helen's of Course in Memphis, Tennessee full time since 1994. I guess people will pay for that, after all.

Assessing Your Skills

When you want to go out on your own, you need to assess which skills you bring to your freelance business. If you were an employer, would you hire you? Make a list of what skills are required in the job you want. You may have to do some research to find out the following:

- ✔ What education is required for the position?
- ✔ What experience do professionals need?
- ✔ Are any certifications required or helpful?
- ✔ What references would potential clients want?

One way to find out more about the essentials is to interview someone who's doing the job. If you're reluctant to call people who may end up being your competitors, call a national association and ask for some contacts in other cities. People are usually happy to talk with you about their careers, and I find that most freelancers are generous people (or maybe they're just lonely!).

After you determine the minimum qualifications for the type of work you want to do, compare them with your own background. Are you already qualified? Will you have to seek additional schooling or other training to meet requirements? As you develop your timetable for going out on your own, you may have to build in a little time upfront to get the training you need.

Aptitude tests, career profiles, and other assessment tools can help you determine not only what you're qualified to do, but also what suits your work style and personality. Check with the career counseling center at a nearby college or university for more information. Your library is another good source of information about these services. A friend of mine also used to work as a freelance job counselor. She provided testing services and offered guidance about careers for a set three-session fee of several hundred dollars. You may find this money well spent.

Doing Your Homework

I've known freelancers who up and quit their jobs and started a whole new life at the blink of an eye. Wow! You may see that as having guts, but I see it more like jumping headfirst into a pitch black pool of water without knowing how deep it is. I personally recommend giving yourself a leg up on success by doing some homework before you make the leap. Give some thought to all the questions in the following sections, and you'll have a better idea of what's in store for you, and you can make choices that match your life goals.

Who is your competition and what do they do?

Take a look around at people who already do what you plan to do. Who are they? Are they national companies, local suppliers, or freelancers like you? Suppose you're in the home-cleaning business. You may compete with a local janitorial company that does primarily commercial cleaning, with a national franchise service, and with other individuals. What they offer and how much they charge affects what you plan to do.

Compare the services you plan to offer with those of your potential competitors.

- Are your services identical?
- Is there something special you can offer, such as free delivery.
- Will your price be higher than theirs, the same, or lower?

Deciding how you will compete is a major step in defining your business.

Can the market support you?

Another important question to ask yourself is, "Is this town big enough for all of us?" In other words, is there enough business for everyone to make a living.

Scope out the number of people in your area doing what you want to do. This takes some research — the following are some places to look:

- ✔ A quick look at the phone directory will tell you about companies you're competing with, but may not highlight other freelancers, who may not pay for a directory listing.
- ✔ Attend meetings of professional organizations to discover other freelancers.
- ✔ Ask business associates whom they know who is also freelancing.

Your potential clients also have access to freelancers who are Web-based. They may or may not be located in your city; the Web makes everyone accessible no matter where they're physically located. It pays to be aware of these competitors, too.

Is there enough business to support a new kid on the block? Or are you planning to do things in a way that's unique, and that will make you highly competitive with existing companies? For example, suppose you want to start a residential lawn service. If your city's economy is booming, with a great influx of two-job — and two-income — families, you may easily land lots of jobs from these busy professionals. They're the people who can and will pay for a service that frees up their time. On the other hand, if your city is in a recession and two of the five major employers have just moved their headquarters out of town, you could be in for a long dry spell.

Think about this: What if you wanted to start a pool service in Tupelo, Mississippi and there were already five pool services in town? Is that a sound business decision?

Can you compete with your former employer?

In some cases, a freelancer becomes a former employer's biggest competitor. Can you do that?

Some employers require employees to sign a *noncompete agreement* that says, "If you leave us, you agree that you won't compete in the same business for (x) amount of time." The agreement may stipulate how far away you would have to locate a competing business, require that you not use information you gained from that employer, or bar you from the business altogether for a certain period of time. If you signed a noncompete agreement, you have to follow the legal provisions of that agreement.

Taking your former boss' clients is a bit of a sticky situation. If a client follows you of his or her own free will, that's one thing. If you solicit business with the specific goal of taking it from your employer, well, you have to be the judge of how ethical that is. At the very least, recognize that absconding with clients isn't a real good way to win friends.

Consider, also, whether you have the wherewithal to compete with your former employer. For example, if you've been working at an advertising agency as a graphic designer, do you have the clout and the capabilities to draw business of the magnitude that your former employer does? Can you handle the demands of a big corporate client?

Unless you're an unusual breed, you probably think that you can do work that's as good or better than your former employer. More power to you! Get out there and compete your heart out.

Asking Yourself Some Tough Questions

After you decide which freelance position you're uniquely qualified for, you must still consider two important issues:

- ✔ Will freelancing meet your life and career needs?
- ✔ What will you do if freelancing doesn't meet your life and career needs?

While some aspects of freelancing look appealing at first blush, given some thoughtful consideration, they may turn out to be the exact opposite of what you really want. I used to think that I wanted to be a full-time meeting planner; after a few jobs, I realized that doing it full time was like being on a treadmill that never stopped. Before you move into a freelance job, compare the reality of the job requirements with your dream of what you'd like it to be.

Major decisions (like changing your career) require some thought to the consequences down the road. Before you decide to freelance, think through what you want to happen, what is likely to happen, what you need to do to make it happen, and what you will do if it doesn't happen.

What are your career goals?

As you consider where your freelance work will take you, take a moment to think about where you see yourself in ten years. The freelance path can be an exciting one, and after you take that path, you may get caught up doing the work and forget your long-range plans.

✔ **Have a sense of career purpose.** Do you want to freelance forever? Is your freelance work just a stepping stone to a bigger business opportunity?

✔ **Include your career development goals as part of your business plan.** If you want to grow as a professional, what type of jobs will (and won't) help you do that? As a writer, after a certain number of years I decided I preferred not to do newsletters because they didn't add to my expertise or challenge me the way my consulting work does.

✔ **Make a list of activities that will contribute to your career advancement.** Can you join certain associations, attend conferences, attack new subjects? For example, as a marketing consultant, I've recently had to learn more about the Internet as a marketing tool.

Does freelancing help you achieve your career goals?

Will your freelancing experience add to your career marketability? What new skills do you expect to gain, and are they skills that you need in the future? What contacts will you make, and can they help you get where you want to go? What subjects will you learn about that make you more valuable as an employee or as a freelancer?

Some of the advantages you'll gain are broadened experience, the chance to become a decision-maker, and the opportunity to be totally accountable for results. Those types of qualities are desirable no matter where you land. And after you've been in business for yourself, you've demonstrated your ability to take risks, manage multiple responsibilities, and be a success. Success speaks for itself and usually contributes to your ability to be a more effective manager.

Doing a stint as a freelancer can even contribute to your being able to move back into a corporate job at an even higher level because your accomplishment gives you enhanced credibility as a management candidate.

Those are some things you gain. What might you give up? Your corporate connections, for one thing. To move up in the corporate world you usually need to gain a foothold and move methodically into increasingly powerful positions. Taking a freelance timeout can result in your losing your place in line, so to speak. After you're out of the loop, you may have difficulty regaining visibility as a candidate for a corporate position.

When people use freelancing as an escape hatch, it can solve some short-term problems but create some long-term career obstacles. You may become so accustomed to working independently that you have difficulty re-entering the structure of a corporate office or taking orders from someone else. You may also be seen as a renegade, someone who is unsuited for a mainstream job. And if you have background in a particular industry and then you work outside the field, you may lose valuable insight and have to work hard to get back up to speed on the specialty area.

Can you sell your skills?

Certain jobs simply don't lend themselves to being sold on the street corner. You don't expect to see a freelance brain surgeon, and you probably wouldn't hire one if you did. People are accustomed to buying certain products and services from large, well-known, and reputable suppliers. For example, you may have difficulty selling freelance driveway repair, because people tend to be naturally skeptical of an individual doing something that expensive and on such a large scale. On the other hand, most people are accustomed to buying from freelance housecleaners and writers.

You must be able to sell your skill, and that means it should meet the following criteria:

- **Relatively easy to describe:** Can you explain what you do in one sentence? Can you write it in a letter? Can you put it on a business card or in a brochure?

- **Something you can demonstrate skill at:** What is your experience in the field? Have you done it successfully before? Can you show some examples of your work? Because I've never done any interior design outside of my own house, it would be pretty hard for me to sell myself as an interior designer. Likewise, I couldn't get an assignment doing computer training because I have no credentials and no experience. Just saying "Trust me, I can do this," isn't usually enough to convince someone to pay for your services.

Can you make the money you want and need?

If you've ever hired a freelancer, you've heard the hourly fees they charge. You may have thought, hey, $80 per hour times 40 hours a week is a lot of cash. That's right. With 2000 hours in the normal work year (with two weeks' vacation), that totals $160,000. Pretty good money for just about anyone.

But here's the rub: Unless you work 'round the clock, you'll never be able to *bill* 2000 hours. About 30 percent of your time will be consumed with administrative work, sales, and other things that you can't charge your clients for. And then with expenses and taxes, you're left with . . . well, less than $160,000.

As you mentally paint a picture of your freelance career, start by figuring out how much money you're actually living on now and project whether you can make that much on your own. Chapter 15 can help you figure out what the real numbers are likely to be.

Can you afford to give up the benefits of working for someone else?

I'm about to make a rash generalization: What freelancers miss most about working for someone else are the benefits. I feel confident about that statement, because I've heard just about every freelancer I know say it.

Here are a few of the benefits you may be accustomed to your company paying for, and which you forfeit when you go out on your own:

- ✔ **Insurance coverage including health, life, and disability:** You'll definitely have to get some coverage, and it may cost an arm and a leg.
- ✔ **Savings and investment plans:** You can start your own, but there won't be any company matching funds.
- ✔ **Vacation pay:** No work, no pay. That's the freelancers' story.
- ✔ **Sick leave:** No work, no pay. Feed your cold, and you starve your bank account.

Companies generally expect to pay about 30 percent or so of an individual's salary to provide them with benefits. If you're making $50,000, your employer is investing about another $15,000 in your well-being for benefits. And because an employer buys in bulk, it gets a better rate than you will. So when you leave, you're giving up a lot more than your salary.

Can you provide the same benefits for yourself and your family as a freelancer? Sure, but you'll have to significantly increase your income to come out even. It helps if you have a spouse who is employed by a company, and you can get benefits for yourself and your family through that organization.

Is the life realistic for you?

My daughter has two small children and runs her own desktop-publishing business from home. When she had her first child, she expected to work when the baby was napping. The only problem was, the baby didn't sleep at night, and he didn't nap in the daytime, either. Her work plans were shot. Working at home was unrealistic in her family situation, and she ended up having to get some help.

A friend of mine and father of four also tried working at home with kids. When clients called, it was impossible to keep the children quiet. Because the sound of kids screaming in the background significantly detracted from his credibility as a professional, he eventually had to rent office space. He found that working at home wasn't a realistic work situation for him.

Will freelancing complement your family's lifestyle?

Few full-time freelancers can afford to live by a rigid schedule, regularly working in their offices from 9 to 5 and taking off every weekend. If your family needs a rigid routine, and is accustomed to having every weekend free to go camping or attend soccer tournaments, you'll need to make a solid commitment to maintain such a disciplined schedule.

By the same token, when you're a freelancer, you can easily take off at unusual times, like skipping work on Wednesday afternoon to attend a kindergarten play. I find it's easiest to take a long weekend or occasionally, a long vacation. Being willing to take advantage of spur-of-the-moment opportunities helps keep freelancing fun.

Another consideration is how your spouse or children's lives will be affected by your out-of-the-ordinary schedule. What if your spouse works the night shift and sleeps during the day? Would that work if your freelance accounting job requires you to work in your home in the daytime? What if your work as an event planner takes you away at night and on weekends? Will you get to see your family enough?

Take your family's needs and habits into consideration and try to envision how they will fit with your working for yourself.

Are you ready and able, but most of all, willing?

You may have the skills, the training, the credentials, and clients waiting in the wings. All these are critical factors in achieving freelance success. More important, however, is that you're willing to give the time and energy to pursuing your new career. In the beginning you may have to work many more hours than you're accustomed to. In fact, your every waking moment may be devoted to thinking about where and how you'll get business and how to satisfy your clients. With passion for what you do, you can go a long way; without it, you may be embarking on a long, hard road.

A freelancer's prerogative

After you've tread the freelance path for awhile, you may discover it's not for you. If that's the case, you can always change your mind. My friend and former associate, Timothy Powell, is a tremendously talented, energetic, organized, and conscientious person who loves to learn. As my assistant, he ran my business and a lot of my personal life, from dealing with financial issues to buying furniture to protecting me from unwanted sales people. He enjoys serving others and decided he would try to work as a freelancer. Everyone predicted that Tim's business would be a raging success.

In a few months, however, Timothy discovered that he wasn't cut out to be his own boss. He became uncharacteristically unmotivated. "I'm probably 95 percent self-directed when I'm working for someone else, but I found it very difficult to create my own structure. To feel comfortable, I needed the five percent push that a boss contributes."

Tim has returned to working for others and says he's not likely to go out on his own again. "I believe I'm a great number two person. That's my niche. But working for myself? Not something I would enjoy again."

Taking Steps if Freelancing Doesn't Work

There is a chance that your grand experiment won't work out the way you hope. Then what? Like a good Boy Scout, be prepared. You're better off thinking about the possibilities now than being caught off guard with no fallback position. You can take the following steps to safeguard yourself in case you need to re-enter the traditional workplace:

- ✔ **Maintain your contacts.** Stay in touch with people who have helped you get where you are and with those you may need sometime down the road. After you've lost touch, it's a lot tougher to place a call asking for a job.

- ✔ **Be positive about the people you work with.** Don't burn bridges, bad-mouth the corporate world, or criticize your old employer. You never know who your boss will be, especially when you're on the outside looking in. You may be surprised at who moves up that ladder while you're gone.

- ✔ **Don't tell people you'd never consider going back.** When people are convinced you are supremely content freelancing, they certainly won't try to lure you into a job. And even though you may not want a job, you'd at least like to know who wants you and what your possibilities may be. What's the worst thing that can happen? You'll be flattered with job offers you don't want.

> ✔ **Keep your portfolio up to date.** Track your successes, your awards, your client compliments, your professional designations, your work samples, anything that shows how accomplished you are today. I've had freelancers come to me with outdated work samples, which don't show me a lot about their work, but does show me that their planning and management skills aren't so hot.

After you've freelanced, you're a more experienced and valuable employee. You can get another job. If you've done your homework, you've developed contacts at a variety of companies. You're in an even better position today to get a job than you were before.

Chapter 4

Laying the Groundwork for Your New Life

In This Chapter

▶ Writing your business plan

▶ Deciding when to make your move

▶ Networking for fun and profit

▶ Making the break from your old work life

*I*f you're considering freelancing, as much as you may want to simply yell "Geronimo!" and leap from your current position, don't do it. Even daredevil skydivers use a parachute. You greatly enhance your chances of success if you have a carefully devised plan for "jumping out" of your job. From doing your research to building a contact list, a lot of safety nets can help you mentally prepare for the change. This chapter helps you think methodically about how to get from your sky-high dreams to solid ground without cracking up.

Scouring the Planet for Information

The first step toward becoming successful in freelancing is to become knowledgeable. While this book is a good place to discover the ins and outs of freelancing in general, to become even more prepared, you must also become a *subject matter expert;* that is, a guru in your own profession.

Read everything you can get your hands on about your area of expertise. Good resources to tap include the Internet, your library, and bookstores. Talk to people, your friends in the business, members of professional associations, and recognized experts in your field. Check out competing companies. Don't leave any stone unturned. Find out everything there is to know on your subject, and you'll be the hottest freelancer in town even before you hang out your shingle. If you're the world's expert in your field, how can you not be a success?

Making a Plan

If you want to get across town, you can zigzag around the streets, or you can look at a map of the city and follow the shortest distance between points. Either way, you may arrive at the same place, but you'll be a lot more likely to get there faster if you know where you're headed.

Start with a *business plan,* which says the following:

- ✔ Here's where I'm going (what I'm going to do).
- ✔ Here's how I'll get there (how you're going to do it).

Don't let the term *business plan* intimidate you. Every company that goes into business needs a business plan. Your plan doesn't need to look like a complicated legal document. It's simply a map or blueprint for making your business run. Check out *Business Plans For Dummies* by Paul Tiffany and Steven Peterson (Hungry Minds, Inc.) for painless tips and tricks on writing your own plan.

Knowing why you need a plan

A business plan can help you do the following:

- ✔ Figure out what you need to do.
- ✔ Point out when you need to do it.
- ✔ Provide signals that help you stay on track.
- ✔ Help you figure out when you've accomplished your goal.

You may think, "I'll never follow the plan." That's okay. Simply developing the plan helps you think through some action steps, and that process alone is worth the effort.

Ideally, you'll develop your business plan before you make your move to leave your job. That's when it can be most helpful. Even if you've been in business for a while, a plan can get you back on track or provide the direction you need to become even more successful.

If you're planning to borrow money to start your business, you need a business plan to show a potential lender why you are a good risk. A business plan demonstrates that you have good critical-thinking skills, substantial knowledge about your business and its potential, and a head for numbers. That's what an investor is interested in: The likelihood that you'll make money and pay back the loan. Even if you're only going to invest your own hard-earned savings in your business, you owe it to yourself to put in the time and the thinking to produce a plan. If you haven't thought things out carefully enough to create a plan, you may not be ready to go into business.

Understanding what's in a business plan

Pretend you're a banker considering whether to invest in You, Inc. You'd want to know how the company will function so you can judge whether it will make money or not. You want to see that the person running the company has carefully considered how to protect your investment. This is what a business plan will do. A typical business plan includes this information:

- ✔ **Description of the products or services:** What will you sell? If it is a product, how will you produce it?

- ✔ **How the company will be organized:** Sole proprietorship, limited liability corporation, and so on.

- ✔ **Legal issues or regulatory agencies that affect or govern your business:** Selling financial products requires licensing; writing press releases about corporate investor relations requires that you follow Securities and Exchange Commission (SEC) rules; and acting as a certified public accountant (CPA) requires certification and ongoing professional education credits.

- ✔ **Explanation of the competitive advantage:** What makes your product or service special? How is it different from other similar products or services?

- ✔ **Competitive information:** Who else provides this product or service? What are their strengths and weaknesses? What do they charge for this product or service? Are the competitors local, regional, or national?

- ✔ **Financial information:** What will your start-up expenses be (include everything, such as legal fees, phone hook-up, computer equipment purchases, printing stationery, and so on)? What will your ongoing monthly expenses be? How much can you charge for your product or service? How many hours per week can you bill in the first month, two months, and six months? Will you need to borrow money to get started? How long will it take you to *break even;* that is, have your income catch up with your expenses? How much do you expect the business to grow, and how long will it take?

- ✔ **Marketing information:** How will you sell your product or service? Who are your key target clients? How will you reach your potential clients? What role will advertising play in your plan? How can you get public relations coverage?

No one on earth should know more about your business and its potential than you. When you've answered all of these questions, you have a clear picture of what your business needs to succeed and how to go about achieving that success.

Finding information

Some of the information you need, you already know, such as what you plan to sell and who will buy it. Collecting other information may take some effort. Your detective skills and curiosity are your best allies in the search for business plan information. Sources I find helpful include the following:

- ✔ The local Chamber of Commerce
- ✔ Small Business Administration (SBA), which has its own Internet site
- ✔ Convention and Visitors Bureau
- ✔ The library, using trade journal articles, *Who's Who in Business,* back issues of your local business newspaper, the business section of your daily newspaper, and other sources your librarian may recommend
- ✔ The Internet, using search engines
- ✔ Government agencies, all of which are available on the Internet
- ✔ Professional associations, which usually have trend reports on their industry
- ✔ Magazines on specific topics, such as advertising or marketing
- ✔ A walking tour through the area where you will be doing business

A success formula

How will you define success? You may be perfectly content if you eke out a living, because being on your own could be reward enough. If you want to borrow money to get started, though, that kind of success formula may not be enough to make your lender happy. When borrowing money, you need to put on your accounting hat (or hire someone who wears one).

Bankers want to know that you'll be able to pay back any money you borrow, with interest. You need to talk in terms they can understand, and that means using their formula for demonstrating how your business will succeed. A key term is *projected cash flow,* which means how much money you believe you will make over the next three to five years. The way you determine projected cash flow is as follows: Show revenues (what you take in) minus expenses (what you pay out). The remainder is your *net cash inflow* (positive) or *net cash outflow* (negative). Believe it or not, many businesses project a negative cash flow at some point, and that's okay as long as you can show that it resolves itself quickly.

Timing Your Move

If you've written a business plan, you have a clear idea of the costs of freelancing and the amount of time you have to wait before money comes rolling in. So unless you're confronted with the possibility of being outplaced — or have already been downsized, reengineered, or merged — make your move at the most advantageous time. Timing can make or break your business for a number of reasons. The following sections explain why.

Counting your money

In order to be able to eat in the first year of your freelance career, you have to stash some money away before you leave your day job. Here's why:

- ✓ **It takes awhile to build a freelance business.** Unless you've lined up specific projects before you leave your company, you may not have any paying work for several months. Table 4-1 shows you that getting up to speed financially takes time. Even if you've lined up work in advance, you're unlikely to jump directly into full-time freelance projects. Expect to slowly build your business over a period of time.

- ✓ **After you send out your first bill, you'll suffer through a lag time of a minimum of 15 to 30 days before you receive payment.** If your clients are slow to pay, you may wait as long as 90 days. Table 4-1 shows that at the end of your first five months, the amount you've received may be substantially lower than the amount you've billed. You expect to collect all of the money eventually, but it may take awhile before you catch up.

Table 4-1	Getting Up to Speed
Billed	*Received*
January 15: $0	$0
February 1: $1,500	Feb 28: $0
March 20: $3,200	March 31: $1,500
April 15: $4,000	April 30: $2,800
May 31: $4,000	May 31: $3,000
Total billed: $12,700	Total received: $7,300

The saying goes, "You can never be too rich," and I like to add that you can never have too much money to get a business started. To be on the safe side, assume you won't make a penny for six months to a year, and set aside enough to live on during that time. Plan not only for living expenses, but also the costs to get your business started. Items like stationery and office equipment can add up fast (see Chapter 6).

Considering your current employer's benefits

Financial reasons can make delaying your move a smart decision. Perhaps you own stock options that are about to mature. You certainly wouldn't dream of leaving your current employer before you take advantage of those. Or maybe you won a sales award and the prize is a cruise that's coming up in two months. Who could miss that? Are you due a bonus at the end of the year? Wait until you've collected. Evaluate anything you could potentially lose by leaving your current job and weigh the potential benefits of freelancing. You may find that temporarily sitting tight can pay off in the long run.

Thinking through seasonality or event relationships

Some businesses are seasonal or benefit from their relationship to certain events or activities. The following are some examples:

- ✔ Florists know that their busiest days of the year are Valentine's Day and Mother's Day.

- ✔ Annual report writers expect to be especially busy around Christmas, because many companies publish their annual reports between March and June.

- ✔ Real estate sales tend to drop off from October to January because people don't want to move after their kids start school or during the holidays.

- ✔ Swimming pool contractors know that summertime generates the majority of their income.

 What seasonal or event timing factors may affect your business? Pick a time that will be most advantageous to you. Give yourself some *lead time* (that's pronounced LEED time not LED time), which is how long it takes between the time you put your name in front of the public to the time it takes to actually get hired to do a freelance job. You may have to contact people several times before they give you a project, so you certainly want more than one chance to sell yourself before your busy season comes and goes. If you write annual reports, for example, start your freelance business no later than July so you'll have time to let everyone know you're available before they're hiring for the next publications. You may be aware of other considerations that may contribute to or detract from your freelance efforts. Build your business schedule to take these considerations into account.

Everything takes longer and costs more than you anticipate. You need lead time between the time you start a project and the time you actually collect any fees, so build in a comfortable buffer to bridge the gap.

You get the least business from the people you expect it from the most and the most business from the people you never expected any business from. Just because your associates say they'll hire you when you leave doesn't mean they really can or will. Don't count any chickens until they've put up the scratch.

Writing a schedule

Because you're about to be a one-person juggling act, plan your time in writing. Create a calendar for yourself showing each week of the first three months of your business. Indicate what actions you need to take each week (from deciding on your company name to having stationery printed), what calls or visits you'll make each week, how you'll follow up, what news releases you'll send out, and so on. You have a lot to do and a short time to do it, so map out your plan. After you've seen it all on paper, you may realize that you need more time to prepare than you thought. Or if you're lucky, you may be able to get everything done and get started freelancing sooner than you planned.

Creating a Strong Network of Contacts

During the time you're preparing to move into freelancing, become a social butterfly: Getting to know people is a vitally important piece of creating your new business. It's not what you know; it's who you know and who knows you! Never forget that. The most important thing you do in your freelance business is to develop contacts.

Networking while in your current job

The time to start building your network of contacts is before you leave your day job. After you leave your job, it will be pretty obvious to everyone that you're calling with an ulterior motive. I don't know about you, but I hate feeling like I'm begging. I prefer to start early to cultivate a contact. Then, when you've established a relationship, you can pick up the phone without feeling like you're obviously selling.

How and where can you find contacts?

- ✔ At your own company, by expanding your contact with your peers

- ✔ At professional association meetings

- ✔ On task forces that bring people from different companies together

- ✔ At other companies, using your existing position as an excuse to call people in similar jobs to share thoughts and ask for advice

- ✔ In volunteer groups that attract professionals

- ✔ At the gym, the golf course, the doctor's office, the grocery store, and so on. You are now in the business of talking to people everywhere you go. Remember, there's a potential client around every frozen food counter.

Business people joke about *rubber-chicken-and-green-pea lunches,* by which they mean awards lunches, not-for-profit fundraising events, and other sometimes tedious gatherings where the food is mass-produced and not so appetizing. As a freelancer or potential freelancer, these events become the most fascinating events in your life. They give you a chance to meet lots of people, many of whom belong in your network.

It takes more than money

I have a friend who has been employed in traditional positions since he started working. I'll call him "Mr. A," because he doesn't want his current employer to know that he's considering other options. "Unfortunately, I don't have much impetus to get out of here, because this is a great company," he says.

Despite his contentment, Mr. A's dream is to be in business for himself. For five or six years, he has been exploring possibilities and trying to create a sensible plan for becoming a freelancer. He has interviewed me and other freelancers, collected ideas in a folder, copied articles, and made a list of ten excellent reasons he wants to become his own boss.

As he has been building his plan — and his courage — to take on the world single-handedly, he's seriously considering making the move. "I've put aside some money for this and having put it on paper, I can see that this is something I could actually do. For the first time, I'm beyond it being just a dream." Still, he has to make the emotional leap to entrepreneurship.

Becoming a freelancer is a process, not a single action. It takes time to work through not only the financial considerations, but also the emotional ones. You have to be ready, and it may take years to reach that point. I'm betting Mr. A is almost there.

Continuing your alliances

After you embark on your freelance career, you must plan time each week to get out of your office. Yes, I know you became a freelancer so you could avoid meetings and work in your pajamas. But you will have to do lunch, take a meeting, and go places. Being visible is absolutely essential, because people need to be reminded that you're around. I have generated huge amounts of business just by strolling through the offices of my biggest client and saying hello to people. As people see me it jogs their memories of projects they've been meaning to call about or of services I offer. They may say, "Oh, hey, I've been wondering, is this something you can do?" The project they have in mind may be an albatross around their necks that they can't figure out what to do with. They see me and suddenly realize that there's someone who can drag that smelly bird off their shoulders.

Meeting strangers

Networking isn't really that hard, even with people you don't know, because as a freelancer, you can meet people from all walks of life by asking for advice. What more pain-free way is there to start developing a relationship? (Translate "developing a relationship" to "making a sales call," because that's what it is.)

Here are a few suggestions for getting your foot in the door by asking advice:

- ✔ **Almost everyone is flattered by a request to interview them as experts.** You can generally get referrals from friends and associates to their friends and associates. Call one and ask him (or her) to lunch so you can pick his brain. (Select a restaurant that's conducive to talking and pay the bill.)

- ✔ **Call total strangers you've read about in business journals and tell them you admire their successes or their philosophies or whatever you can truthfully compliment.** I've done this and have found people who are very receptive. Of course, some people are naturally skeptical, so don't be discouraged if your invitation is met with suspicion.

- ✔ **Develop a *hit list* of managers at the top ten corporate clients you'd like to have.** Call and tell them you're interviewing managers at top companies. Very few people will turn you down.

Whatever you do, don't waste people's time. Make a list of intelligent questions about the person's business, trends they observe in business, what they may use a freelancer for, how they would suggest you market your services, or a million other things. The more prepared you are, the more useful this interview will be for you, and the more likely your new ally will be to take you seriously.

Back in your office, put these people on your mailing list, and make your first mailing to them a brief thank-you note like the following, but be creative!

> Dear Jeff,
>
> Your name will be at the top of my "indebted list" when I kick off my freelance business. You were very kind to take time to meet with me and answer my questions about how you've used marketing to build your decorating business. I'm beginning to appreciate how important time is to a self-employed person.
>
> I plan to try your suggestion about sending out a direct-mail piece to my clients. It's something I hadn't thought about.
>
> Thanks again. I look forward to a time when I can reciprocate.
>
> Sincerely,
>
> Dana Jowers

Everyone's favorite subject is themselves. To be successful at networking, you just have to ask people about themselves and listen. Selling isn't about telling clients what you can do for them. It's about letting them tell you what you can do for them.

Networking acquaintances can help you in two ways:

- ✔ When you're freelancing, they can send you business.
- ✔ If you decide to quit freelancing, they can help you find a job.

When I began freelancing, I had a wide-eyed innocent belief that clients would hire me for the sheer power of my talent. I envisioned that my reputation would be known far and wide because of my high-quality work. Yeah, right. Instead, the majority of my work comes from my established contacts. One person tells another, and another, and so on.

Don't think that corporate clients are the only sources worth pursuing. You may be amazed at the referrals you get from small business connections, as well as people who are at both the top and the bottom of the ladder. Cultivate the approval and support of people throughout your business network, and you'll find that business comes from all corners. Besides, having the help of your client's administrative assistant is a godsend.

Moonlighting for fun and profit

From the time you decide to freelance until you actually do it full time, flex your freelancing muscles by moonlighting. *Moonlighting* — working another job while you're still doing your full-time job — can be a great way to make a transition; it's a wonderful insurance policy against spending several months without income. By moonlighting, you can create a bridge from your old job to your new one and save the extra money you make to cover your start-up costs.

Of course, your current employer may frown upon such a practice. Naturally, the last thing you would ever want to do is conduct your freelance business during your employer's work time or squander all your energy on moonlighting to the detriment of your employer's projects. And ethically, it isn't right to compete with your employer while you work there. But if you can work out a way to do it, moonlighting is a smart way to ease into a freelance career.

Line up projects that you can accomplish in your off time. This lets you test the waters in several ways:

- ✔ You practice your freelance skill without having to depend solely upon it for a living.

- ✔ You try out your organizational techniques, working out the kinks in a relatively safe environment.

- ✔ You set aside the money you make moonlighting as a nest egg for your new business venture. Because you're not accustomed to living on that money, you'll never miss it.

- ✔ You develop clients who may hire you as a freelancer.

- ✔ You build client references for future use.

Making the Break from Your Old Work Life

As you anticipate your new life, you may also feel a twinge of sadness at leaving your old life behind. Initially, you may say, "Good riddance!" but at some point, you may miss some things about your old job. Prepare yourself not only for the joy of a new adventure, but also for the discomfort of change.

Keep in mind that leaving is actually not an event; it's a process. Ease yourself through it and give yourself plenty of time to make the transition to your new environment. Knowing what to expect may help you adjust. The following sections describe some experiences that can be unsettling and give you ways to create more comfort for yourself until you become accustomed to your new way of life.

Leaving friends and gaining friends

You can take your friends with you to some degree, at least for a while. Schedule lunch dates, go out for drinks, or plan social occasions together. You can maintain relationships as long as you put the effort into them, but don't depend on others to think of you. Out of sight, out of mind prevails in these situations. Take the initiative, however, and you'll be rewarded with many lasting friendships.

The flip side is that you may also find yourself drifting away from even your closest buddies. Eventually, you'll be out of the loop on what's happening at your old company. They'll work on projects you're not familiar with, offer stories about the latest office gossip on people you don't know, or discuss company developments that no longer affect or interest you. At the same time, you'll meet new people and travel in different circles, too, and you may find you have less and less to talk to old friends about.

One of my dearest friends refers to the *mobility of relationships,* which means your willingness to let your relationships ebb and flow depending on time and circumstances. When you move from one life to another, try practicing that philosophy. In the long run, you may be able to build an even larger stable of true friends.

Finding new resources

Giving up the resources of a company can pose a challenge, and that's especially true if you've been relying on someone else to take care of the nitty-gritty details. Even the simplest tasks, like sending an overnight package or binding a proposal, can seem like a complicated process to the new freelancer who doesn't know one end of a hole punch from another. Becoming a do-it-yourselfer takes time and practice, and other freelancers can give you tips about where and how to get such tasks done quickly and efficiently. (See Chapter 8 for tips on hiring help.) The result of your helplessness is that you'll soon learn a lot of new skills, and you'll probably appreciate your former coworkers a lot more!

Facing the unknown

Although the corporate world can surprise you, for the most part, life is fairly predictable day to day. You know when to get to work and when to leave, who does what, when your paycheck will arrive, and where the cafeteria or break room is. You can predict who will call you, what they'll be working on, and what kind of raise you can expect.

By contrast, freelancing is just one giant unknown after another. Practically nothing is predictable: your salary, your projects, even your daily activities. Does that strike you as a problem? If so, you can look at this unpredictability in one of two ways:

- ✔ **The unknown is scary.** Something bad can happen any minute.

- ✔ **The unknown is exciting.** You may find a fabulous surprise around every corner!

I actually love the unpredictability of my work because I consider it a gift every time the phone rings.

To combat some of the unpredictability that's inherent in freelancing, create a structure for yourself that allows you to predict certain events. Even setting up a standard lunch time or setting aside time each week to do bookkeeping can help you feel more in control of your work life. One freelancer I know schedules her lunch to accommodate watching her favorite TV show.

Having explained the importance of planning, I must admit something: A large number of the freelancers I know didn't plan a thing. That's right. It is not only possible, but probable, that if you have the personality to jump into free-lancing with both feet, you also have the guts to make it work without putting a single thing on paper.

While I believe that planning is the wisest path, I can't say that you'll fail if you don't plan. I know too many people who are raking in dough just through the strength of their energy and their desire to succeed. I speculate that the explanation is simple: People who go out on their own are action-oriented risk takers who don't take no for an answer. They do whatever it takes to make their businesses work, and when they see something that isn't working, they change it. If you're one of those people who just has to leap before you look, go for it. Just by being tough and unwavering in your commitment, you can probably make it work.

Dealing with buyer's remorse

Have you heard of *buyer's remorse?* This is the time when a person invests in something rather large — like a house — and then questions the decision afterward. At some point, you may have buyer's remorse about your decision to quit your job.

The first few days of freelancing may be totally invigorating as you get settled in your new digs and start cranking up your marketing efforts. Somewhere along the way, though, you may wake up one morning and ask yourself why you ever thought you could be a freelancer. It could be one of those days when no checks are in the mail and no appointments are on the horizon, or it could be the morning after five 14-hour killer days in row, with no end in sight. Either way, planning your move can help you anticipate and cope with those times more easily.

Being a freelancer is like having a baby. It hurts a lot at the time, but most people forget the pain. Hang in there, and one day you'll have beautiful offspring: your very own business.

Part II
Opening Your Doors for Business

The 5th Wave   By Rich Tennant

FREELANCER NED WILLIS CONSULTS WITH A MEMBER OF HIS TECHNICAL STAFF

"...and that's pretty much all there is to converting a document to an HTML file."

In this part . . .

Now that you're the boss, you have the power to decide how your company runs. That means wrangling with a few legal issues, juggling your many roles, and taking some commonsense approaches to protecting yourself and your investment.

This part gives you guidance on how to form your company, organize your office, conduct your workday, get expert help, and take care of some of the not-so-glamorous aspects of minding your business.

Chapter 5

Forming Your Company

*B*eing in business for yourself is more than an exercise in playing house. After you open your doors for business, you open yourself up to some legal issues that can get you in hot water. To protect yourself, you can create a company that can give you both legal advantages and tax advantages. This chapter familiarizes you with the kinds of legal business organizations available to you as a freelancer, the protection they offer, and the best ways to put forth a professional image.

Naming Your Game

If you've never had the fun of naming a child, naming your company is almost as good and is actually more challenging.

For several years, I worked as a sole proprietor, and I operated simply under my own name. When I decided to hire an assistant, we talked about how we would answer the phone. Having him answer "Susan Drake" didn't seem quite right. I also decided to incorporate at this time, and all the forms I had to fill out asked for the company name. I decided I needed a business identity — a name. The following sections help you decide whether you need a business name, and help you choose and test one, should you decide to go that route.

Deciding whether you need a name

Chances are, if you're just starting your business, you'll be getting business on the strength of your own personal name. People know and trust you, and you hope they'll hire you on the strength of your reputation. That's a good reason to use your name as at least part of your company name. I find a lot of freelancers tag "and Associates" onto their names, in an effort to make their companies seem like more than just one person operating out of the basement.

Conversely, using your name makes doing business difficult in some ways. For example, when you open a bank account, it's much clearer to have it under a distinct company name so there's no confusion about it being a business account. And when people ask you for your business name, it's easier to tell them Spellbinders, Inc. (my business name) than to explain that you do business under your name.

Choosing a name

Choosing an effective company name isn't a simple task, as Table 5-1 shows. You want a name that suits your business, that appeals to you, that isn't difficult to say or spell, and that won't be out of style in a few years.

Table 5-1	Do's and Don'ts of Picking a Company Name
A Business Name Should	*A Business Name Should Not*
Be memorable	Be too cutesy or trendy
Describe your business	Limit your business possibilities
Be simple and to the point	Be too long or complicated
Have a long life expectancy	Be hard to spell or pronounce

The following sections discuss several factors to consider: image, descriptiveness, timelessness, uniqueness, and emotional attachment.

Considering your image

Your name is what you are. The name you select should convey the image you want your company to have. Your desired image may be determined in many ways by the business you're in and the type of image someone in your business needs. For example, a financial advisor needs a name that conjures up an image of trustworthiness, prosperity, and other virtues people look for in someone who's telling them what to do with their money. You're well advised to go with something conservative, like "Smith and Adams Financial Services." Perhaps you'd personally like a more exciting name, but you can't afford to serve your own need and ignore what clients will think. A financial advisor certainly wouldn't want a company name like, "Skyrocket Financials," because it doesn't sound stable, and it also promises something you can't necessarily deliver (which is a legal no-no in the financial business).

Your professional or state board of certification may dictate what your legal entity name can be if you're an attorney or a CPA, for example. In fact, the board or state may even specify what type of legal entity you have to organize under.

Conversely, if you're in a business that's supposed to be creative, select something that shows how creative you can be. "Dog and Pony Productions" is a great name for a company that produces presentations (which are frequently called dog and pony shows by business folks) because it's different and it describes what the company does in a memorable way. "Working Behind the Scenes" is a neat name for a freelance video producer who prides herself on invisibly making productions effective. One of the most fun names I've heard lately is "Fireball Express" for a freelance advertising production troubleshooter who specializes in fast turnaround. The owner passes out a flyer that shows a picture of her in a fireman's pants, jacket, hat, holding an axe. It's an apt name for someone whose most important selling point is her ability to fight fires; that is, to troubleshoot problems. "The Quiet Riot" is a team of brothers who do training using theatrical methods and sound effects.

You may be able to express a quality or feature that you're selling in your name. "Cut-Rate Lawn Service" tells people that rock-bottom pricing is one of the features that distinguishes you from the competition. They may not expect quality, but they will expect a low price. "Dinah's Down-Home Cooking" would describe a catering service that features informal, country-style meals rather than upscale cuisine. "Andrea's Couturier" implies a more sophisticated, higher quality (and potentially more expensive) sewing service than "Becky's Quick Changes" alterations, which relies on speed as a primary selling feature.

Choosing a descriptive name

Choose a business name that tells people what you do. A good name for a writer named Bill Smith may be "Word Smith." "Politically Correct Public Relations" or "The Spin Doctor" may be an interesting name for a public relations person who specializes in political campaigns. "Contemporary Interior Design" describes an interior design firm that helps people create modern-looking homes versus traditional or antique looks.

Making it timeless

Assuming that you plan to be in business for a long time, choose a name with long-lasting appeal. Don't use trendy words or phrases that have a limited life or may have a tendency to go out of style. "Fast Fax Research" service would lose appeal quickly and seem antiquated in this Internet age.

Picking a unique name

Make your business name stand out from the crowd so that it will strike a chord with your clients. Run-of-the-mill names tend to be forgotten, and you certainly don't want that. Try it out in this example. Suppose you only use a printer occasionally. Which name would you remember: FRP Graphics, or Print Perfect? Unless the initials FRP mean something special to you, they could just as easily be GSG or DMZ. When a person picks up the phone book, they should be able to find you even if they can't exactly remember your name.

In the interest of creating something memorable or clever, some companies (big and small) reinvent the English language. They spell their names in a weird way, they run words together, or they put small letters and big letters in strange places. For example, you've seen the word "cut" spelled "kut." Imagine a name for a kids store called "JustlittleOnes." It's difficult to spell (and type), which, in my opinion, is a drawback for any company name. It almost ensures that every piece of paperwork you receive will be incorrect in some way!

Unless you have a huge marketing budget and expect to become an icon in your field, steer clear of such imaginative names. No one will be able to spell your name correctly, pronounce it correctly, or type it correctly. And when you answer your phone, the person on the other end will never know that Ready, Willing, and Able Accounting is actually, "RedyWill-ing and Abel."

Blending your emotional needs and your business needs

Choosing a company name is a business consideration, but it's also a personal and emotional investment. You have to choose a name that you can be excited about and live with for a long time.

When I chose the name of my company, Spellbinders, Inc., I argued with myself about using something more conservative, like Drake Marketing and Communications, or something with more pizzazz. On one hand, I felt that corporate clients may prefer the safe, traditional, businesslike sound of Drake Marketing and Communications. On the other, I wanted people to know they could expect something more exciting from our company. I finally selected Spellbinders because I believed it conveyed the kind of marketing and communications I sell: something out of the ordinary intended to "cast a spell" over an audience. I've had great success with that name and the rather Hollywood-esque stationery and business cards that go with it.

Testing your name

Select a few names you think you like and ask people what they think of when they see or hear the names. Request that they tell you what kind of company they expect to work with when they hear the name.

Ask people who may use the service, such as coworkers or potential clients. Although your next-door neighbor may have an opinion, it shouldn't count much unless your neighbor is similar to the audience you want to reach.

Protecting your name and obtaining licenses

If you're a sole proprietor, as long as you use your own name as a part of your business name, you can do so without registering the name. And chances are that unless you have a common name, no one else will be using it for a business.

If you select a business name that doesn't contain your name, you have to register your business name under a *fictitious business name statement*. Sometimes this is called *Doing Business As (your business name)*. You'll also hear this referred to as a *DBA*. More formal legal business organizations, including corporations and limited liability corporations (see the "Organizing Your Company" section, later in this chapter) must also register their names.

Registering your name provides protection to you in two ways:

- ✔ It ensures that you're not infringing on the rights of someone else who may already be using the name.
- ✔ It prevents others from using your name after you've started using it.

Contact your local county clerk or your Secretary of State to find out exactly what forms you must complete. This is usually a rote process of applying and paying a small fee. If you prefer, you can hire an attorney to conduct a search of your proposed name to make sure no one else has already registered it in your state. An attorney can handle the legal aspects of having your name registered (see Chapter 8 for information on hiring an attorney).

You must have a bank account in whatever business name you're using, otherwise you won't be able to cash checks made out to the company name. For example, if you're using a spiffy name just for your clients' sake, and they make out a check to your spiffy company name instead of your own personal name, you won't be able to do anything with the check. It can be embarrassing to go back to a client and ask them to reissue the check. It sort of defeats the purpose of having a spiffy name in the first place. When you're ready to open your account, take your business license with you to the bank.

On a larger scale, you can also trademark your name and any graphics or symbols that accompany it (your logo). Just by using the name and symbol, you establish your ownership of it, although it can be challenged. To formally register your name, you must file a registration request with and pay a fee to the U. S. Patent and Trademark Office. After you've received your approval, you can use the symbol (r) (which stands for registered trademark) with your name.

In addition to purchasing your business license, you may have to have a special license for the type of business you operate. A catering service, for example, may be required to have a health department permit that allows employees to handle food, and may be subject to inspections. A lawn-service employee may be required to have a special driver's license for driving trucks that are loaded with equipment.

Organizing Your Company

With the details of your name aside, you're ready to form your company. You may be itching to put "Inc." after your name, but is that really what's most advantageous for you? You can pursue several legal avenues, covered in the following sections.

Weighing the advantages and disadvantages

You can choose from four types of organizations:

- ✔ Sole proprietorship
- ✔ Limited liability corporation (LLC)
- ✔ Subchapter S corporation
- ✔ C corporation

Maintaining professional certifications

In certain careers, to call yourself a professional you must be a member of a professional association and/or maintain your accreditation by completing specified professional-education classes. This holds true for certified public accountants (CPAs), financial planning professionals, insurance brokers, and so on. If your profession requires such credentials, you certainly want to maintain them, not only to remain in compliance with standards, but also because they make you look good to your clients.

Even if your chosen career doesn't require such accreditation, you may find it advantageous to pursue additional credentials in your field. For example, in the communications industry, you can earn a designation through the International Association of Business Communicators that says you have passed their accreditation test and have agreed to uphold their performance and ethics standards. It impresses some clients that you can put professional letters after your name.

The two areas in which freelancers should compare these types of organization are in the following:

  ✔ Tax consequences

  ✔ Reporting requirements

With regard to tax consequences, you should know the phrase *pass-through entity*. A pass-through entity is one for which the income that the organization makes is passed through directly to the individual's tax return. This is the case with a sole proprietorship, an LLC, and a subchapter S corporation. For a C corporation, the organization is considered a separate entity and is taxed in a different way. The tax rate is typically higher for a corporation.

These vary from the simplest (sole proprietorship) to fairly complex (C corporation). Before you decide which one is for you, call a professional (see Chapter 8 for information on hiring expert assistance). Ask an attorney which legal setup is best, and ask an accountant which one provides the greatest tax advantages. After you know the pros and cons of each type of business organization, you can decide which one is for you. The following sections briefly describe how these organizations work.

Organizing as a sole proprietorship

A sole proprietorship is a simple way of doing business: You own it, you run it, and you have very little interference from anyone else. Legally, a sole proprietorship doesn't require you to form a company. You may need a business license, but that's about all. I ran my business this way for several years and found it to be hassle-free.

The biggest drawback to being a sole proprietorship is that you have no protection against personal losses or liability in case something happens to your business.

If you find it overwhelming to consider forming a legal organization right off the bat, remember that it's easy to start as a sole proprietorship and become a legal corporation later, if you choose. It's a lot harder to go the other way, from a corporation to a sole proprietorship.

Forming a limited liability corporation (LLC)

The limited liability corporation (LLC) is slightly more formal than a sole proprietorship and has become a popular method of organization among small companies. It protects you against personal liability for the company's losses (unless, of course, you've personally guaranteed a debt). Even though an LLC is called a corporation, it really isn't; instead, it's a cross between a partnership (which most experts do not recommend for freelancers) and a corporation. It does, however, provide some of the protection of a corporation, without some of the hassles.

Forming an LLC requires more paperwork than forming a sole proprietorship. Having an attorney do this for you could cost over $1,000. You can actually set up an LLC yourself, but you may find the paperwork quite a hassle. Some states have restrictions on who can form an LLC, so check with your attorney to make sure your business qualifies.

TRUE STORY

Ain't no big thang

As far as Robin Thomas is concerned, forming her publishing company, Black Pants Publishing, LLC, was a non-event. "It was easier than I thought; no big deal," she says.

Robin has been a marketing expert for a number of years, working primarily with financial institutions. She decided one day that she wanted to get into the publishing business. "I didn't know a thing about publishing, but I felt it was something I wanted to get involved in," she says. "Coincidentally, my husband wanted to write books, so it seemed like a good match." Robin spent six months immersing herself in the book-publishing business, educating herself about everything from bar codes to book cover design to distributors. She attended workshops, read everything she could get her hands on, and talked to the experts. With all that information under her belt, she was convinced she wanted to seriously jump in. She was ready to make things official.

"I did the trademark research myself, using the Internet to do most of it. I could've hired an attorney to do that, but there's so much available online now that I decided I could do that part myself." She looked for Web sites with the Black Pants name or a variation, and she didn't find any. She also researched publishing

company names and, not surprisingly, found none by the name Black Pants. ("We chose that because our books are like a pair of black pants — they work anywhere.") She registered the name with the U. S. Patent and Trademark Office at their Web site. The next step was to get an Internet domain name, reserving the name blackpantspublishing.com. Finally, she called a lawyer, who did the paperwork to form her limited liability corporation. "All in all, it was a really simple process."

"Even though I had been freelancing for about a year, I hadn't formed a separate legal entity for that business. Getting Black Pants registered and forming the LLC has given me more of a feeling of commitment to take this endeavor seriously. Psychologically, it would be more difficult to turn back."

Even though the legal aspects of the business were no big deal, Robin is excited about the prospects for her company, especially the name, Black Pants Publishing. "The name Black Pants is weird, but women get it," says Robin. "When Hillary Clinton was elected, she was quoted as saying that during the campaign she had gone through six black pants suits. At that point, we knew we had a winner, too."

Your company can become an LLC in one of two ways:

- ✔ Request information from your state. Fill out the papers very carefully and send them in with your fee.
- ✔ Hire an attorney to file the paperwork for you.

Creating a corporation

A corporation is a legal entity separate from its owners, and for a small business owner, forming a corporation is more trouble and expense than an LLC (see the preceding section). You can form your corporation in one of two ways: Both are legal entities, but they're taxed differently by the IRS:

- ✔ **C corporation:** This is by far the most complex of the potential organizational systems you can choose from. For a C corporation, the corporation itself must file separate tax returns and meet federal and state requirements for reporting results. Not many freelancers consider this alternative.
- ✔ **S corporation:** An S corporation is simpler than a C corporation in that owners (shareholders) report profits or losses from the corporation on their personal income tax returns. Next to an LLC, this is probably the best alternative for a freelancer.

Chapter 6

Organizing Your Office

In This Chapter

▶ Choosing a work home

▶ Furnishing your space

▶ Getting wired

*F*orget that nice, high-speed copier that collates, staples, and practically walks your copies to the mailroom. Forget the interior designer who ordered your desk and hung your paintings. Forget the free cell phone, the corporate credit card, and an assistant who sets up your files. You're working for yourself, and you get to be office manager, decorator, equipment buyer, and file clerk — all in one. Where do you begin?

Begin with this chapter, which tells you how to get yourself ready for the deluge of clients who will undoubtedly knock down your office door (wherever it may be).

Finding Office Space Away from (Or at) Home

Workspace is a special part of a freelancer's life. This is where you spend a sizable part of your day, and you owe it to yourself to design something comfortable and conducive to your work well-being.

The following discusses several factors that come into play when you're deciding where and how to locate your office.

✔ **Your budget:** Money is a pretty big consideration for most freelancers, because without any history, you can't predict how much money you're likely to make. You've set aside a certain nest egg for your first year, so decide how much of that you're prepared to spend on office space. If you don't already have office equipment, that may take a chunk out of your wallet, so think about whether you want to spend another sizable amount on leasing office space. After you're locked into a lease, you won't have the option to change your mind without paying a price. (See the "Leasing office space" section later in this chapter.)

If you have adequate room, working at home is certainly the most economical way to go. At least in your first year or two, being at home gives you a chance to see how things go and how much money you can count on each month. If you decide later that you need to rent office space, you'll have a better idea of what you need and how much you can afford.

I know freelancers who have tried both, and budget constraints usually play a part in their decision. Of course, leased office space looks more official and can contribute to a more professional image. But you are the only one who can decide how much you stand to benefit from that extra credibility, and if the cost is worth it.

✔ **The type of work you do:** Can you actually do your work from home? Most people have limited space in their houses in which they can set up an office. If your job requires a lot of equipment, the way a photo studio does, you may have a hard time making that work in a spare bedroom. On the other hand, many freelance jobs aren't space-intensive. Before you decide where to locate, figure out what you'll need to put in the space and plan from there.

Is your business the kind that needs high visibility? Everyone can use exposure, of course, but some types of business don't depend on it. Consultants, for example, can be hidden away in office buildings where passersby don't really see them much. In fact, many freelancers would discourage *foot traffic,* that is, people who just drop in. Strip mall offices, for example, may get a high number of drop-ins from solicitors as well as from undesirable characters. This type of facility may not be for you.

A different type of business may benefit from being seen. For example, if you operate a lawn service, you count a large percentage of the general public as potential customers. A highly visible office is a way for people to gain awareness of your services.

✔ **Your work style:** I have friends who simply can't discipline themselves to go into their home offices. When they're at home, they lollygag in front of the TV or hang out reading a magazine. They need the structure of an office in another building to feel that they're officially at work.

Are you the type who can comfortably and efficiently work at home? If so, make your office as businesslike as possible. I set up an office that's almost as well equipped as any corporate office. My dad always said you can do any job if you have the right tools, and I insist on having everything I need to do my work. When I "go to work," I have no problem feeling that I'm at my job, and I'm seldom tempted to lie in bed with a book.

Table 6-1 sums up the pros and cons of working at home and working in a leased office space.

Table 6-1	Home Office Versus an Away Office
Home Office Pros	***Home Office Cons***
A three-step commute	Harder to separate work life and home life
Safe environment	May disturb family members
"Cafeteria" onsite	"Cafeteria" onsite can lead to constant snacking
Casual dress code	Must keep home clean for clients
Tax deductions for business-related home stuff	
Away Office Pros	***Away Office Cons***
Separate home and office	Must commute
More professional image	Less control (landlord)
Space designed for business	Higher cost

Leasing office space

As you consider whether to have an office at home or to make your home at an office, be sure to consider all the factors. To lease space, you have to sign a contract that legally obligates you for a certain amount of money or period of time. Most office leasing agencies require some proof of financial stability. In some cases, new business owners are subject to greater scrutiny than existing businesses, because they may have no track record of credit. Be prepared to show your ability to pay.

Most offices require pre-payment of a deposit that amounts to one or more months' rent. Even if your company is formed as a corporation or a limited liability corporation, you may have to personally guarantee the rent for the lease period.

The bullets that follow describe some of the key factors to think about before leasing office space:

- ✔ **Space:** How much space do you need right now? Figure 6-1 can help you determine the space you need.

- ✔ **Growth space:** As your business blossoms, it will probably grow tangibly with files and equipment. If you lease space, take into account the length of the lease and how much additional space you may need during that lease period. You don't want to be stuck in a space that's too small with no way out of the lease.

- **Safety:** Who has access to the building? Is it secure? If you will be working odd hours, will you have to walk through dangerous spaces to get to and from your office? Who else may have access to your space? See the following section ("Staying safe") for more information on putting safety first.

- **Cleaning:** Does your rental fee include housecleaning? Will you have to clean your own area, take out trash, and so on? At home, you must do all the chores unless you have a housemate or spouse who is extremely supportive.

- **Repairs:** Who is responsible for making repairs to the building and the individual offices? How difficult is it to get critical items repaired? Ask other tenants. In some cases, you can simply take care of repairs and send the bill to the landlord for reimbursement. In others, you must wait until the landlord gets around to it.

- **Food and beverage facilities:** Does the office have a break area or drink or snack machines in the building? Are restaurants nearby?

- **Utilities:** Are they included in the rent? If not, what are the average utility bills for the amount of space you want to rent? Ask to see utility bills from summer and winter months.

- **Restrooms:** Will you have a restroom in your space, or will you share a restroom with other renters? If you'll be sharing a bathroom, how close is it to your office? (You wouldn't want to walk up five flights of stairs just to use the restroom!)

- **Lighting:** Do you get plenty of natural light from windows? Do windows have shades that are in good repair? Is the artificial light bright enough to work by?

- **Visibility and appearance:** Does your business need high visibility? The right office space can provide that. Does the area create the kind of image you want with your clients? Is the building attractive, well-maintained, and nicely landscaped? Is it a smoking or non-smoking space? You certainly don't want your office to house lingering unpleasant odors.

- **Contract terms:** This includes all the specifics of your lease, including the size and cost of the area you're leasing, the length of the lease obligation, requirements for notification of cancellation on your part as well as the landlord's, options for renewing, expenses and what they include (such as cleaning and maintenance), credit requirements, and so on. Does the lease specify how potential increases will be handled and how they will be calculated? Have your attorney review a lease before you sign (see Chapter 8 for advice on hiring an attorney).

To help figure out how much space you'll probably need, trace out your space the way I have in Figure 6-1. Using graph paper, assign a measurement — such as one foot — to each block. Measure your room and draw it on the graph paper, indicating exactly where the doors, windows, and other features are located. Then cut out shapes that represent the size of your furniture and place them on the paper. You can easily see what fits where. (Be sure to allow room for doors to open and space around furniture so you can move around comfortably without banging your shins!)

Staying safe

Security is an important factor to consider when you're deciding where to locate your office. At times, when other people may be snug in their beds, you may be cranking to meet a deadline or to put a proposal together. Most freelancers work odd hours — early, late, and weekends — at some point. If you have any inkling that you may burn the midnight oil, you need an office where you can be safe while you're alone and as you arrive and leave.

Laying Out Your Work Space

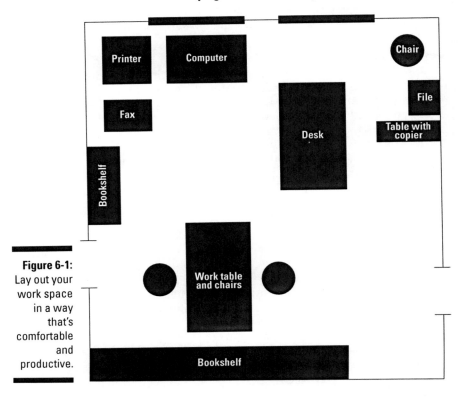

Figure 6-1:
Lay out your work space in a way that's comfortable and productive.

Usually, the safest place you can be is in your own home, where you control who has access to your space. You simply go from one room to another and you're at work! In a leased office space, you have to consider the following:

- ✔ **Parking area:** Is it well-lit? Patrolled by a security agency? Close to the building? Does it have any areas where someone can hide? Will your vehicle be safe?

- ✔ **Building access:** Is the building secure and does it require a special code or key to gain entry?

- ✔ **Security:** Is there a security guard? Alarm system? Video monitoring? What about after hours: Is there a sign-in requirement?

- ✔ **Lighting:** Is the hallway or path you take from the office entrance to your office area well lit and secure?

- ✔ **Office access:** Is your own office area secure?

- ✔ **Visibility:** Can anyone see you from outside the office, or can you close curtains or blinds?

- ✔ **Emergency systems:** Does the building meet codes for fire and safety? Does it have adequate smoke alarms, working fire extinguishers, backup power, and so on?

- ✔ **Elevators versus stairs:** How do you reach your office, by elevator or by stairs? What happens if the elevator gets stuck in the middle of the night? Where are the stairs in relation to your office, in case of a fire or other emergency? Are they locked? Can you go in as well as out? Are the stairs safe, or would you feel insecure walking the stairs at night?

Whether you locate your office in your home or in leased office space, make your space comfortable, spacious, affordable, and convenient.

Furnishing Your Space

Buying the basics — even for a home office — is expensive. You can reduce your costs in several ways:

- ✔ **Do your research.** Compare brands, equipment features, and prices. Check out the discount stores, Internet manufacturers sites, and online auctions where you can bid on name-brand items at a discount. Always take into account the length and coverage of any manufacturer warranties, the validity and price of store warranties, and factors like how easily you can get service or repairs.

- ✔ **Be prepared to wait.** The longer you have to get ready, the better your chances of getting a deal. When you're in a hurry, you won't be able to wait for items to go on sale or to win an auction bid. Give yourself a minimum of several weeks to get your office set up.

✔ **Consider used items.** New file cabinets, for example, are very expensive. Because they're almost indestructible, you can always find used files that are like new. I don't necessarily recommend used equipment unless you know the history of the item, but you're pretty safe buying used furniture, especially if it's a name brand.

✔ **Investigate reconditioned items.** I have found that used equipment isn't often discounted that much, and I'd just as soon pay a little extra for a new piece of equipment. Nevertheless, reconditioned equipment may save you a little, and most of the time, it will have a limited warranty.

✔ **Remember that you don't have to have office furniture.** Garage and estate sales offer some great furniture items that look great with a little paint or elbow grease. You can use a baker's rack for a bookshelf, a dinette set for a conference table, or an old armoire for a storage cabinet. Use your imagination and create an antique office setting.

The more research you're willing to do, the better deals you're likely to get.

Your office is your castle

You've left the four walls of corporate life to create your own unique work experience. Give yourself the latitude to make your office a representation of your adventure. Add touches that make you feel at home, recognize your individualism, and create a space that excites you and gives you energy. Your office is you, and you're no longer bound by the rules for appropriateness that govern people when they work for someone else. Yes, you can keep it businesslike, so that when clients visit, you maintain your professional image. But you can also be yourself. That's what your life is all about!

✔ Decorate in a style and in colors that suit your personality.

✔ Add personal touches that are meaningful to you, such as sculpture, framed awards, gifts, your kids' handprints, or other mementos. I have a photo of a llama next to my computer!

✔ Make it comfortable. Have an area where you can relax and put your feet up, just to think and plan.

Feng shui and office arrangements

You're on the clock whenever you walk into your office, either working for your clients for pay or working for yourself for free. You can't afford to waste your own time (time that you're not charging to a client) because you're missing some equipment or can't work efficiently. How you arrange your office contributes to your efficiency and your well-being. The more efficient you are, the more time off you have.

One thing at a time

Chris Crouch, coauthor of *The Contented Achiever, How to Get What You Want and Love What You Get,* believes in simplicity. After years of corporate success, he left his job as CEO of a division of a *Fortune* 500 company to do something he loved, although at the time, he wasn't even sure what that was. Having been a certified public accountant (CPA) and corporate creature all his life, he had followed others' dreams for him. "One day I was out running, and I started thinking about my life. I had it all, but I was unhappy. All of a sudden, I realized that I simply didn't like what I did." A couple of days later, he quit.

Now building a business as an author, speaker, and consultant, Chris keeps his several undertakings under control by being a stickler for organization. He created a set of files numbered 1–31 to represent the days of a month. At the beginning of each day, he spreads all his projects out on the desk, and prioritizes them. Then he takes the papers for whatever can be accomplished today and puts them in the file that corresponds to today's date. The next most important projects go in the file for tomorrow. He never keeps more than one project on his desk at a time. Chris says this does three things for him:

- Keeps him from feeling overwhelmed by a pile of undone work or a list of projects that can't possibly be accomplished today.

- Helps him stay focused completely on the task at hand, rather than on what may be lurking out there ahead of him.

- Contributes to a neat work space that is much more conducive to good organization than a messy desk.

"I don't believe in spending much time on things that don't enrich my life. Being organized lets me get past the unimportant details and get to the things I love: playing the guitar, traveling, reading, writing, and spending time with my family."

When you consider how to arrange your office, think more about how you work than about following a typical room layout. Your workspace has to be easy for you to function in. I have arranged my desk area in a U-shape, with my reference books to my left, my computer in the middle, and my desk space and phone to the right. When I'm working at my computer, I have everything at my fingertips. I simply turn left to grab a book or turn right to jot a note. Set up your workspace in a way that best accommodates your work style and that saves you steps. Don't create a situation in which you have to leave your desk to get something you often need.

Because I spend a lot of time at my computer, I prefer to face a window, so that when I gaze into space searching for a thought, I have a nice outdoor view to help me along. You may have to experiment with arrangements that inspire you.

Some people swear by *feng shui,* a Japanese technique of arranging living space in a way that helps energy flow and contributes to health and happiness. Check out *Feng Shui For Dummies* by David Daniel Kennedy and Lin Yun, Ph.D. (Hungry Minds, Inc.) for the lowdown on this technique.

Getting Equipped

I have strong feelings about the minimum equipment you need to function properly and convey a professional image. To compete today, you must be fully automated and able to meet your clients' needs for speed and efficiency. Even though you're a one-person operation, clients expect you to be able to make them copies, send and receive faxes, be equipped to send and receive e-mail, and so on. Your own convenience and efficiency also play a role in what you need. In this section, I've included items that I feel are essential to enhance your life and your work as well. The absolute minimum requirements for an office today include the following:

- ✔ Phone
- ✔ Computer with Internet connection
- ✔ Fax
- ✔ Copier

Every day, I see enhancements in office equipment, so I can't possibly tell you which piece of equipment is right for you. Shop for features and the best prices and buy whatever is today's best bargain. With so many items to choose from and so many reasonably priced models, you can probably find several good possibilities. The following sections discuss various types of equipment.

Phone

Every office needs a telephone devoted to business. You can accomplish this in a couple of ways:

- ✔ **Dedicated phone line:** This is a line that's separate from your home line and is devoted strictly to your business.
- ✔ **Distinctive ring:** A less expensive way to create the appearance of a separate line is to have one line with two numbers, with a distinctive ring for calls to your business that's different from calls to your home. When you hear the special ring, you know it's a business call, and you can answer appropriately. You can use the same feature for a fax line or a computer line. In our area, you can have up to three separate rings.

To save the cost of having a separate phone jack installed, you can buy a plug-in remote phone jack for about $70. A remote operates like a radio, with a transmitter and a receiver. You plug the transmitter into an existing phone line, and plug the receiver into an electrical outlet in another area, attaching the phone to that receiver. It doesn't work for more than one phone line. If you have more than one phone line, this can be a tricky process, so you may need some advice from your friendly telephone-jack store.

For an additional charge you may also select additional phone services such as the following:

- ✔ **Caller ID:** You can see who's calling before you answer. Advanced caller ID (also called call waiting/caller ID) tells you who's calling while you're on another call.

- ✔ **Call waiting:** You can put a call on hold to answer another call.

- ✔ **Call forwarding:** Call forwarding lets you transfer your phone to another number. This is convenient when you're expecting an important call and must leave your office. You can forward calls to your cell phone so you won't miss a thing.

- ✔ **Three-way calling:** When you need to have a conference call with more than one person, use three-way calling.

- ✔ **Call-back:** You can automatically redial the last person who called you.

- ✔ **Voice message system (voice mail):** An automated service lets your caller leave a message, and you can retrieve the message from your own phone or from any other phone. You can also buy a telephone with a built-in answering machine, but if your power goes out you may miss some important information.

The greeting you record on your voice message system is a part of your image. When you record it, use a friendly, welcoming tone and deliver a businesslike message. Make sure there's no background noise that would detract from your professional image, such as kids talking or dogs barking. Keep it short: People want to quickly leave a message, not listen to a dissertation on where you are or what you're doing. I prefer a direct approach: "Thanks for calling Spellbinders. Please leave a message and we'll call you back."

Computer

Absolutely no one conducts business today without a computer. What kind of computer you need depends on what kind of business you do. Corporations update their computers and software regularly; but freelancers seldom have the budget to upgrade at the drop of a hat. So as you shop for a computer, consider one of the two following approaches:

✔ Get the latest and greatest computer you can buy, with the maximum capability, and expect to keep it for a long time, which, in computer terms, is about 3 to 5 years.

✔ Get the cheapest computer you can buy, as long as it has everything you need, and expect to upgrade every year or so.

If you use your computer for simple tasks like word processing, chances are, you could use the same one for five years and never feel the slightest bit under-equipped. If you have more sophisticated needs, you may need to update your capabilities more often.

Don't under-buy and don't over-buy. Computer technology changes so fast that whatever you buy will be out of date within a year. Get the latest and greatest in terms of power and memory, but don't worry about all the bells and whistles. If all you use is word processing, you don't need a huge computer. If you do graphic design, you'll need all the power and space you can get.

According to my computer guru (who is an indispensable person in my life), companies make two versions of computers: a *commercial version* and a *consumer version*. The consumer version tends to have cutesy extras like games and special icons that do neat stuff for you. These consumer computers, however, are not as good an investment as the less sexy commercial models.

Printing your work

Having a printer is every bit as important as having a computer. Like your computer, the type of printer you need depends on the work you do. You can get a decent printer — even a color one — quite inexpensively today. The differences in printers tend to be in these areas:

✔ **Quality of print:** If you expect to print finished, high-quality client documents, you need a printer that's up to the task. Quality is usually described as *dots per inch (dpi)*. The higher the dpi, the greater *resolution* (clarity) of the document. And, naturally, the higher the dpi, the higher the price.

✔ **Volume of print:** Printers are designed to handle a certain number of copies each month, with a lifespan dependent upon how heavy your usage is.

✔ **Multi-tasking capability:** Many desktop printers are now combined with fax and copying capabilities.

✔ **Number and size of paper trays:** Printers may have one letter-size paper tray that holds one ream of paper (500 sheets) or multiple trays that handle legal size sheets or even card stock.

✔ **Speed of print:** Speed is expressed in how many sheets per minute the printer spits out. If you print mostly short documents, speed may not be that critical to you. If you process long documents, a higher speed printer may be useful to you.

Two important factors to consider when buying a printer are as follows:

- ✔ **Cost of ink:** The cost of color ink cartridges is higher than black and white ones.
- ✔ **Ease of maintenance:** Can you get your machine serviced locally, or will you have to send it somewhere to have it fixed? What will you do in the meantime?

Adding software

Spend a few minutes in your friendly neighborhood computer store and you'll see a lot of software to help you manage your business and a lot that's totally unnecessary to your business. I know people who are so enamored of electronic toys that they want every new tool that comes along. For play purposes, fine, but you don't really need it to run a business. And you could spend every penny you make on software, which I don't think is a good investment. It hasn't been that long since I kept a spiral notebook of my project income and a file folder of invoices that I hand-marked "paid," and, frankly, that worked just fine. Of course, now I wouldn't think of not being fully automated because accounting software is not only faster, but also allows me greater flexibility. I can generate reports that show my business from a variety of standpoints such as monthly income or expense, weekly hours, and expenses or revenue by project, by client, and so on.

I recommend a few types of software programs that can make your life easier:

- ✔ **Word processing:** If you ever type a letter, a proposal, or anything that's narrative, you need word-processing software that allows you to type, edit your words, move text around, and save documents. Choose software that matches what the majority of your clients use. Even though most word-processing software packages today have conversion features that translate documents produced in different packages, the formatting of documents often doesn't translate perfectly. Your life will probably be a lot easier if you and your clients are using the same software.
- ✔ **Accounting packages:** Some simple accounting packages let you record your income and your spending and can generate reports several ways. Here are some things you can do with the typical package:
  - Keep your books.
  - Pay your bills by writing checks (generated on your own printer).
  - Generate invoices.
  - Produce reports that tell you how much money you've made or how much you've spent in a particular category. This is extremely helpful when you get ready to prepare your taxes.

  You can choose from several formats, and your accounting expert (see Chapter 8) can help you decide which one matches your business needs.

✔ **Project-management tools:** If you do projects that have multiple deadlines with lots of tasks or elements, you may benefit from using project-management software. It will help you track actions items, especially when multiple clients are involved.

Getting wired

To run a business today you must be hooked up to the Internet. Every one of my clients uses the Internet for (at a minimum) e-mail. The Internet is also a handy tool that you can use to do the following:

✔ Buy office supplies

✔ Order magazines

✔ Buy books

✔ Do research for projects or look up clients

✔ Play games

✔ Find freelance jobs

I won't give you a crash course about the Internet, because *The Internet For Dummies,* 7th Edition, by John R. Levine, Carol Baroudi, and Margaret Levine Young (Hungry Minds, Inc.) is an excellent resource!

To hook up to the Internet, though, you need a way to link your computer to the outside world. You can do that in a variety of ways:

✔ **A telephone line to your computer:** You generally find three types of phone lines:

• **A regular phone line:** You can either pay for a separate phone line that can be hooked up to your computer all the time, or you can have a switcher that goes back and forth between the Internet and your regular telephone. I find that clients expect me to be able to look at e-mail while I talk to them, so some form of dual capability is essential.

• **A DSL (digital subscriber line), which is a high-speed connection:** A DSL allows you to use your existing phone line for voice and Internet connection.

• **An ISDN (integrated services digital network), which is also a high-speed dedicated line that costs a lot more than a regular line:** ISDN also allows you to use voice and data transmission simultaneously. It's not as fast as DSL, however.

✔ **A cable connection:** This is just like having cable TV, and it keeps you online all the time. The disadvantage of a continuous connection is that it makes it easy for hackers to use your computer without your knowledge while you sleep.

Cable hookups and DSL lines keep you online 'round the clock, so with either one, you need a *firewall,* which is a software solution that keeps hackers out. (See, I told you that you need *The Internet For Dummies,* 7th Edition!)

For any Internet connection, you need a *modem.* A modem is a mo(dulator)/dem(odulator), in other words, a thingamajiggy that lets you send information over a telephone wire. If you use a telephone line, you may have an internal modem in your computer, or you may have to have an external modem installed. For cable, your cable company will provide a special cable modem.

Fax

Even if you can send a fax from your computer, you may still need a fax machine for sending things that weren't created in your computer, like signed documents. If you're going to get a freestanding fax machine, make sure it uses plain paper and feeds multiple-page documents without your having to stand over it. I have found that few fax machines are good at feeding, and they're a real pain when they're not.

A lot of companies now make combination fax machines/copiers/printers/scanners. I have separate machines for all these purposes, because with a combo model, if one element goes out, you're out of luck all the way around. I prefer to keep my equipment separate; I don't like being just one widget away from a business shutdown. Still, if you're short on space or cash, a combination machine can be a big help.

Copy machines and copy services

When you need to make copies, you have five options:

- ✔ **Use your fax machine, which can usually double as a copier.** If occasionally, you need only a copy or two of a normal-size document, you can probably make do by using your fax machine.

- ✔ **If you need multiple copies of your computer documents, simply print more than one.**

- ✔ **Scan a document and print it.** Of course, you need to own both a scanner and printer to do this.

- ✔ **If you regularly need more than one copy, or you need to copy long documents or oversized documents, invest in a copy machine.** Small, desktop models are moderately priced.

- ✔ **If you don't mind running errands, go to your neighborhood copy center and pay by the page.** These service centers can also add a spiral binder, color cover, and other cosmetic elements to make your documents look spiffy.

Electronic extras

Electronics are your friend. Even though you can live without them, they can make your work easier and help you be more efficient. Three particular types of electronic extras are commonplace, but you can certainly find a wealth of gadgets and gizmos if you're so inclined. Keep your budget in mind; it's easy to get carried away with the appeal of electronic toys.

✔ **Cell phone:** For your own convenience as well as that of your clients, you may want to purchase a cell phone, which allows you to make and receive calls from just about anywhere. Cellular companies sell service in minutes, so compare plans to see which one makes the most sense for your needs. Just be sure to overestimate the time you expect to spend. You may use it more than you think you will, and when you exceed your time limit, the fees can be steep.

Be careful when you use a cell phone. You can put yourself in real danger if you talk on a cell phone while driving. In addition, thieves can *clone* your number, that is, pick your cell phone number out of thin air and charge to their hearts' content on your account. Take a few precautions to reduce the likelihood of cloning: Turn off your phone when you're not using it. If you must leave the phone in the car while you're away, use the keypad lock and also lock the cell phone in the glove box or other secure place. Monitor your monthly bill to see that the calls you're charged for are your own. One signal that you may be getting cloned is repeated hang ups or wrong numbers. If you experience these, report it to your wireless provider.

✔ **Beeper:** Beepers used to have to make noise to tell you someone was looking for you. Now they can do a lot more, like display messages (and even sports scores), or show you the latest stock prices. Some people find it convenient to use a beeper instead of a cell phone because a beeper doesn't interrupt you as much as a phone call can.

✔ **Electronic data system or personal data system:** These handheld computer wannabes are all the rage. They can hold your schedule, let you hook-up to e-mail, and can even be downloaded directly into a full-sized computer. Some people rave about them, others buy them and leave them in the cardboard box. The trick, of course, is building the habit of using it enough to make it pay off.

Office supplies

Shopping for office supplies can be a dangerous mission: You pick up a little of this and a little of that and, pretty soon, the cash register is ringing up hundreds of dollars of little stuff. Remember to purchase only what you need. Table 6-2 gives you a checklist of essential office supplies.

Table 6-2	Office Supply Checklist
Must Haves	**Nice to Haves**
Printed stationery, envelopes, business cards	Personalized invoices and folders
Copy/printing paper, mailing labels	Personalized notepaper and mailing labels
Notepaper and legal pads	Sticky-backed notes
Pencils, pens, highlighters, paper clips	Decorative office desk set (paper clip holder, pencil holder, desk pad, and so on)
Ruler, scissors, stapler, staples	Paper trimmer
Hole punch	Heavy duty hole punch (punches many sheets)
Large white or manila envelopes	Presentation binder
Hanging files and file folders	Colored file folders
Calendar	Day planner, leather portfolio
Contact file (Rolodex-style card file, computer software, or metal file box with business cards)	
Paper shredder	
Dictionary and thesaurus	

As more people create home offices and one-person leased offices, you can find supplies in lots of places, such as the following:

✔ **Local (usually small) office-supply stores:** These stores offer personal service, and they frequently deliver. Prices may be higher than at a discount store.

✔ **Large, discount office-supply houses:** These stores offer a wide selection and are usually open late, which can be a great convenience to small business owners. Some feature delivery within a particular area. Brand selection may be limited.

✔ **Discount department stores:** If you're flexible about what brand you choose, you may find that these stores serve your needs. (You can combine your personal shopping with business shopping, killing two birds with one stone!) The selection at a discount department store is a bit more limited than at a specialty office store, but most people can make do with what they offer.

✔ **Catalogs:** I receive tons of catalogs with a variety of brands and prices. After you become an official business, you will probably get on a lot of catalog mailing lists, whether you like it or not!

✔ **The Internet:** You can order online from the large discount houses, or you can find catalog stores that are limited to online ordering. Remember to check shipping costs and delivery time to make sure that you're getting either a bargain, convenience, or both.

✔ **Grocery stores, drug stores, and other specialty stores:** Some grocery stores, drug stores, and other specialty stores sell office supplies, and are a good source for emergencies. They usually offer a limited selection and higher prices, however.

Protecting Your Equipment

You probably have invested (or will soon invest) some of your money in equipment for your business, whether it's computer equipment, a lawn blower, or a chef's thermometer. As a freelancer, you may not have a lot of money to throw around buying or repairing your equipment, so invest in the proper maintenance to keep your equipment operating smoothly and to extend its life. The following sections tell you how.

Taking steps to prevent electronic disasters

Electronic equipment, including computers, printers, copy machines, fax machines, answering machines, and the like, function best when they're in a controlled environment. Consider whether you can provide appropriate conditions, such as the following:

✔ **Temperature:** Computers like an even, moderate temperature, and they especially dislike being too hot. Keep your room at a steady temperature.

✔ **Cleanliness:** Dirt and dust are equipment enemies. In fact, even a small particle can mess up a computer mouse.

✔ **Non-magnetic personalities:** Magnets have a tendency to erase computerized information, so keep anything magnetic away from your computer's main operating unit (also known as a *CPU* or *central processing unit*).

✔ **Steady power:** Sudden bursts of power through electrical lines can be death to anything that's plugged in. I have a friend who was on vacation when lightning struck a phone line in his home. He lost his phones, fax machine, microwave oven, clock radio — you name it! If it was plugged in, it was destroyed. And keep in mind that even the normal power surges that happen as a routine each day can be damaging.

You can buy a few gadgets to help you create ideal conditions for your very important equipment. Here are a few:

✔ **Surge protector/surge suppressor:** These devices are like big extension cords that serve as a go-between for your plug and the wall outlet. You can plug several pieces of electronic equipment into one.

✔ **Dust cover:** Electronic equipment doesn't like dust. Protect your computer and printer by keeping them up off the floor and covering them with a dust cover when you're not using them.

✔ **Battery backup:** A portable backup system automatically switches your computer to backup power during a power outage. *Uninterrupted power supplies (UPS)* give you 10 or 15 minutes to save your work when the power suddenly cuts out. The first time you sit around waiting for the electric company to restore power after a thunderstorm, you'll appreciate how valuable this can be. If you receive data via modem, it will keep you from losing information in transit when there's a power sag. If you buy a generator-powered model, you can continue working under all conditions.

✔ **Hard drive backup:** The word "crash" strikes fear in the heart of anyone who depends upon a computer for their livelihood. Crash means that your computer suddenly decides to shut down and takes all your information with it — sometimes permanently. To avoid this, buy a computer with a writable CD or Zip drive that allows you to save to an external source. Of course, this doesn't work unless you regularly save your files!

Maintaining your equipment

Almost every type of equipment can benefit from routine cleaning and maintenance. Set up a schedule for checking your equipment at regular intervals and follow all the manufacturer's recommendations for cleaning, oiling, or otherwise taking care of it. Your equipment will last longer and provide better service, and you won't suffer the frustration of having equipment suddenly out of commission when you're working on a big project.

Practicing Good Work Habits

One thing you can do to enhance your health is to control your work environment. Here are some areas to think about when you're planning your work space.

Because I'm tall, I'm aware of the fact that furniture can't be built to fit every body type. If you're of average size (whatever that means), you may find that all the furniture and fixtures are perfect for you. I don't ever find that to be the case, so I shop carefully for equipment and supplies that can be adapted to my needs.

Adjusting your chair

A person who sits at a desk and uses a computer needs a work area built for safety, as well as for comfort and convenience. Select a chair that's the right size, with good back support. While you can cut corners on items such as desks and tables, you can't afford to shortchange yourself when looking for a chair that fits. Try out a variety of styles and models — with and without arms, with tilt and height adjustment, with rollers and without — and choose one that suits your work style. Remember to take into account seat depth, arm height (the chair's, not yours), and other factors that you may otherwise overlook. Try several stores and brands before you make a choice. And whatever you do, be sure that you can try your chair out at home and return it in a few days if it isn't the perfect fit.

If your legs are short, place a footstool under your feet to avoid putting unnecessary pressure on your back.

Fiddling with your computer monitor

Pick a monitor size that allows you to easily see what you're working on and has a clear picture. You can also adjust the type size on your monitor so that you can easily read from a comfortable distance.

- ✔ **Height:** Adjust your desk, chair, and monitor height so that the monitor is just below eye level.

- ✔ **Distance:** Place your monitor so that it's within arm's length when you sit in your chair.

- ✔ **Glare:** Position your computer screen so that glare from sunlight or desk lamps doesn't interfere with your line of sight. If you find yourself squinting, reposition the monitor. You can also buy a *glare screen* for your monitor that eliminates glare from your screen.

Adapting your lighting

To feel comfortable and reduce work strain, give yourself the proper light so that you can see clearly and without glare on your work surface. I prefer lots of light, not only because it helps me see what I'm doing, but also because it makes the office seem more cheery. I've had several fluorescent lights installed in my office to increase the amount of light. Position your light so that it doesn't reflect on your computer screen.

I can see clearly now . . .

Anyone who wears glasses or contacts has to take special consideration when working around computers. While you may think that looking at your computer is just like looking at anything else, it's not.

In the last several years, I've been blessed with the need for bifocal glasses. When I first got them I was excited that I wouldn't have to change glasses to work at my computer or to go to the kitchen for a snack. I was mistaken. After several days of severe neck strain, I realized that to see through the reading part of my bifocals I was craning my chin up and producing constant tension on my neck.

In addition, your reading glasses may not be the right strength for working at the computer. Check with your eye doctor, and be sure to mention that you work at a computer. He or she can direct you to a prescription lens or to an over-the-counter strength that will work best.

Altering your keyboard position

People who type a lot sometimes experience pain from temporary conditions such as tendonitis or from more serious physical conditions such as carpal tunnel. *Carpal tunnel syndrome* is a painful condition that occurs when a particular nerve gets trapped in your wrist by swollen tendons, ligaments, and muscles. It's caused by repetitive activity such as typing, piano playing, or sewing. Take the following precautions with your keyboard:

- ✔ Make sure your keyboard and mouse are positioned at elbow height and type with your wrists slightly above the keyboard tray.

- ✔ Adjust your chair, your body, and your keyboard to a height that allows you to keep your forearms parallel to the floor.

Make sure your keyboard is positioned so that your fingers are held below your wrists. Take frequent breaks and visit your doctor if you experience any pain.

Sitting in one position all day can be a pain, literally. Throughout the day, take breaks to give your body and mind a rest. Stand up and do gentle stretches for your back and neck. Flex your fingers and hands.

Don't rest your elbows or wrists on a hard surface, which can place pressure on a nerve. Look for gel pads that you can put in front of your keyboard to rest your weary bones, as well as one to use with your mouse pad. I've even adapted a set of keyboard pads to put on the arms of my chair.

Cleaning Up Your Act

Cleanliness is not only next to godliness, it's the surest way to feel more in control of your world. Everyone has his or her favorite organization method. The following are a few of mine:

- ✔ **Get a *desk caddy*.** These sectioned organizers fit everything from pens and pencils to paperclips, stamps, and scissors.

- ✔ **Use paper trays as an inbox and outbox.** Keeping your files separate means you handle paper only once and then put it in the out box.

- ✔ **Buy a *cord management device*.** These conceal and control your phone line cords and electrical cords.

- ✔ **Keep client addresses and phone information handy.** Use an address book, card file, or your computer.

- ✔ **Store frequently used computer disks and CDs in holders that can sit on your desktop.**

- ✔ **Use a paper sorter tray to store different types of paper.** You may, for example, use plain white copy paper for draft documents, letterhead stationery for letters and proposals, and envelopes.

- ✔ **Keep the files you're currently using in a file drawer or holder close at hand.** Put your closed files, the ones you're finished with (even temporarily), in a file cabinet.

- ✔ **Use notebooks and dividers as project organizers to keep key information in one place.** At the front of each notebook put a plastic business card insert or sheet to record information about phone numbers and addresses of key project contacts. This keeps information from being strewn about your desk. When you go to a meeting about that project, take along your notebook and you're never without backup information that you may need. If you meet a new person, jot their info in the front of your book. Using different colored folders for projects helps you easily grab the right one when you're in a hurry (and it looks attractive, too).

Making Clients Comfortable

Some types of freelancers routinely go to clients' offices, whereas others expect clients to come to them. If your clients visit, you need to prepare an adequate and appropriate space in which to meet. Your clients' comfort and convenience is of the utmost importance, and if your office isn't set up to accommodate meetings, you'll have to adapt. Here are some suggestions of ways to make clients feel at home:

✔ **Have an adequate and appropriate space in which to meet.** Give clients a table where they can lay out their materials and write comfortably. If you don't have room for a small conference table and you're in your home, meet at your kitchen or dining table. Clear off all the extraneous personal belongings, such as Johnny's school books and your latest utility bill.

✔ **Present a neat workspace.** Clients will judge your mental processes by your physical environment. Clutter suggests disorganization and undermines confidence. Eliminate stacks of folders and paperwork; instead, file them away. Keep books and notebooks on bookshelves, not piled on the floor.

✔ **Have a variety of beverages (diet and regular, with caffeine and without) and small snacks, with napkins, on hand.** Although serving food and beverages isn't necessary, it is a nice extra. Some clients consider time out of the office like a mini-vacation, and the more comfortable you can make them feel at your place, the greater your rapport will be.

✔ **Avoid having children there if at all possible.** Kids need attention, and they probably can't resist interrupting. The distraction will hurt your concentration and may irritate your client.

✔ **Prepare copies and other materials in advance so that you'll look as efficient and prepared as you would if you were working in an office with an assistant.** If you aren't good at operating office equipment, avoid opportunities to fumble in front of your client.

REMEMBER

Home office pet peeves

I once recommended a language tutor to a client who spoke English as a second language. The tutor was referred to me by a friend, and I trusted that the tutor would act professionally. I was shocked to later hear that the tutor's home — where they met — smelled strongly of animals. I never imagined that someone would conduct business in such surroundings.

If you have pets, make the following special arrangements for meeting with clients at your office.

✔ **Keep pets out of sight.** No one wants to be met at the door by a jumping, wagging, barking dog.

✔ **Remember that many people are allergic to animals or their hair.** You can't completely eliminate animal evidence, but you can vacuum and make sure animal hair is dusted away before clients arrive.

✔ **When you're on the phone, be sure animals are where they won't disturb you with their barking.** Lock them out of your office or put them outside when you're expecting a call.

Chapter 7

Budgeting Your Time

In This Chapter

▶ Scheduling realistically

▶ Expecting the unexpected

▶ Guess-timating your workload

▶ Blocking your time

*I*f you don't control your work, your work will control you. It's as simple as that. You go into business for yourself so that you can decide what to do and when to do it, but sure enough, the easiest thing to lose control of is your time. This chapter offers guidance about scheduling, so that you retain the flexibility you love so much.

Understanding a Freelancer's Weekly Activities

When you sit down at your desk that first day of freedom, what will you do? Seriously, do you know what activities will fill your day? As you think about how to block out your time, consider all the things required in your new position and estimate some percentages of time that each of these activities will take.

✔ **Selling:** Selling involves all the activities associated with getting business: from making calls to taking people to lunch; from writing a sales letter to writing proposals. These are things you aren't paid to do, and they usually take up about 25 percent of your time (25 percent × 40 hours = 10 hours per week).

✔ **Administration:** Administration involves all the work you must do to run your business: tracking your work, sending out bills to clients, depositing your money in the bank (the good part!), filing your taxes, ordering office supplies, and so on. You aren't paid for these activities; they require about 15 percent of your time (15 percent × 40 hours = 6 hours per week).

I've never heard any freelancer say, "Oh, boy, I can't wait to do that administrative work." You won't find administrative work to be as exciting as your actual work, but it's every bit as important. After all, money gets from your client's account to yours through administrative tasks. By doing small amounts of administrative work as needed, you can keep it manageable. If you save it all up, the growing mountain of paperwork may paralyze you. Schedule time each week to do your administrative chores such as record keeping and accounting, and when the end of the year comes, you'll be glad you did.

✔ **Personal and professional development:** Developing your skills involves activities like reading, networking, and attending conferences or seminars that will make you a more valuable freelancer.

The amount of time you spend on personal and professional development varies depending upon the requirements of your profession. A certified public accountant (CPA) has to complete a certain number of hours of professional education each year, while a garden specialist may have to read up on new treatments for plant diseases. For the sake of an estimate, plug in 1 hour per week. Counting a 2000-hour work year, that equates to 2 percent of your time.

✔ **Working for clients (also called *billable time*):** You must, of course, do the work your client hired you to do so that you can deposit those checks in the bank. After subtracting time for selling, administration, and development, you'll have about 58 percent of your time left to work for clients (58 percent × 40 hours = 23.2 hours per week).

Consider this: If you charge by the hour, and you can charge only for about half the time you work, how does that affect your income? Chapter 16 tells you more.

Starting Your Day Productively

Before I begin the day, I need to know what's ahead. I make a to-do list of my personal and my professional obligations, and I feel great when I can check things off. Sometimes I begin with less important, easy tasks that I can do quickly, and that gets me off to a successful start. I can work up to the ones that take more concentration.

Don't let a long to-do list overwhelm you. Use it as a tool to steer the ship, not an anchor around your neck.

Remind yourself when you look at your list that the only thing you have to do right this minute is *look at the list.* The next thing you may do is to take out the file you intend to work on. Then open the file, and so on. Focus only on the next indicated step. You can't be in two places at one time or do more than one thing at a time. The to-do list is nice information to have, but use it to your advantage, not to your detriment.

Time is on your side

I have my favorite time management techniques, like setting my clock ahead ten minutes and putting already-done things on my to-do list so I'll have something to check off. My friend Renee Dingler has some more sophisticated ways of controlling her schedule.

Renee has been freelancing for about four years, and she comes from a highly structured finance and accounting background. She uses tried-and-true time management techniques:

✔ Decide on annual goals.

✔ Break them down into monthly, weekly, and daily goals.

✔ At the beginning of the day, make a to-do list that includes at least one personal goal.

✔ Mark the ones that have to get done, and do one of these high-priority items first to give you a sense of accomplishment and keep the momentum going.

Renee doesn't want to work full time, and she has made some rules for herself about managing her time. "I don't schedule more than 30 hours of chargeable (billable) work per week, and I let my clients know beforehand that's how I work. I discipline myself not to work more than that unless I absolutely have to. I just don't accept more work than I can handle. I figure if a client wants me badly enough, they'll wait. And if not, I'm giving someone else a chance to earn some money!"

Budgeting Your Time According to Three Simple Rules

The three most important things to remember in budgeting your time are as follows:

✔ **Count on everything taking longer than you think it will.**

✔ **Be realistic about what you can reasonably do.** Allocate enough time to do what you've given yourself to do. If it takes you 20 hours to write a speech, give yourself 20 hours. Don't block 3 hours, spend 20, and then wonder why you're behind schedule.

✔ **Don't overcommit.** Fear and greed are the freelancer's greatest enemies. You may be tempted to take every project you possibly can because you can't ever be sure where the next job is coming from. But if you take on more work than you can handle, you may be stressed, and your work quality will probably suffer. The bottom line is that you could lose business, leave the client with a negative impression, and create negative word of mouth referrals. Whew! What a domino effect.

When you work from home, clients may assume it's okay to call you at night or on weekends because they figure you're there, waiting for work. If this bothers you, set boundaries by stating your business hours on your answering machine message. Or, have a business line with a special ring, so you know when it's a client (and you can just let it ring). I have one client who deliberately calls at odd hours. He wants to efficiently leave his message and truly hopes I won't answer!

Tracking Your Time

If your time is what you're selling, you must keep track of your *inventory* — the amount of time you have sold and the amount you still have available to sell.

Being able to organize your time isn't something you're born with; it's something you have to put forth effort to do. Time management is a system of good habits, one of which is writing things down and keeping up with things as they happen.

Here are a few tips for helping you organize and track your time:

✓ **Keep a calendar or an electronic scheduler to note all your appointments.** Don't depend on your memory to figure out where you're supposed to be and when. The busier you become, the more difficulty you'll have juggling your time. With all your dates noted, you're less likely to *double book* (make a date to be in two places at one time).

✓ **Estimate how long you believe each appointment will take.** Be sure to give yourself time to get from one appointment to another while driving carefully, and that you build in time in case one appointment runs over. You don't want to have to cut off a client to get to another appointment.

✓ **Include specific appointment times with yourself to complete projects or to do personal things, including relaxation times.** If you don't actually book these times into your schedule, you may find you have to book a lot more than 40 hours in your week to get everything done.

Use a calendar that divides the day into 15-minute increments to accurately track the time you spend on a project. I mark billable time with a vertical line, and unbillable time with an "x." This makes it easy for me to see at a glance how much time I'm spending on unbillable activities in a week. That can be an eye-opening experience.

An accurate calendar can help you estimate other jobs. Better yet, it will come in handy if the IRS ever audits you. It's nice to be able to show on your calendar that you spent time in a client meeting that you deducted mileage for or at a client lunch that you deducted.

Phone calls count. They not only take up the minutes you're actually on the call, but they also consume time afterwards, when you have to reestablish your concentration on what you were doing before the phone rang. Some clients call infrequently; others call a lot. To accurately account for your time, note each call. Ideally, write down how long each one takes, although I have a hard time doing that. While I don't believe in charging minimum 15-minute fees for each call no matter how short it is (as some freelancer do), I do estimate each call for 5 minutes and note the ones that are longer than that.

 Note activities as they happen; otherwise, you won't remember them accurately. Time will get away from you, and you won't be able to account for hours in your week. Chances are good that your lost hours would have been billable hours, but you can't bill for them if you can't remember for whom you were working or for how long.

Coping with Success

Assuming your business takes off like you hope it will, how will you cope with the increase in work? One of the most difficult juggling acts for a freelancer is to manage the amount of business to keep it just right. People who are successful reach a point where they must decide whether to keep their operation small or to expand.

Recognizing the time to change

It's pretty likely that you'll have times when business is excessively heavy and times when it's slow. You certainly can't rush out and hire additional staff just because you have a busy time — the busy time may not last for the following reasons:

- ✔ If you're in a seasonal business, this could be a short-term period of busyness.
- ✔ If it's the end of the year, your clients may simply be winding down, trying to close out projects before the end of the year.
- ✔ If you've recently sent out marketing materials or made sales calls, you could be entering a work burst that will taper off after the initial boom.

When your period of overwork extends to six months or beyond, it's time to do something different.

When friends become foes

War makes for great comrades, and freelancers who suffer together tend to bond like soldiers. Thus, it's no surprise that when a freelancer becomes overworked, the first thought is, "Hey, it would be fun to go into business with my friend Cindy (or Joe or Kerry)." Take a tip from *Lost in Space*: "Warning, Will Robinson." Good friends don't necessarily make for good coworkers. In fact, the more alike you are, the less chance you'll make compatible business partners. Businesses tend to thrive when partners have complementary skills such as the following:

- ✓ Analytical people work well with creative people.

- ✓ Outgoing sales people work well with serious project implementers.

- ✓ Thinkers work well with doers.

Some differences in qualities, however, can incite war: A punctual person working with a person who is always late can be a highly explosive situation. Patience wears thin, and the partnership can turn into a bomb. Choose wisely.

Handling too much work

Steady work is good. Steady overwork is not. You can handle client overload in four ways:

- ✓ **Increase your rates.** Sometimes a heavy workload indicates you're not charging enough. Compare your rates with other freelancers in your field and see whether you have room to raise your fees.

- ✓ **Say no to business.** You can turn down business selectively, which is probably one of the goals you had when you started working for yourself. Turning business down can even be a plus because it reinforces your worth to your existing clients.

- ✓ **Hire part-time help.** I reached a point in my business when I realized that I was spending too much time doing clerical work, when I could have been doing billable business. It made sense for me to hire a part-time assistant, who makes a much lower hourly fee than I do. The type of help you need depends on where you're spending your time. You may find that a bookkeeper is the answer, or perhaps you need an administrative assistant. Analyze your time and your needs before you decide what type of help will contribute most to your business. See Chapter 8 for tips on hiring part-time help. And always consider hiring another freelancer!

- ✓ **Expand your business.** Is this what you became a freelancer to do? Strongly consider the pros and cons before you decide to become a small business owner with employees. This step involves more than simply hiring someone. It can completely change the face of your business and your responsibilities. Being a manager is a lot different than being a lone ranger.

Before you expand your business, try some short-term fixes such as hiring temporary help or using other freelancers. That way, if you've misjudged your needs or the time your business boom will last, you can test the waters and aren't tied to a permanent decision that could be costly and painful.

Continuing to Sell

One big mistake freelancers make is slacking up on selling when things are going well. You can't afford to wait until things are slow to look for business, because if you do, the lag time between asking and receiving may result in hunger.

In some form or another, you must sell all the time, every day, every week, every month. Put selling on your calendar. Take the time you need to sell, divide it by five, and spend that amount of time each day soliciting new business or keeping in touch with old clients.

Selling doesn't only take the form of going out and soliciting business. Sometimes, business comes knocking on your door in the form of requests for job estimates or proposals. This section describes several opportunities you can use to sell indirectly. (See Chapter 11 for more on selling.)

Estimating jobs

An estimate is a prediction of how much a job will cost before it is begun. When a client asks you for an estimate, it may include only the cost for your services, or it may also include the cost of associated things such as reproduction of reports, creation of a product, mailing or shipping, and so on.

In three cases, a client may want you to provide an estimate:

- The budget for a project is already established, and the client wants to make sure your costs will fit within the budget.
- You've already been assigned the project, but the client wants an idea of what the cost will be before you start.
- Several people are bidding on the project, and low cost will be a consideration.

In the last case, what you bid may have a direct bearing on whether you get the project.

Answering a request for proposal (RFP) or request for bid (RFB)

A *request for proposal,* commonly called an *RFP* and also called a *request for bid (RFB),* is a request that organizations send to several people, asking them to present a plan and a budget for completing a project. The RFP generally includes some background information about the project, specifying the desired outcome. An RFP asks you to describe how you would approach the project, how long it may take, what additional resources you need, your estimated costs, and other information important to the particular project. RFPs have deadlines by which all participants must submit their plans.

When all bids are in, the client weighs the pros and cons of each proposal and selects the one best suited for the job according to certain criteria, such as low cost, high quality, ability to meet deadlines, or other important factors.

An RFP is a great marketing tool — a chance to differentiate yourself from the competition. When you're preparing an RFP, be honest, but also sell, sell, sell! Add some features that enhance your value, helping the client understand why you're the absolute best choice for the job.

Preparing an RFP is a time-consuming process. When you do an estimate (see the preceding section), you simply estimate how much time it will take you to think through and complete a project. An RFP requires you to think the project through before being offered the project, so you may invest a good bit of your time for no payment whatsoever. If you really want to win the job, you must put your best foot forward. Only you can decide if it's worth your time to respond to an RFP, knowing that you may not get the job.

Protecting yourself

Every project has unexpected twists and turns and in almost every case, the job will take longer or cost more than you predict. To protect yourself, estimate how long you think the job will take and add some additional time to cover the unexpected. In some professions, it's standard to double or triple an estimate.

As you get to know clients, their company policies, and their work styles and eccentricities, timing becomes more predictable. In the meantime, boost your estimate to protect yourself.

Clients would always prefer that you estimate high and come in below the amount you've estimated than to estimate low and exceed your budgeted amount. Until you've had a lot of experience estimating, give yourself plenty of leeway.

In certain situations, such as government bids, price may be the sole determining factor in who is awarded a project. But in other cases, although price is a factor, the client may not choose the low-cost bidder. Quality and service frequently play just as big a role as price in landing a job. Your proposals should stress the value you provide, not just the price.

Make a table of all the elements of a job and keep the list handy to guide you in doing estimates. Using this checklist approach, you won't have to recreate an estimate list for every estimate or proposal, and you can come closer to making a good ballpark estimate of your time.

You will routinely pay some expenses, like long-distance phone calls, as you do each job, and some clients will reimburse you for such costs when the job is done. Expenses you pay for are called *out-of-pocket expenses*. These may include long-distance calls, copies, travel, meals, and other day-to-day expenses that go along with most jobs, but may not be predictable in the beginning. I simply ask the client to reimburse me (pay me back) these expenses at cost. Other freelancers mark-up the cost of these extras as much as 20 percent. Clients may ask for receipts to show how much you actually paid for these items.

Managing the Delicate Balancing Act

I think most freelancers are slightly off-balance, in a good way. People who choose this life tend to throw themselves into it with reckless abandon, which certainly makes them highly committed individuals. (As I said, they're off-balance and perhaps need to *be* committed!) Such enthusiastic pursuit of goals leads to some awesome results. It can, however, also lead to anxiety and overwork.

It has taken years, but I've finally learned that I have a biological project rhythm that hums along quite nicely on a schedule that suits me, but that wouldn't fit someone else. It works like this: I work intensely on a project (like writing a book) for a few months, working against a deadline. When the project is done, I need a couple of weeks of downtime to recover. If the project takes less time than this, I can't get as fired up as I'd like, because I build momentum over time. If it lasts longer than that, I fizzle out. My husband has an opposite rhythm. He functions best working in a balanced way each day. He doesn't function well without sleep, and he paces himself each day. He prefers projects that are short-lived, because they complement his physical and mental makeup.

Everyone has a rhythm that's most conducive to health, productivity, and happiness. Perhaps you already know what your optimum work schedule is. Are you a morning or a night person? Do you prefer a five-day workweek, or would you rather work fewer hours and more days? Don't try to go against your natural rhythm. Your body and spirit will show it.

If you've been working according to someone else's ideas of when you should work, you may only now have a chance to find out what feels natural to you. Try a few different approaches and see what feels comfortable. Don't be led by what is "the norm." I know of one creative company at which the employees don't come to work until 11 a.m., because that's what works best for them. This schedule makes it a challenge for their clients; nevertheless, clients are usually willing to go along.

Find your own balance, and you'll find you're a happier freelancer.

Cutting corners

Part of balancing your schedule is figuring out what to do yourself and what to pay someone else to do. Freelancers who are just getting started are prone to do everything themselves. They make copies, deliver projects, and do all sorts of things for clients that are outside the realm of their actual profession. They do this because they think it will save them money and because they can charge the client for their time. Think carefully about this practice, however.

- **Saving money:** Since I started my freelance business, I have used courier services to deliver packages to clients. I do, however, know freelancers who make their own deliveries. Consider the actual cost of doing that. In our city, a typical delivery probably costs about $10. As long as the delivery is directly associated with a project and you've worked out this arrangement beforehand, you can bill the client for that out-of-pocket expense. Assume the delivery would take 30 minutes out of your day. Could you actually bill the client for 30 minutes of your own time for a delivery? If your hourly fee is $20, maybe it's worth it. If it would cost more than a courier fee to do it yourself, it's not worth it. (Unless you make the delivery in order to make a sales call, too.)

- **Charging the client:** When your charge for a delivery is higher than it would be to send a courier, you're not spending your client's money wisely. For example, if your hourly fee is $60 and it would take you 30 minutes to make the delivery, that's $30. Why should your client pay $30 for a delivery when they could pay only $10? It doesn't make sense to spend your time or your client's money doing something you can pay someone else to do less expensively.

Consider two important reasons not to do tasks that you can pay someone else to do:

- **It interrupts your day.** Cost-saving tasks cut into the time you could be spending selling or doing other activities that increase your business.

- **It can reduce your value as a professional.** If you're a consultant who makes copies, you send a message to the client that you don't have more important things to do. (Even if you're licking envelopes, don't broadcast it.)

Now that's corny

Here's a bizarre project rescue I worked on that shows how you can do two things at one time. A manufacturing client was planning an open house for employees' families and people in the neighborhood where the plant was located. We had printed 4,000 copies of a company overview that included a description of the products they made. One of the products described was made from corn. In the printed piece, it incorrectly said "bran." We only had overnight to fix it, and we couldn't afford to eat (no pun intended) the cost of reprinting. I called on close friends and family to help me repair it. We created an assembly line. One typed the word "corn" on a long string of correction tape. The next person cut sections of the tape with just the one tiny word on it. A third person opened the print piece to the proper page. A fourth pasted the tiny word "corn" in the proper spot. Because the word "corn" was in the middle of the sentence, each piece of tape had to be very carefully cut to fit. All 4,000 of them. Pretty tedious, to say the least. Fortunately, we multitasked: We ate pizza, laughed a lot, and made "corny" jokes. The whole event has become legend in my company. I love it when potentially disastrous situations become fun. They always will if you approach them with a light heart.

Doing two things at the same time

Another way to balance is to *multitask* — a fancy corporate buzzword for doing more than one thing at a time. Handling five or six projects or tasks simultaneously is a realistic expectation for freelancers. If you make a habit of never doing just one thing at a time, you'll accomplish a lot.

Some activities are simply not compatible. Don't balance your checkbook while you drive. Don't do noisy things while you're listening to a client on the phone (they can hear the peck-peck-peck on your keyboard or the clank-clank-clank of dishes being washed and will realize you're not giving them your full attention). And never use your laptop computer while you engage in any water activities!

The following are some activities, however, that you can combine:

- ✔ Check your e-mail as you call your mother to wish her happy birthday or return a call. You can also write checks, lick stamps, file your nails, polish your shoes, or fold laundry while you talk on the phone.

- ✔ Combine your professional and personal errands. Drop off your shirts at the cleaners and the client bills at the post office on the way to a meeting.

- ✔ Dictate notes to yourself on your handheld recorder while you cook dinner or drive to pick up the kids.

Finding Time to Stay Healthy, Wealthy, and Wise

The need to budget time doesn't just apply to budgeting work time; it also applies to making time to take care of yourself. When you're the star athlete of your team, you must stay in peak condition. After all, every day is the big game, and no one can stand in for you when you're injured or ill. You can't afford to be on the disabled list, so take extra measures to ensure your health.

You went into business for yourself to create a more pleasant work situation. As you work, you should feel relaxed and comfy. Every so often, stop and pay attention to how your body feels. Are you relaxed? Are your shoulders tense? Are you frowning or squinting? By being aware of your body, you can adjust your surroundings — or your mental state — to create a more enjoyable situation. (See Chapter 6 for more information on adjusting your office equipment.)

Guarding against illness

Freelancers tend to come into contact with people from a variety of areas. If you contract a cold or the flu, you may actually be like typhoid Mary, carrying illness from one client to another or getting sick repeatedly. You can take steps to reduce your susceptibility to whatever's going around:

- ✓ **Wash your hands often.** Shaking hands is the surest way to exchange cold and flu germs.

- ✓ **Get plenty of rest.** Overwork can lead to illness because, when you're tired, your body can't defend itself against potential invaders.

- ✓ **Avoid stress.** Being in a stressful situation is another condition that can lower your ability to fight off disease. Stay cool, calm, and collected and don't put yourself in highly stressful situations. When your work gets a bit intense, take breaks. Walk around the block, take deep breaths, or get a massage.

- ✓ **Keep your hands — and pencils — out of your mouth.** It's true. Germs travel on people's pens and pencils. Use your own and don't use it as a pacifier.

- ✓ **Eat right.** The fast pace of some freelance jobs can lead to grabbing food on the run. That can also mean you're eating fast food or unhealthy snacks. Try to maintain a balanced diet.

- ✓ **Drink right.** If you can't get revved up without your daily cup of caffeine, indulge, but try to moderate your caffeine intake. Caffeine is addictive:

too much can make you jittery, make your heart race, cause gas, and keep you up nights. And remember, caffeine doesn't just come in coffee and tea: It lurks in some soft drinks and in chocolate.

✔ **Exercise regularly.** If your office is in your home, you can probably find a convenient time to plan to exercise. Incorporate regular exercise into your day. Taking a brisk walk can clear your mind and help you maintain a trim, healthy body.

✔ **Take time off.** You may feel extra excitement when you get your freelance business off the ground, and the energy can keep you going for quite awhile. Even after you get past the initial high of running your own show, you may get on a fast track to keep up with clients' demands. Whoa! What happened to time for you?

For your physical and mental well-being, regularly take some time off. This may mean a long weekend; a half day in the middle of the week to go to a movie; or a whole week or more off. Whatever you do, build in time to reclaim your peace of mind and your physical strength. In the long run, it will make you work smarter.

Weighty matters

Normal, corporate jobs build in a certain structure to the day: breakfast before work, lunch midday, and dinner after work — with, perhaps, a snack in between. But what happens when you no longer have that structure? Some freelancers find that their bathroom scale mysteriously inches up a few pounds when they start out on their own. Why?

Mostly, it's because of your constant access to food. When your office is at home, the refrigerator is just steps away, and you don't even need quarters to put in the machine. Getting started in business can also mean more social events associated with wooing clients. Business lunches, cocktail time, and social occasions can all lead to increased food intake or poor food choices.

To maintain control of your new freelance appearance, try the following tips:

✔ **Set certain times for your meals and don't allow yourself to wander into the kitchen at other times.** Keep something crunchy (and healthy) at your desk so you won't be tempted to sneak into the food danger zone.

✔ **Fill your refrigerator with healthy snacks like veggies.**

✔ **Plan your at-home lunches.** Shop for healthy food so that you don't just grab any old thing for lunch (like potato chips and chocolate chip cookies).

✔ **Plan your client lunches at places where you can make healthy food choices.** Most restaurants will accommodate special requests such as grilling fish instead of frying it.

Protecting your body parts

Aside from staying healthy, you can practice work habits that will contribute to your continued good health. Try the ones that follow:

✔ **Protect your back:**

- Don't lift anything too heavy. If your job requires frequent lifting, invest in a hand truck: They're not that expensive, and they can save you plenty in doctor bills!

- If you must lift that 10-ream box of copier paper, do it right. Crouch down first, use both hands, and lift with your legs.

✔ **Protect your neck:**

- Avoid holding the phone between your head and shoulder; it's sure to create a pain in the neck.

- Buy a headset that allows you to have both hands free while you chat. Some convenient models clip to your belt so you can even walk around while you talk.

- Use a telephone that has a speakerphone built in (another way to talk hands-free).

✔ **Protect your eyes:**

- If you must sit at the computer for long periods of time, take breaks to rest your eyes. When you look at a computer screen for hours, you blink less frequently, which leads to dry, irritated eyes. To remedy this, look away from your screen every 10 to 15 minutes, focusing on something farther away to let your eyes rest. Blinking helps create tears, which moisturize your eyes. Non-prescription moisturizing eye drops can also help.

- Use the proper lighting to avoid eyestrain, and take breaks to rest your eyes.

- Wear the proper glasses for the work you do. If necessary, use a magnifying glass when looking at small parts or small text at close range.

- If your job involves activities such as welding, mowing, or other potential hazards to your eyes, wear safety glasses.

✔ **Protect your skin (if you work outside):**

- Wear long sleeves and a hat.

- Wear sunscreen on areas you can't cover up.

- Use protection to keep your lips from becoming chapped.

- Dress in layers when it's cold.

- If the weather has dried your skin, put a cup of salt in your bathwater; my dermatologist recommends it as a cure for dry skin (and it works!).

✔ **Protect your feet (if you have to be on your feet a lot):**

- Wear comfortable, practical shoes that are the right size.

- Give your feet a soothing soak at day's end.

No matter what your job, indoors or out, drink plenty of water to keep your body well hydrated. Getting dehydrated is generally bad for you and can lead to fatigue, which is one of the freelancer's worst enemies.

Mixing Kids and Clients

Did you start a home office so you'd have more time to spend with your family? Small children and business don't mix very well unless you have a plan for every situation. The following sections can help.

Scheduling child care

Anyone who works at home must have some time dedicated to getting work done. Even if your spouse has agreed to watch the kids while you work, it's almost impossible to avoid interruptions.

Mondays and Fridays are the days when business clients seem to have the greatest need. They're coming back after a weekend and are fired up about getting things accomplished, or they're desperately trying to wrap things up before they leave for the weekend. If you're considering when to arrange childcare, strongly consider doing it on at least these days.

Phoning while at home

Talking on the phone with kids around can be a harrowing experience, no matter which end of the phone you're on. Spare yourself and your clients a potentially unnerving experience by trying the following:

✔ **Try not to take calls when your children are at home and awake.**

- If the phone rings when your kids are home and awake, let voice mail or your answering machine pick up calls. Return them when your children aren't around.

- If you can return calls by simply leaving a message, do it when the kids are in bed.

✔ Schedule interview or conference calls at certain times when you know your kids will be at school or daycare.

✔ Have a cordless phone so you can quickly move to a quiet room when a client's call comes in.

✔ Set up a table in your office as your children's desk, and have them work at it quietly when you're on the phone.

✔ Keep a special box with activities your kids are allowed to do only when you're on the phone. This will keep them intrigued during important calls.

Taking an honest approach

Believe it or not, clients can be more accommodating and understanding than you may suspect. Work/family programs are among the most popular benefits that corporations offer today; in fact, they're becoming a necessity at companies that want to attract and retain the best workers. Most of your clients probably have families, too, and they can understand your need for time to care for your kids.

For example, if you work only until 2:30 each day and then leave to pick up your kids from school, let your client know that you're not available after that time. Be honest (but brief) about your childcare issues. Reassure them that you will deliver a quality product in the timeframe they require, and they may be perfectly willing to accommodate your schedule.

Working parents often suffer the trauma of children in the home begging for attention when they really need to work. Instead of asking children to wait until you finish work to receive attention, childcare specialists suggest that you give kids undivided attention first. This takes the edge off kids' needs and may buy you the time you need later.

Be realistic about what you can accomplish with your children around. It's silly to expect to complete a full day's work with children in the house.

Avoiding guilt

A friend of mine feels like a bad mom when she sees other parents spending time sewing Halloween costumes, making homemade Christmas ornaments, and serving pancakes decorated with sprinkles for their children and friends. Guilt be gone! Parents who demonstrate good work habits and can healthfully balance both work and play also contribute to their children's development.

Chapter 8

Building an Extended Staff

*I*f you knew everything about everything, you may be in a different business than you're in today. So I assume that, even though you're highly qualified in your field, in some areas, you can use expert assistance. You don't have full-time vice presidents working for you like a big company does; nevertheless, you need that same range of expertise.

Instead of actually hiring a staff, surround yourself with a diverse group of competent freelancers, consultants, volunteers, and part-time employees. This chapter helps you figure out what your pretend organizational chart should look like, what skills your ideal staff needs, and where to recruit an expert team.

Getting Expert Advice

Your income and livelihood is involved in your freelance business, which means you want the best advice you can get. As you seek advice, you may find that everyone has an opinion and is more than happy to offer it — whether you want it or not. Even if your brother-in-law is an armchair expert, or your sister "knows all about that," you're probably better off finding someone who gets paid to advise small-business people. What works in one type of business doesn't necessarily apply to another. Likewise, what's best for Joe the barber may not be the wisest course of action for you, the consultant.

How do you find the perfect expert for you? The following sections show you how.

Finding an expert

I like to get referrals from other small business people who have had successful relationships with lawyers, accountants, and other experts who understand a freelancer's unique needs. The following are some guidelines for hiring an expert:

- ✔ **Call the local chapters of professional associations** such as the American Bar Association or the American Institute of Certified Public Accountants. They can give you a list of members and can explain which credentials you should ask for. Local people are more likely to know local professionals than national groups are.
- ✔ **Ask for references, and then call the references.**
- ✔ **Interview the person face to face.** You need rapport with someone who will guide you in your business, and the only way to establish that is up close.

Working with an expert

Even though you're hiring experts, you need to guide them. It helps to give your new expert the lowdown on what you do.

- ✔ Invest the time in acquainting the expert with your business.
- ✔ Explain what you think your needs are. To use everyone's time wisely, have a clear idea of what you want. Gather any necessary background information and have it ready at your meeting.
- ✔ Listen to their recommendations.
- ✔ Let them know when you have questions or reservations.
- ✔ Let them do their jobs.
- ✔ Review their work.

Don't relinquish responsibility even for the areas in which you don't feel confident. Keep your eye on what's being done, and you'll learn as you go. Who knows, you may even become an expert in that area, too!

Bartering 101

Bartering is easy as long as you and the other person agree on the value of the services offered. The easiest way is to determine value according to your hourly rate or service fee, trading one $50 hour for another $50 hour, trading two $50 hours for one $100 hour, and so on. It's best to trade based on a specific monetary amount versus exchanging service for service. When you trade service for service, you may be swapping services that are of unequal value. For example, is a one-hour massage equal to one sales letter? You be the judge.

Because you're undoubtedly a versatile and resourceful person, you're probably capable of handling many diverse roles. The question is: Can you afford to spend your hours doing something you're not an expert at, or could someone who is an expert do it more efficiently? You may initially say, "Hey, I'm doing it for free, and someone else would charge me." Not so fast. Have you considered how much your time is worth? Assume that you're a graphic designer and you charge $75 per hour. You've been freelancing for a year, but you've decided you need to form a limited liability corporation. Here are two examples of how you could accomplish that:

✔ You don't want to spend money to hire an attorney, so you decide to file the paperwork yourself. You contact your state, get a copy of the forms needed, read all the directions, fill out the forms, send them in, and follow up on it. It takes you three hours. Even though you paid nothing, you spent three hours of your time. If you had worked three hours for a client at your hourly rate of $75, you could have raked in $75 × 3 hours = $225. Translation: You've actually lost $225.

✔ You hire a bookkeeper for $75 per hour. It takes a bookkeeper 2 hours to do what took you three hours. You pay the bookkeeper $75 × 2 hours = $150.

Compare the $225 you could make with the $150 you would pay, and you can see that you'd still be ahead $75. On the flip side, remember that if you didn't hire the bookkeeper, you'd be out $225 (and, perhaps, the price of several aspirin).

Of course, if a bookkeeper charges more per hour than you do (or is exceptionally slow), you may be losing money. Figure out the math to make sure, but many times it makes sense to pay someone else.

Bartering your services for theirs

Before I overwhelm you by telling you how many experts you need, let me introduce you to some payment alternatives. Small business people are like a clique. They share secrets with each other, offer tips, and warn each other about pitfalls. They also sometimes swap services. When freelancers don't have cash, they do have time. Granted, a freelancer's time may be limited, but it is something you can substitute for cash. All you need is a willing teammate. Swapping products or services for products or services is called *bartering*. For example, if you are a CPA, you may need a sales brochure, a snappy sales letter, a letterhead design, or a marketing plan. You could work with a writer or a graphic designer, offering to do his or her taxes, conduct an analysis of that person's business, or set up a bookkeeping system. A writer or designer may be happy to have your expertise in exchange for theirs. See the "Bartering 101" sidebar for details.

I've heard people get all excited at the prospect of trading services because they assume that they won't have to worry about paying taxes. In a sense, they feel like they're getting something for nothing. Wrong! According to the tax code, bartered goods and services are considered income to both parties, and they have to be reported to the IRS. Not only that, but backup withholding may also apply. The IRS has publications that explain what the ins and outs of bartering are. Or, to be safe, you may want to check with an accountant. (Maybe you can barter for the advice.)

Understanding which experts you need

You don't necessarily have to have a host of professionals at your beck and call, but you'll benefit from developing a relationship with a select group of specialists. The following sections describe a few of the basic advisors you may need to call on occasionally.

Hiring legal eagles

How much you actually use an attorney's services depends on the type of business you have. When I worked as a sole proprietor, I didn't really need an attorney's services. My writing business seldom requires legal help. Later, when I decided to incorporate, I had an attorney file my incorporation papers. Even now, I don't usually need a lawyer, but I still have the advantage of knowing someone who is there if I need him. One time, when a client *stiffed me* (that's freelance talk for "refused to pay a measly $250"), I called my attorney to find out my options. After he explained the process, I decided it wasn't worth my hourly rate to go to small claims court for $250, much less the aggravation I would endure. Ultimately, I let it pass.

A lawyer can help you do the following:

- ✔ Help you with the legalities of starting a business.
- ✔ Recommend contract terms or help you prepare a standard services contract.
- ✔ Advise you about your rights in a legal situation.
- ✔ Wade through negotiations for office space or other business negotiations.

Establishing a relationship with a lawyer is a good idea for when you may need one, for example:

- ✔ When someone sues you, and you aren't guilty of anything.
- ✔ When someone sues you, and you are guilty of something (but didn't know it, of course).
- ✔ When someone doesn't pay you.

✔ When you don't want to pay someone who didn't provide a service or product you felt they should have provided.

✔ When you need advice about a contract.

✔ When you want to change something about your company, such as becoming incorporated or taking on a partner.

Accounting for your money

An accountant is a freelancer's best friend. Your accountant can help you in important areas, such as the following:

✔ Deciding what business structure is most financially advantageous to you.

✔ Explaining tax consequences of various decisions and recommending tax-filing methods.

✔ Setting up an accounting system that gives you the information you need and is easy enough for you to manage yourself.

✔ Assisting you in filing tax returns and being present if the IRS decides to audit you.

I am a real scaredy-cat when it comes to tax liability and other things for which I could suffer severe penalties (such as financial setback or jail — see Chapter 17). In my book, an accountant is a must-have expert.

While you may think that an attorney is an attorney is an attorney, there are actually a huge number of specialties in the field. Someone who specializes in tax law may not know much about contract negotiation. In both accounting and law, be sure to go to someone who is an expert in the particular area in which you need help.

Finding resources

Small business owners can find free assistance from organizations that specialize in providing advice on planning a business, getting financing, and other key areas of running a one-person show.

✔ Your local bank can be a great resource for information and suggestions on financing and credit opportunities. They may have a special division for small business.

✔ The Service Corps of Retired Executives (SCORE) is an agency under the auspices of the Small Business Administration (SBA) that provides free advice and assistance to start-ups. Look for additional help through the SBA, which arranges loans to small business owners, especially women and minorities.

✔ The Chamber of Commerce has a variety of services for business owners and, if you join the group, you have access to networking opportunities, too.

Speaking financially

Because freelancers don't have the same savings and retirement options that other employed people have, they must use creative approaches to prepare for the future. If you're a student of financial strategies and investment opportunities, you may feel comfortable managing your own finances. If you're not sure about the ins and outs of financial planning, a financial advisor can help.

You may want to use financial vehicles designed especially for self-employed people, or you may choose traditional investments that anyone can make like buying stocks or bonds. (See Chapter 19 for details.) Whether or not you trust someone else to advise you, you can at least learn the options from a pro.

Marketing your business

When I say, "Hire a marketing specialist," you may have visions of fancy advertising agencies and big bucks. Not necessary. You can get help from a number of sources that are likely to be very reasonably priced.

You may feel that you know your business better than anyone and that you know how to sell You, Inc. So why would you need marketing assistance? Because you're probably not an expert at marketing, and even if you are, you can't be objective about your own business. Doctors don't operate on family members and lawyers don't represent themselves. Naturally, I'm biased, because marketing is my line of work, but I have seen too many small business people waste their money on useless marketing materials.

Who can help you with marketing? You probably don't need a guru. You need someone who understands how to effectively and efficiently reach potential customers. Lots of freelancers have expertise in areas related to marketing, and if they're not experts, they probably know people who are. Here are some of the people who could direct you to helpful sources:

- ✔ Writers
- ✔ Graphic designers
- ✔ Public-relations specialists
- ✔ People in the marketing and communications departments at your clients' offices
- ✔ Marketing professors at colleges and universities. Introduce yourself to the marketing teachers; you may find that they'll take on your business start-up as a student project. Otherwise, they may offer to do the work themselves as a freelance project or refer you to someone they know.

You need a name for your business and business cards and stationery, but those are barebones marketing tools. Add to that a Web site, brochure, presentation folder, invoice template, and a host of other selling possibilities, and you could be looking at a substantial investment. You don't want to spend your money on things that don't work. You need a plan that defines which marketing tools give you the biggest payback. Consider, therefore, a marketing professional for the following:

- ✔ Identifying the vehicles that will reach your potential customers.

- ✔ Creating a family of materials that complement and reinforce each other. (Too many freelancers I know have a hodgepodge of materials that look like they're just thrown together.)

- ✔ Suggesting ways to stretch your marketing dollar.

In short, hiring a marketing professional increases the likelihood that the materials you use will actually generate business.

Looking for Junior Partners: Administrative and Clerical Help

In addition to needing professional advice about business issues, you may need an extra hand for routine office duties or special projects.

Having a full-time administrative assistant can be a pretty big luxury when you're on your own, yet you may need help with tasks such as filing, sending invoices, or doing other clerical jobs. After you get busy with your own work, you can easily let your clerical tasks slide. Pretty soon you're buried under a mountain of paperwork. Before that happens, think about lining up some help.

Sometimes, I simply can't do it all. After struggling on my own, I finally decided to get an assistant. I tried a full-time person, but then I was spending half of my time working to pay her salary. It works out better for me to have a part-time assistant. Mine works about 12 hours a week sending out invoices, paying my bills, doing Internet research, ordering client gifts, and completing other assorted tasks that I don't have time to do.

Getting help on an as-needed basis

Putting someone on the payroll may be overkill for a freelancer who needs assistance on a now-and-then basis. Consider hiring help by the project or by the hour for jobs you find just too time-consuming or tedious to deal with. You can find such help in the following places:

- ✔ Copy shops, office supply stores, mailing houses, and others advertise a variety of services ideal for small businesses — from printing to renting conference rooms to sending faxes and doing desktop publishing.

> ✔ Personal-shopping services charge by the hour or the job for gift buying, dropping off and picking up cleaning, and performing myriad jobs that require running around.
>
> ✔ Freelance bookkeepers send invoices and keep up with your incoming and outgoing money.
>
> ✔ Typists or transcribers type up notes you dictate or format documents to make them look attractive.
>
> ✔ Researchers charge by the hour for digging up information on anything you need.

Look for these services in your local newspaper, on grocery bulletin boards, in your city's business newspaper or magazine, or by asking around. And what about your freelance friends? If they need the same kind of assistance, why not go in with them to group jobs and share the cost?

Working with an in-house assistant

Before you hire someone to work in-house for you, check out the various responsibilities that suddenly land in your lap when you have employees: tax forms, liability, insurance issues — the list goes on. Having an employee brings with it complications that you may not have bargained for when you chose your independent life. If you decide you do want an officemate, be prepared for a change of life by reading Chapter 17.

Finding a terrific assistant is no easy task, and it may take time. Having a big mouth works to your advantage: Tell everyone you know that you're looking for help. Everybody knows somebody who knows somebody, and this method is safer than finding someone who doesn't know anyone at all.

Here are places to look for an assistant, some good, some not-so-good:

> ✔ **Your clients' human-resource department:** This is my number one recommendation because this is how I found my assistant. Susan (yes, we're both named Susan) was working part time at the client's corporate office, but her job had been eliminated. One day soon after that, I was in the director's office and I mentioned that I was looking for someone. The director thought of Susan, who is an accomplished person who wants to work part time so she can spend time with her children. Her needs (part time work and flexible hours) and mine are a perfect fit, so after four years, we're living happily ever after.
>
> ✔ **Colleges and universities:** Students are cheap labor, and you can usually find plenty of them to go around. In fact, if you offer an internship in your profession, you may even get them for free. Students looking for

work experience may be willing to do administrative work just to be exposed to their career area. Hiring a student, however, has three potential disadvantages:

- You may have to work around your assistant's class schedule.

- They may not have the maturity and experience level to be as professional as you'd like.

- You could have to break in a new assistant at semester breaks or at graduation.

✔ **Temporary agencies:** These groups charge a premium for part-time temporaries (called *temps*) because they must make money off the placement and, in some cases, because they're paying the temporary worker's health care and other benefits. Because temps move around a lot, you could get in a training merry-go-round, which is not a good use of your time. The only assistant I ever tried from a temporary agency told me that she couldn't be friendly to my clients unless they were friendly to her first. Needless to say, this isn't my favorite source.

✔ **Secretarial schools:** These schools have students and even graduates who need experience. They're already trained and could very much appreciate getting a break. A potential down-side: These are not seasoned assistants, so you may spend a lot of time training them.

✔ **Newspaper ads:** This is one of my least-favorite sources because ads usually generate lots of nuisance calls and few qualified applicants. Try placing an ad in your local suburban weekly newspaper. Ads are cheaper and more likely to net you some results among stay-at-home moms looking for part-time, flexible work.

✔ **Senior citizens groups:** Even though they're retired, a lot of over-65 people want to continue working. Try your local seniors' groups to find people who may not want a full-time job, but who are experienced and can be a great asset to your business.

✔ **Church groups:** Ministers or other church leaders may be aware of someone who could use a new start or who needs to make additional money. Check with nearby organizations for able and willing people.

✔ **Job-counseling organizations:** Job counseling groups look for placements for all types of workers: mothers rejoining the workforce, people changing careers, widows who need to stay busy. Give them your name and number, and perhaps you'll get a call.

✔ **Mothers' groups:** This could be your best bet. Some women who have left the workplace to care for their children eventually want to work part time for sanity and/or money or because they need mentally stimulating work.

Scratching backs

You'd probably like to take all the work that comes your way — maybe even take every freelance job in your field in the city. But you can't. Unfortunately, sometimes you may feel as if you have taken them all. You hate to turn anyone down, especially new clients, because after they've gone elsewhere, they may not come back. At the same time, you can't do everything. Now what?

This is when you need a cooperative friend in the business. I hire several writers from time to time when my workload gets out of hand. I act as the liaison with the client, but I subcontract the actual work. I make sure the work is up to my standards, tweak it with my special finishing touch, and hand over a completed job. Sometimes I let the client know that I'm working with someone else; sometimes I don't. The important thing is that the client gets a satisfactory product.

In other cases, I may hire someone who can do the job better than I can. My friend, Laura, is a great ad copy writer, and I love to get her help on those kinds of jobs. I think the client actually gets a better product in that situation than if I did it myself. (But I'm certainly not telling the client that!)

Sometimes, when a client asks me to take on a project that's vaguely related to what I do, I take on the work, find someone who is an expert, and sub-contract with that person. I regularly work with graphic designers, video-production people, market researchers, human-resource consultants — whomever I need so that I can act as a one-stop-shopping service to my clients. Using other people's talents, I expand the scope of services I offer, which makes me a more valuable resource. It's good for my business, and it's good for the other freelancer's business, too. This kind of arrangement can go both ways. When you're willing to share the wealth, others will rely on you as a resource, as well. Informal working partnerships are a very good thing.

Sometimes, a client may want you to do a *speculative proposal,* meaning that you must submit a bid and get paid only when the client hires you for the job. Most freelancers are happy to jointly prepare speculative bids with you, as long as you're willing to reciprocate when they need a bid from you. For more information, see Chapter 7.

In the long run, whether you actually work with another freelancer, developing these relationships is fun and worth the effort. After all, we may want to be independent, but no one wants to feel as if he or she is in this freelance business alone.

If you're planning to hire someone part time, keep in mind that you could get away with paying only a small amount of money. At a low rate, however, you won't necessarily get the highest quality help. Ask yourself the following questions to help you decide what you think you need to pay:

- ✔ Will my assistant answer the phone and deal with my clients?
- ✔ Will my assistant handle sensitive information?
- ✔ Will I supervise this person closely, or will he or she need to work on his or her own?

✔ Do I want someone who will stay with me, or do I expect this person to leave after a short time?

✔ How much training will get this person up to speed?

✔ How important to my success is the quality of this person's work?

If you want the crème de la crème of the workforce, you can't pay skim milk prices. Decide for yourself how much this person will contribute to your image and pay accordingly.

 Give your assistant — and yourself — the greatest possible chance for privacy, comfort, and success by providing a practical space where he or she can work. Everyone needs a corner to call his or her own and, in business, that includes a desk, a computer, a phone, and any others tools required to do a good job.

Making Work a Family Affair

You may feel that the most logical way to build an extended staff is to add family members. That way, you keep the wealth in the family, right? Certainly, many family-owned businesses thrive; but others squeeze the life out of an otherwise happy relationship. The following sections take a look at some of the plusses and minuses of bringing family members to work.

The devil you know

Working with people you know and understand can provide shortcuts: You don't have to spend time wondering, "What did he mean by that?" or dreaming up how to motivate someone. With family members, a lot can go unsaid. What are the other advantages of working with someone you love? Here are a few:

✔ **Understanding:** Just as you know them, family members know you. They can read your moods, needs, pain, and happiness better than a stranger can.

✔ **Commitment and loyalty:** Family members may be more committed to your success than an employee may be. They'll withstand hard times and keep coming back for more simply to help you get a foothold in the business.

✔ **Ownership:** It's easier to ask someone you love to "take ownership" of the business, because they may have a personal stake in your success.

- ✓ **Temporary help:** You can easily hire a family member as a temporary helper, without expectations that the job will last forever.

- ✓ **Cheap labor:** Family members may work cheap, which can be very helpful in the beginning. Paying people "slave wages" isn't a good idea in the long run, though, because eventually they will feel resentful.

The devil you don't know

Strange things can happen when family members work together. Adding the burden of a professional relationship can create tension in a relationship. You may suddenly see a side of people you never saw before. Good relationships can go bad when some of the following things happen:

- ✓ **Hurt feelings:** Family members may take it personally when you "order" them around or give less-than-positive feedback.

- ✓ **Stepping out of bounds:** Family members may feel more entitled than an employee would to take liberties with decision making, spending money, or otherwise running the show. It can be hard to reel in a loved one who has gotten out of control.

- ✓ **Unrealistic expectations:** You expect family members to support you, and you may even expect them to go above and beyond what you would expect of an employee. Could you be taking advantage of a relative's commitment?

- ✓ **Slacking off:** Loved ones may not have the same level of commitment to work that they would have for a regular employer. The phrase "getting away with murder" comes to mind. Insist on putting your school-age children to work? Expect a challenge as you try not only to get them to do what you need, but also reinforce good work habits. This may not be the place for training.

The most dangerous area of combining family and work can arise when things don't go well, and you need to "cut bait" as they say. How do you fire a family member and maintain a loving relationship? That's something to think about *before* you hire him or her, not *after*.

The double-edged sword

Some of the benefits of working with family may also be some of the drawbacks. Two old sayings may apply: "Familiarity breeds contempt," and "The same things that you love about a person are the very things that ultimately drive you crazy." When you apply those to work/family relationships, they can be magnified many times.

For example, family members may be more inclined than regular employees to work at off times. Great. But what about when you want them to work 8 to 5? And do you really want them around all the time? Wouldn't you sometimes like to escape? I would! Suppose you love working with your brother because he's an independent thinker and a take-charge kind of guy. When he works for you, though, he may decide that he has some great ideas for your business and take it upon himself to implement them.

It's hard to keep family members at arm's length the way you would an employee. Your closeness can be a blessing and a curse. You may have an easier time talking honestly with them, or you may have a harder time.

The solution — good communication

You can take steps to enhance the possibility of working well with your family members. I've been working with my daughter for years, and we've ironed out some of the kinks. One of the first things we had to overcome was her reaction when I used my "business voice" with her. She was accustomed to my speaking to her in loving tones, whereas my business voice tends to be direct and no-nonsense. That wasn't what she was accustomed to from "Momma," and I had to explain that it wasn't personal.

The same techniques for good communication apply to working with family members as employees: Listen and hear what people say.

- ✔ **Be honest.** Don't be afraid that you'll hurt each other's feelings. When things aren't going the way either of you prefer, say something.

- ✔ **Give your best.** Recognize and reward your family members the same as you would an employee. (You would recognize and reward employees, wouldn't you?) Everyone needs a thank you on a regular basis, and even small rewards go a long way toward encouraging people to help.

- ✔ **Don't take things for granted.** Just because people have been living around you and your work for a long time, they may not completely understand what you do or how you do it. You may have to explain things just as you would for any newcomer. And don't assume that family members will jump in and take charge; you'll probably have to provide the same training you would for anyone else.

Working with the people you love can be gratifying and fun as long as you keep things in perspective. If your relationship is always first and foremost, you may have to make some business sacrifices to keep it that way. You have to decide if this is worthwhile or if you'd rather hire someone else.

Part III
Bringing Your Work to Life

In this part . . .

You are your most valuable product. How do you let the world know you're here? You're unlikely to have a multimillion-dollar marketing and advertising budget, but you can still create a buzz about the yourself. This part helps you spread the word in order to land the most desirable projects and hang on to the best clients.

Chapter 9

Creating a Professional Image

*L*ove at first sight is a concept that works pretty much the same in a business setting as it does in the romantic realm. Your potential clients size you up in seconds, deciding that you have (or don't have) the potential to be a good mate. To ensure that you're a match made in heaven, you must present a proper image. This chapter helps you develop an attractive package that any client will want to buy.

Of course, love pairings come in all shapes and sizes, and you can't fit everyone's idea of the perfect freelancer. My goal in this chapter is to steer you away from some glaring errors and to give you guidelines about the less clear-cut decisions you can make.

Creating a Total Package

As I began writing this chapter, I had an experience that will tell you the bottom line of presenting a professional image in about one minute's reading time. I've been preparing to sell my house, and a service representative came to perform our required termite inspection. He was dressed in a crisp white shirt and clean, pressed pants with a neat, business-like tie. He introduced himself and explained how the inspection would proceed. During our conversation he asked me where I was moving. When I told him the street, he said, "Oh, yes," and he named the address, the current owners, and the address that they were moving to! He even told me who previously had owned their new house! I praised his phenomenal memory, and he said, "That's my job. Doesn't it show you that I know my customers? It's all about making a good impression." It certainly is, and he certainly did.

In the course of one brief conversation, I had an impression that this man really knew what he was doing. How did I come to that conclusion?

- ✔ His appearance
- ✔ His friendly attitude
- ✔ His professional approach to introducing himself and explaining why he was there
- ✔ His knowledge of the market

I still know absolutely nothing about his ability to detect termites. My whole opinion of him has come from the image he projected.

Absolutely everything you do adds to or subtracts from your reputation. Your image either confirms what people have heard about you, negates what they've heard, or totally confuses them. For example, if you have a reputation as a highly skilled consultant, but you dress in a sloppy way, people may say to themselves, "These two factors aren't consistent. I wonder which of them is wrong."

People judge a lot by your image. In fact, in the first minute they meet you they will have a perception of the following:

- ✔ Your business know-how
- ✔ Your credentials
- ✔ Your ability to fit into their corporate culture
- ✔ Your personality and how it fits with theirs

Your credibility is on the line the moment you meet someone. Is it fair for someone to judge you on the basis of appearances? Perhaps not, but they do.

Understanding the Factors That Contribute to Your Image

Image isn't only about your physical appearance. Impressions result from a combination of the following factors:

- ✔ How you look: your clothing, posture, and hygiene
- ✔ How you sound: your grammar, your accent, and your use of slang or profanity (Heavens, no!)

✔ How you act: your demeanor, manner of approaching the project, and personality

✔ How your materials look: professional appearance and quality

Any of these factors alone can be the one that makes the client choose you. At the same time, one false move, and you could be out of the running.

A lot of image consultants tell you how to create an outstanding image. I believe something a little different: Don't do anything to create a negative image. In evaluating your professional appearance, think of all the factors that contribute to your image and examine your checklist to determine the answers to the following questions:

✔ Is there anything about you that would definitely be a turnoff to anyone?

✔ How can you create a neutral impression that won't offend anyone?

✔ Can you think of anything that doesn't enhance your credibility?

✔ What can add to your credibility?

Your goal should be to eliminate anything that could be a turnoff and to add elements that will be advantageous.

Maintaining your best appearance

Consider the following basic rules for your appearance:

✔ Wear clean, pressed clothes.

✔ Wash and style your hair neatly; sport a current style.

✔ Trim facial hair.

✔ Polish your shoes.

✔ Wear unobtrusive jewelry that doesn't jangle.

✔ Don't wear perfume or aftershave.

In addition, dress in a way that makes your clients comfortable. I find that means dressing at least as formally — or more formally — than the person I'm doing business with. In some ways, your clothing should match your job. For any traditional office position, standard business attire is most acceptable. See Table 9-1. If you're in a non-traditional role, such as photography or video production, or another profession that requires you to lug equipment, steer clear of clothing that interferes with your ability to work. You get a hall pass from wearing a business suit or high heels.

Improving your surroundings

A couple of other things contribute to how people see you. They are as follows:

✔ **Your office:** A client may never darken your door, but what if they unexpectedly do? Sure, you know you can find everything on your desk, but a client may not understand that. Your office must give the appearance that you are organized, clean, and that you have everything under control. And if you smoke, try not to do it in your workspace. A non-smoker may be very sensitive to the smell.

✔ **Your car:** Do you ever take a client to lunch? If so, your car should be clean outside and clean and fresh-smelling inside. Before you go to a client's office, get rid of last week's burger bag, the kids crayons, and the smashed bugs on the windshield. If you own an animal that regularly takes a spin with you, be sure to get rid of all pet odors or stray hairs. Take good care of your car and your clients will feel safe with you, too.

Many companies today have switched to what's known as *business-casual* attire. I've also heard this called *snappy casual* or *dressy casual*. What business casual means varies from company to company, but it generally indicates that you don't need to wear a business suit. In some companies I've seen this taken to the extreme of women with bare legs, wearing sandals and spaghetti-strap dresses, and men in jeans. More often than not, business casual means something along the lines of khaki pants with a golf shirt or sweater for men and dress slacks (that is, front zip, pleats, pressed pants — no jeans, stretch pants, party pants, shiny fabrics, or animal prints) with a blouse or sweater for women. See Table 9-1 for a list of business-casual attire.

Never, never, never wear jeans to a client's office. Even if they're wearing jeans, you should be one level more formal than they are.

Table 9-1	Dress Code Standards
Men's Standard Attire	*Men's Business-Casual Attire*
Suit	Sport coat
Dress pants and sport coat	Trousers
Long-sleeve dress shirt	Knit shirt with collar
Tie	No tie
Matching belt and shoes (brown with brown or black with black)	

Women's Standard Attire	Women's Business-Casual Attire
Skirt and jacket	Jacket or cardigan sweater
Dress or a pants suit	Slacks (khaki, gabardine)
Short- or long-sleeve blouse	Short- or long-sleeve blouse or shirt (but not sleeveless)
Dress pumps or flats	Closed-toe and closed-back shoes
Pantyhose	Pantyhose or knee-highs

You may have heard that you should wear conservative colors, but I don't follow that rule because I look like death in colors such as brown, gray, and mauve. (Black, of course, works anywhere.) In certain professions, you may get away with "expressing yourself" through creative attire or unusual accoutrements. Graphic designers or interior decorators, for example, are expected to dress in somewhat less mainstream attire than accountants. In fact, because their selection of clothing in some ways represents their creative flair, eccentric clothing may be advantageous.

You can go to a professional wardrobe consultant and buy a lot of expensive clothes, or you can follow these simple tips to look your best on a budget:

- ✓ **Buy a few basic quality items, rather than a lot of inexpensive things.** As a freelancer, you probably won't see the same people every day, so you can get more mileage out of your clothing than if you had to switch outfits five times a week.

- ✓ **Buy clothes that fit.** Nothing makes clothing look cheap more than a bad fit. If your clothes are too tight, you will look bad and feel uncomfortable — and that's not a good combination. And no high-water pants or short skirts allowed!

- ✓ **Stick with items you can mix and match.** A tweed sport coat can coordinate with several colors of pants. Black is a standard that mixes with just about anything.

- ✓ **Make sure your accessories match.** For example, pair a black belt with black shoes, black handbag, and black pumps. Simple is better.

Finding sound reasons to sound your best

Your voice is your instrument, so use it carefully. What you say — or don't say — can get you in a lot of trouble. The first rule is to listen more than you talk. Any good salesperson knows how important that is. Then use the following rules to play beautiful music.

✔ Use the words "please" and "thank you" liberally. Thank you for the glass of water, for lunch, for meeting with me, for giving me the project, for driving to dinner, and so on.

✔ Speak clearly and in a medium tone. Don't talk too loudly or too softly.

✔ Use proper English. Don't use big words to impress others; instead, talk in a way that an eighth grade student could understand.

✔ Don't tell dirty jokes.

✔ Don't use profanity.

✔ Don't make ethnic or religious comments.

✔ Laugh modestly.

Stereotypes exist. As a woman with a southern drawl, I make a very distinctive impression over the phone. In some cases that's positive; in others, it's not. Be aware of your accent and try to imagine how it comes across to the person on the other end of a phone or even in person. Listen or watch for any signs that the listener doesn't understand. Slow down, enunciate, or otherwise change your style to make yourself clear.

To improve your sound, have a friend rate you on each of the qualities in Table 9-2.

Table 9-2	Talking Points
Attractive Speaking Qualities	***Rating (1=lowest; 5=highest)***
Having an enthusiastic tone	
Using a varying speed and rhythm	
Pronouncing words clearly and distinctly	
Unattractive Speaking Qualities	
Talking at a fast pace	
Using a loud voice	
Speaking with a heavy accent	
Using slang or jargon	
Using profanity	
Interrupting or talking over another person's statements	
Finishing the other person's sentences	
Putting your hands in front of your mouth when talking	
Mumbling	

Your slip is showing

I've seen lots of what I consider unacceptable business garb over the years, from tube tops and mini skirts to dress shirts with sweat stains under the arms. I've also heard horror stories of clothing incidents such as the one in which a woman returned from the bathroom with the back of her skirt stuck up in her pantyhose waist. As she walked through the office (totally unaware of her exposure), she drew looks and laughs, and not a single soul told her about it.

The best clothing story, however, happened to my friend Willy Taylor. She was selling trade show displays, and part of her job was to demonstrate how easy they were to set up. During one sales call, when she raised her arms to put a section in place, her half slip slid down around her ankles. The five men to whom she was presenting remained silent. Ever cool, she simply stepped out of the slip, bent down, picked it up and put it in her briefcase. And then she went on with the show. Smooth move, Willy.

Acting the part

Just because you select a proper wardrobe and speak well, you haven't automatically passed the image test. Your actions still have to match the great appearance you create with the right clothes and sound.

Never, never, never do any of the following when you meet with clients:

- ✔ Bite your nails.
- ✔ Chew gum.
- ✔ Pick your teeth with a toothpick or other implement.
- ✔ Adjust bra straps or other clothing.
- ✔ Smoke. This is seldom an issue in today's smoke-free offices, but some consultants I know ask for smoke breaks or ask to smoke in the car on the way to lunch with a client. Unless your client is a smoker and lights up first, don't do it.
- ✔ Complain about other clients or disclose information about them.
- ✔ Make sexual comments or tell off-color jokes.
- ✔ Make a negative reference to any gender, racial, ethnic, religious, or political group.
- ✔ Fiddle with anything, click your pen, or crack your knuckles.

Pure gold

I have a good friend with whom I sometimes do joint projects, and we once decided to pitch a new client who had just completed a company merger. (*Pitch* means we were approaching her to try to get her business.) This was a potentially lucrative customer, and we were going all out to impress her, sparing no expense. To pique her interest and to make us stand out from the crowd, we did what we call a *teaser*. This is a selling trick in which you send out an unexplained gift item or clever promotional piece in advance to make the client curious. What we created was a small black velvet pillow, with one edge stitched with a 14k gold needle, threaded with gold metallic thread. We wrapped the gift box in handmade paper, and attached a card that said, "Let us help you put the finishing touches on your merger." Every tiny detail of the teaser was of the absolute highest quality. (We actually didn't get the business, but we sure felt good about our creativity. One day we'll use that idea again.)

Above all, don't do anything that could make others feel uncomfortable. Being negative in any way is potentially a put-off. Keep your attitude and your comments positive. You may have your own pet peeves. The best way to identify how you should act is to think about how you would react to someone who was *your* supplier. What would make you feel most positively inclined to hire someone?

Making the grade with presentation materials

Your image rests not only on how you look but also on how the things around you look. Every item associated with you sends a message. That includes the following:

- ✔ Every printed item you use, such as sales brochures, letterhead, and fax sheets
- ✔ Gifts to clients
- ✔ Audiotapes or videotapes

 At the very least, you must ante up for professionally designed and printed business materials. Any freelancer worth his or her salt needs these basics not to appear amateurish and considered a "fly by night." The materials don't have to be expensive. If you're on a really tight budget, check prices at a quick printer. I recommend the following as a minimum way to secure your professional image:

✔ **Business cards:** These should include your company name, address, phone number, fax number, and e-mail address.

✔ **Letterhead stationery:** You need a first page with your company information and a blank second sheet of matching paper.

✔ **Envelopes:** Use matching *number 10 envelopes* (this is a standard-size business envelope) printed with your return address information. If you send a lot of packages, you also need a mailing label for larger envelopes.

✔ **Fax cover sheets:** Type your contact information on fax cover sheets, including what number to call if the fax is unreadable. Fax sheets don't necessarily have to be professionally designed, but they should be standard and neat. Do include your logo, if possible.

Forget everything you ever heard regarding one-, two-, and four-color printing unless you're a graphics professional. These terms don't belong in the hands of an amateur; only a professional designer has the expertise to decide how many colors in which to print a design.

Perfection counts! I've seen resumes with misspelled words, incorrect grammar, spacing errors — you name it. What that tells me is this: If a person won't take pains with the most important selling document they have, they won't be meticulous in their work. You can never be too neat, clean, or accurate. Errors in your materials or in projects you do for a client show the following traits:

✔ You don't care.

✔ You aren't paying close attention.

✔ You're in too big a hurry.

✔ Their opinion doesn't matter.

✔ You don't know any better.

Find the "f"s

As an exercise, read the following paragraph and count the times you see the letter "f."

If you've ever wondered about the origin of the microwave oven, you'll enjoy this story. A scientist was working in a lab, and he was carrying a piece of candy in the pocket of his lab coat. When he stood next to a microwave source, the candy melted. From that he figured out that microwaves create energy from within, and realized that you could use it to cook food.

Although he wasn't the true inventor of microwaves, he did see the possible application of microwaves for a cooking device. The father of the microwave oven: an accidental inventor.

How many times did the letter "f" appear? The answer is 13. What was your answer? Did you count the words "for," "from," and "of"? See how easy it is not to even read those little prepositions? Proofreading takes more concentration than you think.

None of these is a good sign to someone who's considering hiring you.

The worst mistake I've encountered was a letter to me with my name misspelled. I consider this a sign of extreme laziness. (All you have to do to check a spelling is call a person's office and ask.) Here are some tips on making your materials perfect:

- Use your computer's spelling- and grammar-checking features.
- Get a dictionary and a spelling guide and keep it by your side as you read. Don't trust your memory; look up any word that could be wrong.
- Proofread one time for sense.
- Proofread one time for accuracy.
- Read it out loud.
- Proofread backward, word by word.
- Have two other people proofread it.

If that seems like too much trouble to go to, consider that one small mistake could cost you an entire job. How much is the job worth? How much will taking these steps cost you? Go figure.

Maintaining Proper Etiquette

You may not be Amy Vanderbilt or Miss Manners, but you still need to know basic etiquette to create a proper professional image. The following sections share a few of the areas to be concerned about.

Introductions and handshakes

- Stand for introductions.
- Introduce the person who is the higher-ranking, or the one who is the guest, first.
- Offer a firm handshake, whether the person is a man or a woman.

In any business setting, your first goal should be to make the other person comfortable. But have you and your spouse ever walked into a room and run into someone who you've met before, but whose name you can't remember. Help! What do you do? Here's a trick I learned: My husband and I have a pact that if I don't introduce him within the first few seconds, it means I don't know the other person's name. He extends his hand and introduces himself, which prompts the other person to do the same. Problem solved.

If you don't have a husband or business partner, the put-others-at-ease rule still applies. Immediately acknowledge that you've forgotten the other person's name. The other person may say, "Hi, how are you?" And you say, "I'm doing well, thank you. I'm so sorry, but I've forgotten your name. I'm Susan."

Another way to help get others off the hook is to introduce yourself first: "Hi, Linda. Good to see you. I'm Susan Drake."

Mealtime rules

You probably don't need reminders of basic mealtime etiquette such as, "don't chew with your mouth open," "don't put your elbows on the table," and "put your napkin in your lap." If you feel you need coaching in the basics of mealtime etiquette, stop by your library for books on the subject.

In business, however, keep a few rules in mind when sharing meals with clients.

- ✔ **The host picks up the check.** If you invited your client, you pay. If your client invited you, he or she pays.

- ✔ **The person who is the highest ranking official sets the pace.** Follow their lead according to what to eat (price-wise), when to talk business, and when the evening is done.

- ✔ **Use caution when drinking alcoholic beverages.** The safest route is to avoid them altogether when you're with clients.

  - Never order a drink unless your client orders one first.

  - If you're hosting the dinner, offer your client a drink.

  - Limit your intake. Alcohol leads to bad judgment, and when you're with clients, you need all your wits about you.

Good manners should always prevail, and you may be surprised at some of the things that break the rules. Here are two that could surprise you: When eating a roll or bread, break off a small piece and butter it; never butter the whole piece and eat it as a whole. And don't pick your teeth in front of other people, with or without a toothpick. If either of those comes as a surprise, you may want to brush up on your etiquette by reading *Etiquette For Dummies* by Sue Fox or *Business Etiquette For Dummies* by Sue Fox and Perrin Cunningham (both published by Hungry Minds, Inc.).

Electronic etiquette

Even though electronic gadgets help you save time, you can't afford to cut corners on etiquette. Review the following key points to make sure your cutting-edge technological solutions aren't cutting down your image.

Telephone, cell phone, and pager manners

As accustomed as everyone is to using a phone, some people do forget common courtesies.

- When you call someone, introduce yourself before you ask for information or to speak to anyone. Nothing is more annoying than a voice without a name.
- Say goodbye before hanging up.
- If no one answers, don't just hang up; leave a message. People hate hang-up calls.

Cell phones and pagers pose their own etiquette issues, as follows:

- Turn off your cell phone when you're with a client (and at the movies and in restaurants).
- Always use a lower voice when you speak on a cell phone to avoid broadcasting your conversation to everyone in hearing distance. Loud cell-phone conversations are annoying to those nearby.
- Use the silent page feature to avoid interrupting business meetings or social occasions.

Voice mail messages etiquette

Keep the following in mind when you use voice mail:

- Identify yourself. Don't assume the person will recognize your voice.
- Leave your number, even if the person calls you regularly and you think they have your number memorized. Under pressure, people do forget even common things.
- Keep your message brief; leave only pertinent details.
- Offer what would be a good time to call you back or suggest when you will try to reach that person again.

E-mail manners

E-mail is one of the greatest conveniences of this century, but it can detract from communication. Because it's designed to be a quick way of sending a message, it can lead people to not take the time to compose something that's friendly or even correct.

✔ Put a clear identifier as the subject of the e-mail.

✔ Read your note for tone. E-mail can easily sound terse and dictatorial.

✔ Proofread your work. Check your spelling and punctuation.

✔ Include your contact information in every e-mail. There's nothing more frustrating than having someone e-mail you, asking you to call, fax, or mail something, and then having to search for that information elsewhere.

✔ Include a greeting and a closing.

Chapter 10

Finding Clients

. . . .

In This Chapter

▶ Looking for work in all the right places

▶ Juggling for dollars

▶ Keeping up with the Joneses

. . . .

*I*n the movie musical *Oliver!,* the cast sings the song, "Who will buy?" Indeed, when your copy machine's all warmed up, and your new phone line sits ready for calls, who will buy your services? This chapter is all about where to find willing customers and what tools to use to attract them.

Remembering That Selling Is a Full-Time Job

Everywhere you go, everyone you see, and every job you do presents a selling opportunity. Passing an acquaintance in the hall at a client's office can lead to an offhand comment about how the person is swamped with projects and could use some help — that's a selling opportunity. Bumping into an old friend at the movies can lead to a conversation about how the friend has changed jobs and is at a new company — that's a selling opportunity. Sitting next to someone on a plane can result in a conversation about what you do for a living — that's a selling opportunity. In fact, sometimes your leads come from the most unlikely places. One of my longest running associations came from a chance meeting my daughter had at a fitness facility. The key is to recognize opportunities and to follow up on them. Strike while the iron is hot!

 ✔ **Commit to spending the time to find clients.** Devote 15 minutes a day to some form of client communication and, in one week, you'll have a long list of prospects. Contacting even one client per day puts you in touch with 20 people every month!

 ✔ **Keep your ears open.** Train yourself to listen for clues that will tell you that someone needs your services. When Bob sits next to you at the Kiwanis luncheon, listen to what he complains about. Can you solve his problem?

> ✔ **Make sure you follow up at least five times on any lead.** There's a
> reason advertisers run ads repeatedly. One shot doesn't get it. Call,
> write, or visit until you get the business.
>
> ✔ **Ask for the business.** Introducing yourself isn't enough. You must say
> those dreaded words: I'd like to have your business.

The question is: Where should you invest your time for the most likely sale?
Not every opportunity is as lucrative as every other. For example, I can try to
sell my services to a corporation that has lots of money and does many projects each year. Or I can sell to a small company with a limited budget that
will send only a handful of small projects my way over a period of years.
Which one should I spend my time and money to attract? The large company.

Mining for Diamonds with Your Existing Clients

Where miners find one diamond, they know they're likely to find others. The
same is true of clients. It's a lot easier to keep digging in the same spot than it
is to blast out a whole new mine. When you've had success freelancing for an
organization, there's no better way to build a client base than to solicit business in the cubicle next door.

Word-of-mouth is the most effective way to gain clients, and people tend to
trust the people they know inside their own company. What better endorsement could you have than a coworker?

Assuming you're satisfying your clients, they should be happy to refer you to
their friends and coworkers. Everyone looks smart when they send a great
resource to their friends. Ask your clients outright for referrals to their contacts in other departments or other companies. Couch your request with, "If
you'd feel comfortable referring me . . .," so they understand you're sensitive
to their need to maintain their reputation.

Start with a specific request. "I'm hoping to establish relationships with XYZ
company. Do you have any contacts there that you believe could benefit from
my services?" Depending on the answer you get, you can expand to a more
general question. "Are there people in other companies you think I should
contact?"

When you've been referred, thank the person formally for recommending
you. Send a handwritten note on a card. The next time you see or talk to the
person, use subtle follow-up tactics to make sure they know you satisfied
their associate. "Thanks for referring me to Joe. It was a great project, and

I think Joe was pleased. We're getting started on another project in May."
This lets the person know that you've protected their reputation by doing
outstanding work for their friend.

Your own friends can be a source of business, but watch out. Simply because
you enjoy people in a social setting doesn't mean you'll like working with
them. It's fun to tease Betty about always being late to a party; that same
eccentricity isn't so amusing when she's constantly late for your business
meetings. How would you tell a friend that his judgment is poor, or remind
her that she hasn't paid your bill? And if things go awry, you may have a hard
time firing your friends.

Asking for more business

How do you "work" a company to find more business? Here are some tips:

- ✔ **When you're in meetings, strike up conversations with other participants to find out more about what they do.** Ask for business cards and hand out your own. Follow up with those people to explore possible project needs.

- ✔ **Ask your current clients to refer you to others who may need your services.** Be sure to tell them, "If you feel comfortable doing it, I'd appreciate your recommending me to others." Assuming they say, "Yes," ask for names and departments.

- ✔ **Take advantage of any opportunities to meet with other people, attend company functions, participate in workshops or seminars, or go to any social functions.** Familiarity breeds business.

- ✔ **When you're visiting one client, walk around the office and say hello to others you've met.** Visibility is a form of unspoken endorsement, too. If you're hanging around, people will know you're there for a meeting, which means that they've hired you.

- ✔ **Deliver doughnuts to a client and offer them to surrounding departments.**

- ✔ **Invite non-clients to lunch to pick their brains about a project you're working on.** In my business, I can kill two birds with one stone: Gather book material and flatter people by asking them to be involved!

Staying on their minds

Clients are like geese: They wake up in a new world every day. Yesterday's
freelancer is out of sight and likely out of mind. Clients tend to hire
whomever is in front of them at the moment. The flip side of that is that they
tend to *not* hire whomever *is not* in front of them at the moment. To stay on
clients' payroll you have to stay on their minds.

Five quick ways to destroy client communications

Want to do repeat business with your client? Avoid the following at all costs:

✔ Don't return calls.

✔ Spend all your time talking; don't listen to what the client wants.

✔ Try to give clients what you're selling, instead of what they're asking for.

✔ Say you can deliver something you can't.

✔ Be right all the time.

No matter how great a job you've done for a client in the past, to retain their business, you have to stay in front of them regularly. The following sections share ways to stay in touch without constantly bugging your clients for business.

Saying thanks

Mom was right. The two most important words you can say are "thank you." Clients need to hear that you appreciate their business. After all, they've put their credibility in your hands and have paid you for the privilege. Consider the following good ways to thank your clients:

✔ **Tell them in person.** Come right out and say, "I want you to know that I appreciate your business. I enjoy working with you and I hope you'll let me know if there is anything I can do to improve my service to you."

✔ **Take them to lunch just to say thanks.** Have non-business conversations and show an interest in the person. Ask about the kids, dog, bowling team, and anything else that's meaningful to them.

✔ **Send them handwritten notes.** A handwritten note is more personal than a business letter. It's especially meaningful if you mention something about the person. For example, "Dear Bill: Thank you for your continuing business. I appreciate your personal involvement in the market research project we did. Your clear direction made it easy to get the job done right the first time. It's a pleasure to work with you, and I hope we have many more opportunities to solve problems together." Everyone likes a compliment, and clients certainly enjoy feeling that they've made a contribution.

Sending gifts

It's not necessary to send anything elaborate, but some small remembrance makes a great impression. It helps if the gift is related to the project you've done. For example, I once worked on an orientation project in which we used lots of colorful balloons, foil confetti, and other festive elements. Afterwards, I sent the client a small wooden desk box filled with tiny metallic confetti words inside including "congratulations" and "thank you." The gift served four purposes:

✔ It said, "I appreciate your business."

✔ It recognized the client's own success.

✔ It tied me to the client's success (this is most important!).

✔ It sat on the client's desk as a constant reminder.

Most companies have rules about the maximum value of a gift an employee can accept from a freelancer, so be sure to keep your spending conservative. Even without spending a lot of money, you can select something that has meaning to the individual. Creativity definitely counts, and makes your joint efforts more memorable. A job applicant once delivered homemade miniature chocolate éclairs to our office; she was an instant hit, and one I remember many years later.

Saying "hi"

Let clients know that you're always thinking of them and looking for ways to help them, making their lives easier and more fun. Keeping in touch can be a simple matter.

✔ Send e-mails from time to time just to say hello and ask how they're doing. Mention something personal that you remember from their lives, such as, "Have you been back to the mountains lately?" or "How did your daughter enjoy the surfboard you gave her?" I try to stay in touch with former clients about once every couple of months. They appreciate my thinking of them, and I have fun hearing how they're doing.

✔ When you see articles that you think they would enjoy, send them with a handwritten sticky note.

✔ Call them simply to ask how things are going.

Sending greetings

Everyone likes to be remembered as an individual, and I've found that people are extremely grateful (and usually surprised) to receive a greeting that just wishes them well or lets them know I'm thinking of them.

✔ Send a card for an unusual holiday such as Columbus Day. Regular holiday cards such as New Year's cards get lost in the shuffle. When you send something at an unusual time, you have less competition for attention and you demonstrate your creativity.

✔ Send a birthday card.

Your clients undoubtedly represent a spectrum of religious beliefs. Keep your greetings generic, offering wishes such as, "Happy holidays" or "Peace on earth." Offering a wish that has religious overtones — "Merry Christmas" or "Happy Easter" — presumes a certain belief and can be offensive to people who don't share that belief.

Asking for feedback

You need to know how a client feels about the work you've done so that you can keep doing what they like and stop doing what they don't like. I recommend sending a written evaluation asking for feedback. While you can ask your clients for their opinion in person, it could be uncomfortable for a client to give you negative feedback face-to-face. By sending a written form, you give them time to think about your questions and to reflect on what they'd like you to do differently. (Best of all, the survey is one more reminder of the great job you did.)

Your request for feedback should be:

✔ Short

✔ Easy to fill out

Never ask a client's opinion about something that you aren't willing to change. For example, if you ask, "Is my price fair?" you must be prepared to do something about it if the client says, "No." That means you'll have to either renegotiate your fee or provide more service for the price. If you're not prepared to do something about their suggestions, don't ask.

You can ask for feedback on several areas in your client surveys:

✔ The quality of your service

✔ How well the end result meets their needs

✔ Your willingness to be flexible, and your effectiveness at solving problems

✔ The value they feel they receive

✔ Their overall satisfaction

Figure 10-1 shows you a sample evaluation form. You can tailor it to your specific clients, asking questions about any particular projects you've recently completed. Start with some easy questions that you feel sure you will get positive answers. A client will feel more comfortable being able to say something positive first.

Be sure to include a self-addressed, stamped envelope for them to return the survey to you.

Surveys like this one are an easy way to find out what clients think. With their input, you can look at each score for which you fall below your goal and work on that area. You may have to delve more deeply to find out specifics, but you can do that by taking a client to lunch for a one-on-one discussion. To improve their satisfaction, you may have to change some of your procedures, add more services, look at pricing, or address other problems.

Freelancer Evaluation Form

Please rate the service that I provide. Circle one of the numbers for each question: 0 means "not at all" and 5 means "all the time."

Do you feel that I respond in a timely manner to your needs?	0 1 2 3 4 5
Does the service I provide live up to your expectations?	0 1 2 3 4 5
Is my communication with you clear and concise?	0 1 2 3 4 5
Do I live up to your expectations when compared to other freelancers?	0 1 2 3 4 5
Do you feel that you receive a good value for the price?	0 1 2 3 4 5
Would you feel confident referring me to your associates?	0 1 2 3 4 5

What other services can I provide that would be of value to you? *(List some related services that you may actually offer and let them check yes or no. Give a place to write in suggestions.)*

What can I do to improve my service to you? _____

_____

Thanks for your suggestions and feedback!

Figure 10-1:
Sample
evaluation
form.

Some companies send surveys at the end of every project they do. I find this to be a burden, and I never fill these out unless I'm extremely pleased or extremely displeased. I think that the most effective times to send out feedback requests are at the end of a long project or no more than twice a year. If you ask for feedback more often than that, people start to ignore your surveys. At that point, the survey isn't an effective way to get information, and it's not effective for reinforcing your great work, either. In other words, it's a waste of their time, and of your time and money.

What if a client says you didn't live up to their expectations? Follow these steps:

1. **Decide what you're willing to do to fix the problem.**

   You must know how you want to handle the situation before you call the client. To decide this, think about how important the client is to you and how much your reputation is worth.

2. **Call the client.**

   Express your regret that your product or service was lacking. Let the client know that you're grateful to know about the problem and that you certainly want to make it up to them.

3. **Tell the client what you're prepared to do.**

   You may have several options:

   - Do the job over.
   - Reduce the price.
   - Change the way you do things to make the process work better in the future.

4. **Apologize again and thank the client for giving you a chance to make things right.**

   Tell the client how important he or she is to you.

5. **Fix the problem immediately!**

   Good follow-up is essential to show that you take the issue seriously and will do better in the future.

Dissatisfied clients tell lots of people about bad experiences. After the word gets out, you may have a difficult time overcoming a negative impression. Better to nip it in the bud. Fix the situation, and you can turn a dissatisfied client into a loyal one.

Defensiveness has no place in freelancing. I work with lots of freelancers, and I'm not shy about giving negative feedback. Nothing turns me off more than when someone responds to my concern by denying that he or she has done anything wrong or by trying to talk me out of my position. You may be able to prove that you're right, but it will leave a bad taste in a client's mouth. This is a classic case of winning the battle and losing the war.

Understanding the pitfalls of success

Successfully mining for diamonds in one company can be a heavenly experience. The clients keep multiplying, the work gets easier because you know the ins and outs of the company, and you can achieve lots of visibility with one trip to a client's office. One corporate diamond mine can keep you in full-time work, which is wonderful, unless the company merges with a competitor, moves to another city, or lays off all your contacts. As advantageous as it may seem, putting all your eggs in one basket is an extremely risky proposition. No matter how much you like working with one client, you must diversify your client base to protect yourself.

A moving story

Denise Temofeew has moved to new cities four times in her ten-year freelance technical-writing career. Each time she has moved, she has called me soon after and talked excitedly about a potential new client. If she meets someone who may be a future business contact, she lets them know early in the conversation that she's a freelancer. "They often know someone who is looking for what I do," she says. She doesn't usually have to look far. Her magnetic personality and natural selling skills have landed her work with the real estate agent from whom she bought her home, the contractor who built her house, the medical group her husband works with, and the physician recruiter who helped her husband get placed.

Just because she changes addresses doesn't mean she has to give up her loyal clients, either. She can handle most work easily through fax, e-mail, and phone. "I don't make a big deal about moving out of town, because clients tend to panic at the thought of not being able to keep you close at hand. I explain that I have a new set of phone numbers, and that they'll be able to reach me as easily as they always have. If you're reliable, clients don't need to see you face-to-face to do business with you."

How can you find the time to seek other clients when your current client monopolizes your time? Force yourself to accept projects from other clients and build your schedule to accommodate them. Of course, every client wants to feel as if he or she is your only client, and maintaining a high performance standard is difficult.

Expanding Your Base of New Clients

Existing clients are great sources of business, but how can you expand your base? Lots of ways. The following are some places to start:

- **Your clients' friends or associates at other companies:** Ask your clients about their peers at other companies. If they belong to an association or business group, they undoubtedly know people who can use your services. An endorsement from a well-placed client means a lot.

- **In related industries:** If your clients need someone like you, so do their competitors. Specialize in an industry to expand your customer base to other cities.

- **In similar companies:** If one manufacturing company needs employee communications training, so do other manufacturing companies.

✔ **At businesses that are related to yours:** For example, businesses associated with my writing business include the following:

- Printers (who print what writers write)

- Video studios (who shoot scripts that writers write)

- Graphic design studios (who lay out what writers write)

- Event planners (who set up speeches that writers write)

- Advertising agencies (who create ads from the copy that writers write)

The people in each of those businesses have customers who hire writers. What companies are in businesses related to yours? Find them, and you'll find good potential sources of additional business.

✔ **At association meetings:** Almost every profession has a national association that also has local chapters. Attend their luncheons to meet potential clients.

✔ **At local business groups:** Groups such as the Rotary Club, Kiwanis, Chamber of Commerce, and civic organizations have member directories, as well as meetings where you can network and meet other business people.

✔ **In the newspaper:** Read the newspaper and note articles about people who are promoted, accept new positions, receive honors, start new companies, or have articles written about their companies. If your city has a weekly business newspaper, use it as an invaluable source of information about current business needs. Most of these papers also periodically publish special issues that relate to particular industries or subjects, such as health care, and these issues provide in-depth information that can spark ideas.

✔ **On the Internet:** Internet-based business is becoming more and more popular as a way for people to do business without ever even seeing their clients and is another source for finding work. Try a search of your profession, along with a descriptor such as jobs, freelance work, or another indicator of independent working arrangements. Searching for the right freelance assignment may take some detective work, but it can pay off nicely. (Keep in mind, however, that Internet jobs aren't always the highest paying.) You must thoroughly research the source — just because you're a respectable Internet job seeker doesn't mean all the work you find is equally legitimate. See the "Landing Jobs on the Web with e-Lancing" section, near the end of this chapter, for more information on getting started on the Internet.

✔ **In positions that are similar to your clients' positions:** If you do work for one vice president of human resources, you can probably find work for another vice president of human resources. People in similar positions are likely to have similar needs. It can't hurt to ask.

Cold calls leave me cold

I've made few cold calls in my life. *Cold calls* are when you just pick a company or a contact and try to get in to see someone without any previous introduction through associates or friends. I don't like cold calls, so I don't make them, but I probably should. Especially when you're getting started, cold calls can be a way of getting your name in front of people. I'm not saying you shouldn't make cold calls; I'm saying that I know how hard it is.

People who try to make an appointment to see me for a cold sales call usually sink to the bottom of my priority list. It could be weeks or months before I find the time to see them. After I've talked with them, I usually file their information away and never think about it again. Only when they keep calling do I consider giving them a chance to show me their stuff.

If you make cold calls, you must follow up. Unless you're extremely fortunate or call on someone who's in a crisis and hands you a bomb to defuse on the spot, you probably won't get business from cold calls without calling again.

Your job is to know your clients like the back of your hand, which will help you know where to find more people like them. If all the people in an office belong to a bowling league, the place to find clients is at the bowling alley on league night.

Landing Jobs on the Web with e-Lancing

E-lancing is a new twist on the idea of online auctions — and your services are on the block. E-lancing means using the Internet to post information about your skills and your fees and competing with other freelancers for work. You bid on projects or let potential employers contact you if your skills match their needs. Some Web sites charge a nominal fee to the freelancer, but most charge a fee only to the employer.

If you're just starting out, e-lancing may be the quickest (and least painful) way to land jobs. You may even end up working on a team with other freelancers your electronic employer has brought together to tackle a big project.

E-lancing jobs are available in many fields, from accounting to legal services to photography to Web design. Go to an Internet search site or job site and search on the name of your field.

Chapter 11

Landing Business with Advertising and PR

*H*ave you ever wanted a career in sales? Whether you ever have or not, you have one now. Fortunately, you have a product that you absolutely believe in: You!

Perhaps you've met natural salespeople, those who have an outgoing, positive personality, who are talkative, and who smile a lot. You may assume they feel completely comfortable in any situation, able to sell themselves and what they do with ease. It ain't necessarily so. You can become effective at selling, advertising, and promoting your business. This chapter tells you a few of the ins and outs.

Most of the freelancers I know don't have a lot of money to invest in sales, advertising, or public relations (PR). So how much should you spend? Each time you consider an investment, try to project how much business you'd need to get to pay for the project. For example, if you place an ad for $500, how many new clients would you need to offset that $500 investment? If you gain at least $500 worth of business, you break even. If you sell more than $500 worth of products or services, you've made money. At the end of every month, quarter, or year, look at your sales budget and see where you made investments that paid off. Those are the areas where you will probably want to invest again.

Selling Benefits, Not Products

If a client wants to know why she should buy you instead of someone else, what will you tell her? When you know the answer to that question, you will know your *unique selling proposition* or USP.

What makes any product or service better than any other? Take toothpaste as an example. Think of all the ways a toothpaste manufacturer may say, "Our product is better." They may promise any of the following:

- ✔ Whiter teeth
- ✔ Fresher breath
- ✔ Fewer cavities
- ✔ Protection against gum disease
- ✔ Minty fresh taste
- ✔ Tartar control

All these qualities are USPs, things that make one product different than another. Every product, including yours, needs something that differentiates it, something that gives it greater value than the competitor's product, something to boast about that gives a customer a reason to buy. It should be something you can say in one sentence that sums up your outstanding point of difference.

The following are some qualities you may offer that could be your USP:

- ✔ Your product or service is of higher quality than your competitors'.
- ✔ You have more impressive credentials.
- ✔ You have a better track record of results.
- ✔ You have more experience.
- ✔ You provide a service that has more features.
- ✔ Your service is easier to use.
- ✔ You provide faster service.
- ✔ Your cost is lower.
- ✔ You offer a satisfaction guarantee.

Keep two important qualities of USPs in mind:

- ✔ It must be true.
- ✔ It must be something that's important to the customer.

Notice that in the case of the toothpaste, the company sells something that provides benefit to the customer. Whiter teeth and fresher breath, the customer assumes, lead to being more attractive. Fewer cavities lead to fewer painful trips to the dentist. Likewise, tartar protection, gum disease prevention, and so on all have their benefits. In each of those cases, the company sells the benefit to the customer. Focus not on what you are selling, but on how your product or service will make the customer's life better.

What benefits do customers want? Customers want to be liked and respected, they want to make more money, be more secure, make better decisions, keep their jobs, make friends. Do you notice anything about that list? In every case, the outcomes relate to personal benefit. Always remember, your customers are people first and customers second. Appeal to their personal wants, and you will have the foundation for a loyal customer.

Creating a sales presentation

The most important thing to remember in creating a sales presentation is that you should focus on what the client wants to buy, not what you want to sell. Did you get that? Focus on what the client wants to buy, not what you want to sell. Repeat that over and over. Think through the benefits you provide to the client. I've seen sales pitches from hundreds of vendors, and they fail most often because they talk too much about what they do rather than what I need.

A sales presentation can be a formal speech that you deliver standing up in front of a group, using visual materials, or it can be an informal one-on-one discussion. A typical sales presentation includes the following:

✔ A description of your company

✔ A listing of your services

✔ Background of other projects you've done or clients you've worked with

✔ A description of the client's needs

✔ A proposal of what you can do for the client

✔ A timetable for implementation

✔ An estimated price

No proposal is etched in stone. Your proposed elements, timetable, or cost may be estimates only. That's okay. You're creating a place to start. Welcome client revisions — it's a way of increasing their belief in the project plan.

Listen for buying signals. When a client asks questions like how much the service costs or how long it will take, you know they're ready to buy.

Painting a picture of yourself

Potential clients want to see proof of your expertise. People applying for traditional jobs present a résumé outlining their work experience. For freelancers, it's a little different. You're trying to create a picture of what you do, and you can use a couple of tools to do that. The following sections share two effective means of showing off your abilities.

Writing a professional summary

A *professional summary* is similar to a resume, except it showcases your talents and projects instead of your positions (see Figure 11-1). When you first begin your freelance career, you may have to include a good bit of your corporate background in your summary, because you may not have sufficient project material to make an impressive case for yourself. After a few years, however, you should have a lot of ammunition for a great summary.

No matter how pressed for time I am, I always tailor my professional summary to the project I want to land. Because I have background in writing, training, consulting, planning, and several other fields, I try to figure out what will be most important to the client and emphasize that area. Even though I may have many skills, I know that the client has limited time to consider my credentials. I want them to spend their time looking only at things that are useful to them. By narrowing the focus, you're helping the client before you even get the job!

Do personal photos have a place in professional summaries? In some cases, a photo can be necessary and desirable. If you're a public speaker, for example, you certainly need to show that you are a person with a pleasing appearance and a professional image. My own reaction is this: If your appearance has nothing to do with your qualifications, why bother? Are you trying to cover up lack of experience with a glamour shot? If you do use a photo, have a sitting with a professional photographer who can advise you about what to wear and what pose is most appropriate for your needs.

Building a portfolio

A *portfolio* is a collection of representative samples of your work, presented in an organized and attractive fashion. Creating a portfolio may be somewhat expensive, but it's worth the cost of creating a professional image. You can purchase a carrying case (also called a portfolio) that's designed specifically for the purpose of holding printed materials. To save money, you can also use a notebook if you assemble it carefully, putting work in protective sleeves and making it look attractive.

Sample Professional Summary

Professional Background and Accomplishments

Paul Hawthorne is a graphic designer and creative director who has worked in commercial art and advertising for more than 20 years. He spent 6 years with Michie, Charles and John, a New York-based advertising agency, before relocating to Minneapolis to form his own company in 1985.

As a consultant to medium-sized companies, Paul now devotes his creative energy to help growing organizations achieve success in both business-to-business and community-relations activities. He specializes in developing campaigns with measurable results and has recently been named "Most Practical Designer" by the Minneapolis Rotary Club.

Paul also is a contributing cartoonist to *Designs* magazine and has published several technical articles for trade publications.

Sample Results

* Minneapolis Motorama: Increased attendance by 225 percent in one year.
* Children's Hospital Doctors' ads: Increased patient count by 32 percent in six months.
* Automotive Parts Company's Talking Heads campaign: Raised awareness by 68 percent at campaigns' end.

Awards and Recognition

* Best of Show, 1999: Advertising Federation of North America
* Gold Quill Award, 2000: International Association of Business Communicators
* Refined Design Award, 2000: Design Association of America

Professional Designations

* Certified Marketing Designer
* Certified Auditor, Greater Minneapo

Partial Client List

* Bartow and Belk Attorneys
* Holiday Lighting
* General Insurance Agency

Figure 11-1:
The professional summary is similar to a resume, but the narrative format allows you to sell yourself.

Choose the most outstanding examples of
Keep the following in mind:

✔ **Quantity is not as important as quality.** Choose your best work and include a variety of project types. Don't overwhelm the client with a hodgepodge of samples that would take hours to peruse.

✔ **Be sensitive to your previous clients' need for confidentiality.** Never use a sample that exposes confidential client information in a portfolio.

✔ **Whenever possible, show originals of your work.** A copy never conveys the same level of importance or sophistication as the real thing. This is especially true for four-color pieces. Reports should be shown in their actual binders, along with any company material used along with it. This gives the job more credibility.

✔ **Use up-to-date work samples.** Dated material gives the impression that you either haven't done anything lately or that you haven't done anything lately that you're proud of. It's okay to use a few older samples if they are particularly noteworthy because they won awards or were done for an impressive client, but keep those to a minimum.

Sometimes a client will ask that you leave your samples behind so they can be shared with others in the company. I try not to do this. First, it depletes my supply of originals. Second, without my sales narrative, the materials can lose their punch. I graciously explain that I'll be happy to meet with anyone else who would like to see my samples, but I expect to be showing my materials again soon and can't leave them behind.

Preparing sales materials

In the course of your business, you'll meet people whom you want to remember you and know how to reach you. It's a good idea — a necessity, in fact — to have printed materials with information about your services and your address, phone number, and any other pertinent contact information. These materials don't have to cost an arm and a leg; you can probably produce them inexpensively. This section describes some useful sales materials that are a part of your image and should portray you and your business briefly but in a highly favorable light.

Start with the basics — letterhead, business cards, a professional summary and/or a portfolio. You can always produce other materials as necessary; but before you invest in them, wait and see what you need. Several years ago I invested in a brochure because I felt I should have one, and I still have hundreds of them gathering dust. My calendar has always been busy, and I don't believe I've ever gotten one piece of business from that brochure! Besides the basics, other sales materials include the following:

✓ brochure

✓ top presentation

- ✔ Overhead transparencies, which I feel are somewhat outmoded and not very attractive

- ✔ A slide show or computer-generated presentation

- ✔ A video: This isn't appropriate for everyone and is too costly for the average freelancer. I recommend it for public speakers, for audiovisual producers, for event planners to show examples of their events, or for others whose work is highly active and visual.

- ✔ A CD, which is easy for most people to use now that computers are a staple in any office

Your sales materials speak for you. They remain behind after you're gone. Sometimes they get handed to others who don't have the benefit of your personal sales pitch. Everything you use to promote your business should be of the highest quality you can afford. After all, when you're not there, the sales materials represent the quality of your work. The five following rules can help you create professional sales materials:

- ✔ **Have a plan.** Preparing sales tools should never be a haphazard activity. You should make deliberate, well-thought-out decisions about what you want to say to your potential clients and how you say it.

- ✔ **Keep your message simple.** Focus on benefits to the client and reinforce the same points many times.

- ✔ **Create materials that won't quickly become outdated.** Avoid using information that's tied to a date. Use a modular approach of individual materials that you can print and assemble individually. If one piece becomes outdated, you can reprint it by itself or simply not use it in your package.

- ✔ **Maintain a consistent look for all your sales materials.** Your materials should look consistent so that you can begin to develop a name and an image for yourself. You do this through using a constant color theme, typeface, and style of artwork. Anything you do that's visual should convey the same image.

- ✔ **Don't skimp on production.** Use designers, typesetters, printers, and other vendors who are known for quality.

Certain colors, typefaces, types of paper, and other qualities of your sales material contribute to the impression your clients have of you. Be sure your materials say what you want them to say by considering what personality your materials convey. Think about what's important to your clients. If you're offering financial services, your clients probably want someone stable who will protect their interests. Choosing lime green and purple stationery won't send that message. Of course, if you're in a creative business, your client may want someone out-of-the-ordinary, and those colors may be right up your alley. Sales materials aren't a matter of your favorite color; they're a matter of your clients' comfort level.

Using a professional to produce print and electronic materials

In the olden days, people used to tell sad stories about the poor children who had to wear shabby, homemade clothes to school. I feel the same way about freelancers who create their own marketing and sales materials. They look homemade.

No doubt I'm prejudiced in this area because I do it for a living, but I've seen some very smart freelancers look very un-smart because they got the desktop-publishing bug. In this area, a little knowledge is a dangerous thing. Get professional help for any print or electronic materials you intend to produce:

✔ While you may think you'll save money making your materials yourself, a professional

can actually offer money-saving tips that will spare you headaches and cash down the road.

✔ Professionals know where and how to get the highest quality for the best price.

✔ Professionals can be objective about your business and how to showcase your talents.

✔ Professionals can offer advice about alternatives that may be more effective than what you've considered.

Using a specific service to open the door

I like to change the saying, "Familiarity breeds contempt," to "Familiarity breeds business." Sometimes all it takes to get a customer for life is a little painless introductory offer. Most customers just need a chance to see what you can do. You can help them find out about you by giving them a taste of your talent and letting them see a small part of what you offer. After they have a good experience, they will likely come back for more.

People like tangible stuff and they like not being committed to a long-term situation. I can sell writing a brochure pretty easily, because people know what they're getting into. It seems affordable and it has a short timeframe. I have a more difficult time selling communications consulting, because it's not as clear cut. People don't have a picture of what communications consulting looks like, what it will cost, how long it will last, or what they're likely to gain from it. They get nervous at the idea of a long-term commitment. So, why try to sell something that's hard to sell? I sell the brochure writing, and as I work with people, I gain their trust and cleverly find ways to let them know what else I do. One successful project sells another.

You can also pique people's interest by selling them one very specific piece of what you do and letting them grow to depend on you for broader services. Here are some examples:

✔ An accountant could sell a one-time tax return preparation, with the ultimate goal of gaining a client for ongoing accounting work.

✔ A computer consultant could sell an on-site software training class to introduce clients to their need for network management.

✔ A photographer could do children's school photos with an eye toward getting a foot in the door for family portraits.

✔ A landscaping and lawn maintenance company could do a free landscape design to gain ongoing landscaping and maintenance business.

One way to gain exposure is to offer a free service. You see this in department stores in the cosmetics area. Makeup salespeople do free beauty makeovers with the idea that customers will look fabulous and will want to buy the magic products that transformed them. It works with certain types of businesses.

You have to balance the business you may get from a free offer with the perception you're creating for yourself. Sometimes customers can be leery of a cut-rate service. You're unlikely to go to a discount doctor, aren't you? Only you can judge how your client will perceive a free introductory offer.

Calling all sales calls

Hundreds of books talk about how to make a sales call. In my opinion, every contact you have with a client or a potential client is a sales call. Good business practices make for good sales calls. It's mostly a matter of good manners and good habits. Here are a few tips:

✔ Always spell the client's name right.

✔ Be on time.

✔ Dress appropriately.

✔ Thank the person for their time.

✔ Follow up to say you enjoyed meeting them, and you want to work with them soon.

I'm not sure whether to recommend you call the day of an appointment to confirm or not. I consider it good manners to call ahead, as well as a way of demonstrating that you're organized and you respect the other person's time. I've also heard sales gurus say, "Don't call to confirm, because it gives the person a chance to reschedule." I call to confirm.

The most important thing you can say in a sales call is nothing. Being able to hear what your client says will be a better determinant of whether you get the business than anything you say. Your goal should be to identify what the potential client is working on, getting them to tell you as many details as possible so you can be informed about what their needs are. Get them talking, and they will undoubtedly tell you where they need the most help. Listen carefully for comments about being understaffed, needing to solve a problem, being dissatisfied with service they're getting from another company or from internal departments, or other indications that they could use your services. Knowing what they need is vital to your ability to offer help.

In your interview you find out what the client needs. Don't wait for a client to offer you the business. Be direct in asking for it. Try saying the following:

- ✔ I've always admired your company and would like to develop a relationship with you. I'd like a chance to show you what I can do. Can I help you with (name a project they've described)?

- ✔ I'd really like to help you (fill in the blank with the project they've been discussing). Can I give you a proposal?

- ✔ This project sounds exciting. How can I help you with it?

- ✔ I've done a number of similar projects. It's one of the things I specialize in. Can I put together a plan for you?

- ✔ If you're ready to get started, I'd like to work with you on this.

- ✔ I've always enjoyed working with you, and would like to do business with you again. Are there any projects coming up that I can help you with?

Asking so directly may feel uncomfortable at first. Practice makes perfect. And don't think it's presumptuous to ask for business. That's a freelancer's job.

Dealing with rejection

No matter how good you are, occasionally, you will be turned down. The main thing to accomplish when you're rejected is to keep the door open for future sales opportunities. Handle a rejection gracefully, and you will have other chances to land the business. React with indignity, and you'll close the door on your future with that client.

Here are some things you can do to improve your chances for future work:

- ✔ Thank the client for the chance to present your product or services.

- ✔ Ask the client to suggest how you can make a more acceptable bid in the future.

  ✔ Ask for the business. Tell the client directly that you would always like to be considered for future work. Ask if other projects are coming up that they feel you may be suited for. If so, what is the timing and when may you follow-up?

  ✔ Follow up with a thank-you letter and wish them well with their project.

  ✔ Call in two months to see how the project went and to offer your services again.

Always let the client know that their well-being is your first concern. You only want to work on projects for which they believe you are the best choice.

Using Advertising and Public Relations Tools

According to a former advertising executive, the only reason to advertise is because you can't go see people personally. As a freelancer, you certainly "go see" a lot of people face to face. Sometimes, however, you need a more efficient way to let people know who you are and to build your reputation. This is where advertising and public relations can help. It's a fast way to reach a lot of people. But what kind of advertising should you use, and when, and how? And isn't advertising expensive? And how do you get public relations coverage? This section covers some basics, helping you decide what's the best way to promote your services and describing how to get the greatest results for each dollar you invest.

Knowing your audience

To reach your potential clients, you must know whom you're trying to reach or, in other words, who will buy what you sell. This group is your *target market,* because they're the people you aim your sales and marketing efforts at. As you define your market, consider which of the following you want to know about them:

  ✔ Are they men or women?

  ✔ How old are they?

  ✔ What is their education level?

  ✔ Do they have children?

  ✔ What is their lifestyle like?

  ✔ What do they need?

Going for *The Golden Ring*

John Snyder was a perfectly successful advertising and PR professional. He owned a 13-person firm that specialized in sports marketing, handling NASCAR racing teams, Washington Bullets basketball, and international running events. Then he decided to write a book. Inspired by his grandmother, John completed a labor of love entitled, *The Golden Ring,* and set out to sell it. After all, who could be more qualified? He was already a pro. Besides, "I love doing PR for myself, because there's so much client appreciation," jokes John.

At first, John tried the traditional route: trying to get an agent and approaching publishers. He found that to be a vicious cycle. "You can't get an agent unless you've published, and you can't publish unless you have an agent," he says. Undaunted, John decided to publish the book

himself and to take on the job of marketing it. For the last two years, he has pursued agents, publishers, media people, reviewers, distributors, bookstores, and everyone else he can think of who could move copies of the book. He has created media kits wrapped like gift packages and created a Web site. After two years, he's in the black. His book is a top seller with his distributor and is in bookstores nationally. He has a 90-store book-signing tour on his schedule.

John's background in PR certainly taught him not to take no for an answer and, in this case, his dedication has paid off. But not without a lot of rejection. He admits the process of promoting this project has taken a toll. Nevertheless, he won't give up. "I intend to keep writing books. The only alternative is to have a part of my brain removed!"

The more you know about people, the better able you'll be to reach them. My target market, for example, is a corporate manager, because they're the people who need my communications consulting services. In planning how to market my business, I ask myself, "Where can I find corporate managers?" and "What needs do they have?" Then I try to get my name into all the nooks and crannies where they are.

Figuring out WIIFT

The best way to sell anyone anything is to answer the question, "What's in it for them?" That's what every audience wants to know. Show them a product, and they'll instinctively want to know how it will serve their purposes. No matter what type of advertising, sales, and public relations you do, you must always look at it from your customer's standpoint, and ask yourself, "What's in it for my customer?"

Defining where they are

You have numerous ways to "go see" people — think of all the places you see advertising:

- Newspapers, magazines
- Television

- ✔ Radio
- ✔ Internet
- ✔ Brochures
- ✔ Bus benches
- ✔ Billboards
- ✔ Sides of trucks and buses

I could go on. You can think of a million ways to reach your audience. The trick is to narrow down the field to a manageable and cost-effective system.

One of the biggest mistakes people make in trying to advertise their products and services is to try to reach too many people at one time. The key to successful advertising is to reach only the people who will buy what you're selling. Better to find three people who are predisposed to buy than a million people who aren't interested.

When you consider any type of advertising, ask yourself two primary questions:

- ✔ Is this a good place to reach the people who are most likely to buy my product?
- ✔ Is there a faster, cheaper, more effective way to reach them?

Most people take one of two approaches to selling, and I describe them both in hunting terms:

- ✔ **Shotgun technique:** In this method, you close your eyes, fire a shotgun toward the woods and hope to hit something. You may hit the big game you're hunting, but you're more likely to miss the big game and just hit a few armadillos. The shotgun method of advertising is pretty inefficient, because a lot of your ammo gets wasted on people who aren't even potential clients. Sometimes you completely miss the people you're after. For a small business person, television advertising is an example of a shotgun approach. It covers a huge audience, but most of them aren't the people you need to reach.

- ✔ **Rifle or sharpshooter technique:** A rifle is a much more accurate and efficient method of bagging game. You know exactly what you're hunting, you aim only at that select target, and you fire carefully to hit that single target. In advertising, when you target your efforts to clients, you carefully focus on a select group of clients who are most likely to buy your goods or services. Sending a mailer offering a special to a particular group, such as doctors, is an example of a rifle technique. It is much more accurate and effective.

The best advertising is no advertising. By that I mean that the most targeted way of selling your business is to let your business speak for itself. Word-of-mouth is the most effective way to get new clients, so rely heavily on this method. The second best advertising is the rifle technique.

Using multiple channels

The chances that anyone will buy your service the first time they hear of you are very slim. More than likely, you have to keep getting your name in front of people and keep it there. In many cases, people buy whatever is in front of them at the time they need the product or service. Your chances of being in front of people at that moment increase if you're hitting them with messages many times.

While you may find that one channel works well, you may need to actually use a variety of avenues to keep reminding people who you are and what you do.

While you may rely on the newspaper for information, another person may use the Internet, a cable TV news channel, or the radio. People receive messages in different ways: through sight, sound, and touch. To broaden your appeal, you must reach people in a variety of ways. In addition, people have to be exposed to a message multiple times for an impression to stick. Movie screenwriters know that an audience must see something at least three times to make it believable; the same applies to marketing. Get your name in front of your target audience in at least three different ways, so that they will be more likely to believe you are an expert.

Making sure your advertising and PR works

No matter what kind of advertising or public relations you choose to do, decide on a way to measure how effective it is. To me, "effective" means one thing: It brings in at least enough business to pay for itself. If so, it's worth it. By tracking how effective your efforts are, you can decide whether your money is well spent.

How do you measure your results? When clients show up at your door, be sure to ask how they heard about you. This gives you a chance to see if people actually call you as a result of an ad or a public relations effort. When you need to renew your ad or send press releases again, you'll know whether those efforts are likely to pay for themselves. If you consistently buy ads and don't get any clients from them, reconsider your strategy.

It may seem backward to explain how to measure results before describing what you should do. Isn't that putting the cart before the horse? Not at all. You have to decide how you plan to measure effectiveness before you actually do the advertising. Most of your measurement tracking must be set up in advance, because some information can't be captured after the fact. The point of measurement is this: Keeping track of where your business comes from tells you where to spend your money in advertising.

The following are some examples of ways to measure your results:

- ✔ **Using a different offer in different ads.** If you offer $10 off in one ad, offer $20 off in another. You can then easily see which add generated more sales. While you may think that the $20 off would logically result in more sales, that's not necessarily true. Consumers are an odd breed; you never know what will strike their fancy. Take, for example, two fliers or brochures. One offers a videotape for $9.95; the other offers the video-tape for $9.95 or a video-plus-cassette for $19.95. The flier with the two offers not only sells some of the higher priced item, it also sells more of the lower priced item than the flier with only the videotape.

- ✔ **Put a special number on coupons that distinguishes where the coupon was placed.** For example, suppose you put an ad in the local newspaper and in a weekly business paper. You certainly want to know which one generated more interest, as well as actual sales.

- ✔ **Ask each customer how they learned about your service.** What if you were a massage therapist, and you required new clients to fill out health-information forms. You could also include a question about how they learned of your service. By keeping a record of their answers, you could find out how you were receiving the majority of your business.

Advertising yourself through traditional means

Certain businesses benefit from advertising, while others do not. A simple way to test your own business is to ask yourself: Would an advertisement get me interested in my service? If the answer is yes, you can begin to narrow down where to advertise. If the answer is no, you need to consider some other ways to sell.

I don't advocate advertising for freelancers who are just entering the inde-pendent market, because I think advertising is an expensive route to take. Wait until you have a year or so under your belt to decide what advertising you need.

Consider the following forms of advertising:

- **Yellow Pages:** Being listed in the Yellow Pages of the telephone book is a way of giving your business credibility. If you're paying for a business phone number, you get a simple listing free of charge. If you decide you need a more prominent ad, with a box around it, bold type, or a drawing or picture to draw attention to your business, you pay extra for it. Extravagant ads are a pretty expensive proposition and are probably unnecessary for a freelancer.

- **Classified advertising:** Classified ads are the ads you see in the back of your daily newspaper or in a specialty paper such as a weekly business newspaper. I tried an experiment recently putting a classified ad for a career workshop in the newspaper. I had about two calls, and they were from people who showed only moderate interest in the class.

  Use yourself as a guinea pig. If you needed what you sell, would you look for it in the classifieds? If you offer a service such as lawn care, the classifieds may be a helpful place for you to advertise. Keep in mind, though, that someone must be specifically looking for the service you offer in order to find you in those ads. The casual reader will never see your placement.

  Like TV ads, classified ads tend to blanket a lot of people who aren't qualified to buy your service.

- **Newspapers (daily, business, and suburban):** Buying a newspaper ad is a shotgun approach. When you think of all the people who read newspapers and what a small percentage of them are your audience, you can see that your dollars are not well spent. The high cost of newspaper advertising is clearly not something the average freelancer can or should afford.

  In the case of a targeted newspaper, such as the business weeklies in some cities, you may have opportunities to benefit from advertising. Check with the newspaper's sales department to find out who their readers are and how big their circulation is. That will help you judge the likelihood of it being a good tool for you. Expect the cost to be pretty high. In Memphis, we have specialty tabloid newspapers for career women and other groups. These can be effective if your service is targeted to a very specific group.

  When you judge a newspaper as a potential outlet for your advertising message, find out what the *readership* is — that is, how many people actually read the paper — and find out who those people are. Do they match your target profile? The newspaper advertising department can help you figure out how long your ad should be, what section would be most effective for your subject matter, and other relevant issues. There is, after all, a big difference in the readers of ads on the society page versus, say, the sports page.

- ✔ **Magazines:** I'd like to advertise in *Forbes, Fortune,* and other prestigious business magazines, but ads in those publications cost thousands of dollars. I'd have to generate a lot of business to make it worth my while, and I'm not willing to take that financial risk. Aside from national media, you may find that advertising in a local magazine is a worthwhile investment.

- ✔ **Radio:** Radio ads are an effective way to get in front of a large group of people without spending an arm and a leg. While you can certainly buy radio space, you're also likely to get on the radio for free. Check out the PR opportunities (see the "Generating PR opportunities" section later in this chapter) before you buy time.

- ✔ **Television:** The same thing applies to TV as newspapers: lots of money, little control. The TV remote control allows viewers to tune you out in favor of another channel with a quick little click. When selecting television as an advertising medium, choose programs that your potential clients are likely to watch. If you sell fishing lessons, a local fishing show would certainly be a program to choose.

Using direct mail

I find that direct mail can be an effective method of keeping in touch with clients. *Direct mail,* which is sending a selling piece to your potential client's home or office, allows you to target only those people you want to reach, and it can be done in manageable numbers. This, of course, helps cut cost. For the price of the mailer, plus a postage stamp, you can send whatever message you like to exactly the person you want to receive it.

In designing a direct mail piece, be sure to keep it simple and brief. Direct mail should do one of two things:

- ✔ Make people aware of a specific event, offer, or piece of information such as "We're moving."

- ✔ Make people say, "Oh, yeah, I remember them." Your hope is that they need your service at the exact moment they open their mail!

Check your own mailbox for a couple of days and notice how much junk you receive that you never look at. When you send mail to clients, you're competing with all that paper. Yours had better be different, eye-catching, offer something fabulous, or otherwise get their attention.

Keeping a little green book

The heart of your advertising, public relations, networking, or other marketing efforts is your *little green book.* This is a list of the people who are going to put green stuff in your wallet. It could be a list of all the people you've ever met in your whole life. At the very least, it should contain the names, addresses, phone numbers, and e-mail addresses of all your good potential business contacts. Keep a list in your computer so that any time someone moves or changes numbers you can quickly update their information. If you keep the list in a database, you can generate different lists from one master list. That way, you can pick and choose who should receive certain mailings or phone calls. For example, if you want to do a holiday mailing, you can select certain important clients to receive a gift, while others get a card only.

A good salesperson who calls on you more than one time will usually mention something personal about you. You may be impressed by conversation openers like, "How did your son's soccer game go?" and "Did you enjoy your vacation?" Such comments don't necessarily indicate their sincere personal interest in your personal activities, and you don't have to have a memory like an elephant to use this trick of the trade. Do what a pro does: Jot down notes about clients in their files. This may include the name of a client's spouse and children, special hobbies or interests, awards the client has won, trips he or she plans to take, or other details about his or her life. People do business with people they like, and people usually like people who take an interest in them.

Cruising the Internet

Besides being an absolute necessity as a business communications tool, the Internet offers possibilities for letting people know about your company. While it can be an exceptionally useful channel, it can also be a huge waste of time and money. It all depends on what your business is and how you use the Internet.

Faxing and legal implications

Every sales technique has fans and detractors. I may be in the minority on this issue, but one method I find particularly irritating is the message that arrives under dark of night on my fax machine. This is the unsolicited pitch that uses my ink, my paper, and my equipment to try to sell me something. Faxes can be programmed to automatically deliver these messages to large numbers of potential clients, all with the punch of a button.

Be careful if you choose to do this. Your state may have laws about sending this type of information.

A friend was sending these out, and one of the recipients asked that my friend remove him from the list. Through an error, my friend sent a second solicitation to that person. The next phone call was from the angry recipient who threatened a lawsuit. Would my friend have won or lost? Who knows. In any event, it could have cost him money to defend himself.

For some reason, people are less sensitive to junk mail than they are to faxes.

Think of the Internet as a gigantic television, and your mouse as the remote control. You have at your fingertips millions of shows, and you're in charge of when and how long you choose to watch them. Now imagine that you're an advertiser, and consider these issues:

- ✔ Viewers could look and look for you and never find you.

- ✔ Your ad is competing with millions of other visual stimuli and, unless it's fantastically interesting, most people won't even see it.

- ✔ The average time a person looks at one Internet site is very brief. Each site may have fifty different images, all competing for the viewer's attention.

These are only a few of the challenges that face Internet advertisers. How can you use the Internet to your advantage?

Creating a Web page

A Web page is like a brochure on the Internet; a reference where people can go to find out about your company and its services and to see how to get in touch with you. Although having a Web site may not be an invaluable marketing tool, it enhances your credibility among people who have come to expect to access everything on the Internet.

While some freelancers may not need a Web page, anyone who is in a technology business must have a page to be considered up to speed in his or her field. To be a techie without a Web page is like being a computer salesman who uses a pencil and paper.

You don't have to be a technical expert to create a Web page.

- ✔ If you have a technophobia, hire an expert who can create the page for you.

- ✔ If you're one of those curious souls who loves dabbling with new toys, check out one of the free programs on the Internet.

- ✔ By a software program that teaches you how to create a Web page.

You have to *post* the page, meaning you place it on the Internet. In some cases, you can do this for free. Posting isn't the end of the Web page story, however: You also have to maintain the page (meaning you have to regularly update the information), and you have to host the site, which you must pay for monthly.

Having an out-of-date Web page is worse than not having one at all. When people go to your page, they get an impression of your professionalism, your attention to detail, and other factors that show how you approach your business.

Becoming master of your own domain

On the Web, a *domain name* identifies you. By typing in your domain name, anyone will be quickly transported to your Web site.

Ideally, your domain name will be the same as (or a short version of) your company name. Unfortunately, many common names are already reserved, so if your company name is a common one, you may not be able to get one that matches it identically. Start by doing a quick Internet search, typing in the name you think you want. If it doesn't turn up, you have a good chance of getting it.

To own a domain name, you must register it. A number of companies register domain names, and fees vary considerably from free to $50. Find a company by searching through any Internet search engine.

Linking up

Unless someone is looking specifically for your site, people may only happen upon it accidentally. That's not good enough. To get more mileage out of your Web presence, you should link with other sites. *Linking* means that people on other sites can click on your Web site name and get transported directly to your site. Arrange links with companies whose customers are likely to be interested in your service or product. To make the link idea appealing, you can offer a link from your page to theirs, as well. You'll need to contact the person who maintains the Web site for the company you want to link with.

Generating PR opportunities

You may have heard public relations (or PR) called free advertising. Baloney. Public relations takes time, and to a freelancer, time is money. What exactly is public relations? PR is exposure in the media that you generate through your efforts. It may be by doing something newsworthy, like starting a new company. Another way to get publicity is to participate in something that creates coverage for you indirectly, such as participating in a spelling bee for literacy.

Reaping the benefits of PR

Public relations has several benefits that advertising doesn't have:

- ✔ It can create an impression of a *third-party endorsement,* which means that it makes people think you're great because someone else is tooting your horn. Endorsements from people who are perceived to be objective tend to have more credibility than if, for example, your mother brags about you.

- ✔ It tends to cost less than advertising.

Avoiding the drawbacks of PR

Unlike advertising, PR is, for the most part, out of your control. The media determines:

- ✔ If and when they talk about you.
- ✔ What they say. It may be positive, and it may not.

You can pitch all you want to the media, but you have no guarantee that they will be interested in your story. If more interesting news comes along, you can be bumped without a thought.

Locating media who count

We'd all love to be on *The Today Show,* but low-key media can actually be more useful to you in delivering business if it reaches the audience you need it to reach.

Consider these very useful outlets:

- ✔ **Local business newspapers:** Many cities have weekly business newspapers that are usually easy to get coverage in. They have a lot of space to fill up every week, and are continuously looking for interesting stories about new companies.

- ✔ **Trade publications:** Trade publications are news media that specialize in a particular industry or subject, for example, monthly magazines that are devoted to hotel and motel management, accounting professionals, doctors, sports and fitness, hunting, and other narrow topics. These publications are feature oriented and tend to have more lenient editorial policies than strict news media outlets do. Stories that wouldn't be of interest to a daily newspaper or a major publication, such as *The Wall Street Journal,* can find a home in a trade publication. In some cases, trade media will even let you write your own story.

- ✔ **Association publications:** Groups, such as the Society for Human Resource Management (SHRM) or the American Automobile Association (AAA), have magazines for their members. They're on the lookout for timely topics that are of interest to their readers.

- ✔ **Radio talk shows:** Imagine how many guests daily radio talk shows must line up to keep their shows stocked with interesting topics. You can easily be one of these if you have a decent speaking voice and can talk in quick, interesting statements.

Considering what makes for good PR

The media is interested in selling advertising, and to do that, they need a big audience. They have to sell a lot of newspapers, get a lot of people to watch their TV shows, or generate a lot of radio listeners. They want to fill their pages or programming time with items that lots of people will be interested in. This means they're most interested if your suggestion is any of the following:

✔ **Unusual:** The biggest, the first, the best, or the worst. A common description is that the media isn't interested in a dog biting a man, they're interested in a man biting a dog.

✔ **Visually interesting:** The world's longest hot dog, a super colorful bouquet of flowers forming the word *Mom,* or a group of employees throwing pie in the mayor's face.

✔ **Of human interest:** A heart-wrenching story of saving a life, donating to a children's foundation, a mother and child reunion, or a cure for a dreaded disease.

✔ **Affects lots of people:** You've just discovered a cure for the common cold, are donating millions to a foundation that helps the needy, are teaching reading to inner-city children, or will in some way affect a large part of the population.

My former boss was trying to get the national media to cover a hotel chain's opening of a new property. Rather than send out a news release about how many hotels were now in the chain, which was of interest to almost no one, he suggested having a Clydesdale horse lying in a hotel room bed. Now that was visually interesting!

Achieving good PR takes imagination. Set yourself apart from the hundreds of requests the media get by giving them something that sells newspapers.

Getting the media to cover you

Pretend that the media is a potential client: You're trying to sell them an idea. Drag out all your professional selling skills and use them for this situation.

✔ **Do something interesting.** Don't try to get the media to cover something mundane or that is interesting only to you and your family.

✔ **Do your homework.** Call and find out their deadlines, who to contact for specific types of stories (business, community involvement, announcements of achievements, and so on), and how to correctly spell their names. When you're ready to send information, be sure it goes to the right person, otherwise your press release or other information could wind up in the trash can without even being considered.

✔ **Be available.** When the media calls, listen. Most media people are working on deadlines, and if you don't get back to them right away, they move on to someone who can meet their timing needs.

✔ **Be on time.** Media people work on deadlines, so find out what they are and deliver your information on time. You may be surprised how early the deadlines are.

✔ **Be accurate.** Nothing makes a reporter or other media person look worse than not having the facts straight. Don't invent numbers or other "facts" that you think may be true. Check your own sources to be sure you're providing useful and truthful information.

✔ **Be helpful.** Media people are looking for quotable quotes or sound bites, which are brief, punchy statements that get the audience's attention. Develop your own sound bites so that whenever you talk to the media, you won't stumble around looking for the right words. Always be prepared to deliver a punchy statement, such as, "Kids today are smarter than they've been in 100 years." Catch the media's attention by giving them something that is sure to catch their audience's attention.

Don't expect to have *approval rights* (the opportunity to review the story before it's printed) on anything the media writes about you. Asking to read a story before it's published is considered an insult to a newsperson.

Avoiding trouble

The media representatives aren't there just to record what you want them to record. They are there to get a story — and everything they're interested in may not be favorable to you. An old saying is that there is no such thing as bad publicity, implying that having your name in the public eye always helps your business. But that's not quite true. Your reputation is all you have to build your business on, and you need to guard it with your life, using the following tips:

✔ **Be careful.** Never think you're talking off the record. Everything you say is fair game to a media representative.

✔ **Be positive.** Negative, inflammatory information makes news, but you don't want this kind of publicity. Keep your comments positive and never be disrespectful of your competition.

✔ **Be quiet — sometimes.** It's not your solemn duty to tell the media everything, no matter what they ask you. You are not obligated to answer their questions or to know everything.

Writing a good news release

Media people like to have written information to use as a reference, and they want "Just the facts, ma'am." A news release is a concise description that includes five important pieces of information that are often referred to as the *5 Ws:*

✔ **Who** is involved in the newsworthy event?

✔ **What** is the event?

✔ **When** does the event take place, including time, day, and date?

✔ **Where** does the event happen, with the specific street address, city, state, and zip code.

✔ **Why** is the event taking place? If it's a fund-raiser, who will it benefit and how? If it's a party, is it celebrating the opening of your new business?

Keep news releases to one page or less. If you must provide background or other detailed information, you can make the news release longer. Be sure, however, to put the 5 Ws up front where the reporter can get to them quickly.

Providing quotable quotes

Quotes from key people are the backbone of every news story. You can make a reporter's job easier by providing one of these in your news release. Although an in-person interview may be ideal, sometimes a reporter doesn't have time to locate you and get a quote firsthand. In those cases, being able to cite a quote from a news release comes in handy.

To make news, a quote must be interesting. Avoid a typical, "We're very honored to be here," kind of statement. Try to compose a statement that has some m eaning, states some unknown fact, or provides other unexpected bits of information. Keep it short. Rambling, self-serving statements get you nowhere.

The following sample news release shows you how to organize information to make the facts as easy to find as possible.

For immediate release

Contact: Susan Drake

Phone: 999-222-4444

LOCAL BUSINESS LANDS TOP NATIONAL CREATIVE AWARD

Memphis, TN — Thursday, Nov. 30, 2000:

Spellbinders, Inc., a 15-year old local communications firm, was named most creative company in the U. S. at the Best Businesses 2000 awards ceremony in Washington, D.C. The award, presented by the AAA of Communications Businesses, is the result of an annual competition involving advertising and marketing companies that work in the mid-sized business-to-business arena.

"This is a win for Memphis as well as for Spellbinders," says Susan Drake, founder and president of Spellbinders, Inc. "Our team went head to head with much larger big-city firms, and we've proven that Memphis groups are a force to be reckoned with."

Spellbinders, Inc., located in Memphis, TN, specializes in corporate internal marketing and business-to-business communications.

Notice that the quote in this release plays on the pride of the city and its ability to compete with big-city firms. That type of competitive statement makes the item appealing to more readers.

TIP

> # But what I really mean is . . .
>
> If you've ever watched a political debate, you may have noticed that, on occasion, a reporter asks a question and a candidate answers something that seems totally unrelated to the question. This is a well-practiced technique for accomplishing two things:
>
> ✔ Evading a subject the candidate wishes to avoid
>
> ✔ Making sure they get across a point whether the media asks about it or not
>
> Before you participate in any media interaction, you must know what points you want to make, and what points you want to avoid. Know how you intend to respond to a potentially negative question so that a reporter won't catch you off guard.

Never pump up your news release with a lot of self-promoting blather; the media sees right through this. They know you're just bragging about yourself and won't pay a bit of attention to it.

Booking speaking engagements

Organizations are always looking for speakers, especially those who will speak for free. Get yourself booked by calling groups where your potential clients congregate. This may be a civic group, such as the Kiwanis Club or Rotary Club, or a professional association, such as the Public Relations Society of America.

- ✔ Pick a topic that will be helpful to the group.

- ✔ Provide a biography of yourself so that the group's leader can introduce you the way you want to be introduced. This means putting in a plug for your company.

- ✔ Write and rehearse your presentation so that it's entertaining and professional. Don't bore people with an hour of jargon or lecturing. Keep it fast-paced and use a lot of light-hearted expressions.

- ✔ Be on time.

- ✔ Never speak for more than the allotted time. An ideal presentation is never longer than 20 minutes. Don't try to teach people everything you know. Give them a little information that makes them want to talk to you some more.

- ✔ Stay after so people can talk to you in depth about your subject — or hire you!

- ✔ Write down names and contact information of people you meet and use them in your little green book (see the "Keeping a little green book" section earlier in this chapter).

- ✔ Follow up with a thank-you letter to the organization.

Getting involved in an association

It could be to your advantage to actually join an association, whether it is a civic group where you will meet diverse contacts or a professional organization where you will rub shoulders with your associates. Some groups are fairly pricey; pick and choose the ones you can afford, both fee- and time-wise.

Sponsoring something

Becoming identified with a worthy cause can be beneficial not only in getting your name out but also in creating a positive image. If you already have a favorite charity, you can kill two birds with one stone by donating money or services to an event that raises money for that group.

For pure sales purposes, sponsor an event that your potential clients support. For example, if you sell a service that's particularly appealing to women, you may choose to underwrite or be involved somehow with a breast cancer group. A graphic designer could donate the design of a T-shirt for a fund-raising walk; a bookkeeper could volunteer to keep track of the money raised.

Not-for-profit organizations are generally good at giving credit to the people who work on their behalf, but you may suggest to them how you prefer to be recognized. Nine times out of ten, they'll accommodate your request.

Winning awards

Winning awards is a nice ego boost, and it can also be a feather in your cap to clients. It never hurts to be perceived as outstanding in your field, so consider competing in professional association competitions.

It takes quite a bit of time to create an award-winning entry, so prepare for some intensive, non-paying work. If you're going to bother to spend the time, you may as well give yourself the best chance possible of winning. Here are a few tips to enhance your chances:

- ✔ Carefully follow all the contest rules.
- ✔ Make your entry look professional. Use high-grade paper, put it in a binder (or whatever format the contest requires), use high-quality photos or other materials, and explain the results of your project.
- ✔ Ask a professional writer to look it over for accuracy and clarity.

When (not if) you win, get the most from your efforts, as follows:

- ✔ Send a news release to the local media announcing your award.
- ✔ Order a second trophy from the organization (if possible) and send it to the client whose project won the award. If you can't get a trophy, buy one yourself and have it engraved for the client. (After all, you didn't get there by yourself.) If the client displays the trophy at the office, it will serve as a reminder to everyone who did the great work. What a great billboard, sitting smack dab in the middle of your target audience.

✔ Send an announcement to your other clients.

✔ Send a release to the national trade media.

✔ If it's financially feasible, take out an ad in the business paper or other appropriate channel to say thanks to those who helped you win.

Chapter 12

Evaluating Jobs and Projects

*T*he phone rings. It's a potential client. You have three seconds to decide whether you want to take the job. Your first thought is, "Yes, yes, yes!" You figure that any paying job will be worth it.

But remember that while making money is one goal of freelancing, another is usually freedom — freedom to choose which projects you work on, which clients you work for, and so on. If you're taking a job only for money, you may find that your work eventually becomes less fun.

So when your phone rings, make a decision instead of simply reacting. This, of course, is easier said than done. I'm always flattered when a client wants to use my services, so the following responses often run through my head in the space of a single moment after a client asks me to take a job:

✔ "Oh, good — they're a multinational corporation with big bucks, but I'm on deadline, and they want to meet tomorrow morning at ten. No way I can make it!"

✔ "They think I'm wonderful and they're anxious to hear my ideas, but I'm also bidding against another freelancer and I can't be sure of getting the job."

✔ "I'm sure I could win them over, and it would be a terrific project that would really enhance my portfolio, but where will I find the time?"

As you may imagine, these responses could go on indefinitely but (thank goodness), eventually I have to give the client an answer!

Can you accept every project offered? I hope not. I hope your marketing efforts are bringing you multiple opportunities that require you to pick and choose. Regardless of your profession, every project you take should lead you closer to your goals. This chapter shows you how to do that.

Weighing Factors That Affect Your Decision

In the course of your business, you probably will be offered a variety of projects. Some will be perfectly suited to your skills; others will be out of your league; still others may be only vaguely related to what you do. Some will be phenomenally profitable, and some will not. Believe it or not, some projects simply clutter up your day and never bring you closer to your financial or career goals.

TRUE STORY

A freelancer with a mission

No matter where she has worked, Dusky Norsworthy has been a free spirit. As a freelancer, she's known for not taking projects she doesn't like: Dusky is a tough-minded professional who knows what she wants and, after more than 15 years in business, she has learned how to get it.

At 23 years of age, Dusky was working for a TV station as a camera person, but she knew then that she wanted to be on her own. She recognized an opportunity to do corporate video production, but that took equipment — expensive equipment. That proved to be no obstacle to Dusky. She moved back to her mother's house, took a job selling cars, and in six months had saved $72,000. Soon she was on her own.

Since then, Dusky has managed projects and clients with style. Perhaps one reason she's so good at her job is that she's selective about what she undertakes. "I accept projects either when the work itself is something I'll enjoy or when it's someone I enjoy working with. I bring more to the table when I like what I'm doing."

Dusky relies on her instinct to guide her. "When I first started, I didn't trust my gut. Now I realize that if something doesn't feel right, it probably isn't. I can tell in the first couple of meetings if a job is a good fit."

What does she look for in clients? "I look for people with integrity; those who are open to ideas and change. I also look for those who are open to my mistakes. They need a sense of humor and reasonable expectations. I can't work with people who are just big dreamers."

As a video and meeting producer, Dusky relies heavily on other freelancers, from writers to directors, from camera crews to actors. Picking teams that are compatible is one of her strengths. "You have to be part psychologist to know who will fit with whom. And there have been times I've had to let crew members go because they couldn't get over their personal attachment to the work. At some point, we all have to give up our emotional investment and do what it takes to suit the client."

Those moments when projects come together and click are her most satisfying. "There's tremendous energy and drive when you bring freelancers together. When we're all working on a project, everyone is motivated, and that creates a great synergy."

Projects can contribute to your business success and well being in a variety of ways, and money is only one of them. I believe that projects can bring four benefits:

✔ Money

✔ Additional business in the future

✔ New or improved skills

✔ Fun

To decide which projects you want to take, consider which factors are most important to you. You may have periods in which money is vitally important; other times, you may sorely need some fun. In some cases, the reward may be short-term; in others, the payoff may not be immediate, but may be considerable down the road. The following sections tell you how to look at each factor and determine its importance in your decision-making process.

Making money

The most obvious and usually most important factor in your decision to take or reject a project is how much it will contribute directly to your bank account. All money is good money; however, you must set a minimum amount that you require to make a project truly worth your while. Ask yourself the following questions:

✔ Does the amount offered meet or exceed my going rate?

✔ Is the project big enough to be worth my time and effort?

✔ Does the client pay reliably?

✔ Is the payment schedule long or short? If the project has a long-term payback, do I have the luxury of working on a long-term project that won't pay until it's finished.

If the money isn't sufficient to meet your rate, other factors may still make it worth your while to accept.

Creating a foundation for future work

One project can lead to another, which means that even a not-so-lucrative project can be dramatically important if it puts you in a position to get other plum assignments. Which projects are likely to lead to more work? Ask yourself the following questions to help you qualify new business as potentially profitable:

- ✔ Is this a new company with the potential for growth?
- ✔ Is this a division I've never worked in at an existing client's company?
- ✔ Does this project let me demonstrate skills that I haven't exhibited before?
- ✔ Does this project have high visibility in the company or in the community?

If you can answer "yes" to any of those questions, by taking on this project, you may be creating new opportunities for yourself.

Learning new skills

Clients hire you as an expert, but be honest: You're more expert at some things than at others. Luckily, in the freelancing game, you'll probably find chances to add to or refine your skills. After you've established a trusting relationship with your clients, they may ask you to take on work at which you may not have a lot of (or any) experience.

TIP

Spotting great clients

Sometimes I get what I consider a gift from heaven. I usually know it right away, because heavenly clients have unmistakable traits. Here are some of them:

- ✔ **They respect your time.** They keep appointments and arrive on time.

- ✔ **They give clear direction.**

- ✔ **They set realistic expectations.** They change deadlines if you tell them something's un-doable.

- ✔ **They listen.** They respond positively to good ideas and disagree respectfully.

- ✔ **They tend to attract great employees.**

- ✔ **They make themselves available.** They answer phone calls and e-mail and find answers to your questions.

When I find a client who's heaven sent, I bend over backwards to please them. These are the clients I want to keep forever.

I almost never pass up a chance to be more valuable to my clients, even when they're asking me to do something I'm not (yet) an expert at. Unless I feel I'm compromising my ethics or risking my reputation by taking on a job I'm not capable of handling, I usually take on work that builds my skills, which may be the following for you:

- ✔ The project requires research that expands your knowledge.

- ✔ The project exposes you to other experts from whom you can learn.

- ✔ The project gives you the chance to practice skills that need honing.

Any job that teaches you a new skill has value. After all, the client is essentially paying you to go to school. You can't beat that!

Having fun

I like money, but I also put a high value on projects that make my life more fun and interesting. Consider the following factors that make a project fun:

- ✔ **Great people:** Some of my clients are so much fun that the money is almost secondary (almost!).

- ✔ **Challenging, interesting work:** Of course, you have to define this for yourself!

- ✔ **Opportunities to travel:** Seeing the world on your client's expense account is a big plus.

- ✔ **Being respected and trusted:** What could be more fun than having someone ask and follow your opinion?

What makes work fun for you? Think about it. After you understand the factors that make a job fun, you can try to select the assignments that include those factors. At first, you may not be able to work solely on jobs that are fun, but eventually, you should be able to partake of some kind of fun in every job you take.

You may equate fun with money, in which case you should just make sure all your projects pay a lot!

Taking fun projects that don't make money can breed resentment. As you invest more and more hours at low compensation, the fun margin narrows considerably. Before you accept a low-paying project just for fun, be prepared to keep reminding yourself how much fun the project is. Enlist a buddy to jog your memory about why you took the project in the first place.

Avoiding the friendship trap

The phone rings. It's not a client, it's a friend or family member with a project, a referral, or a need. Warning: You are about to fall into the friendship trap. Before you accept a project from a friend, consider a few possibilities.

✔ What will you do if the friend expects a cut rate or a free project?

✔ How can you be honest with a friend if his or her idea is bad?

✔ If the friend is hard to please and the project drags out longer than you think it will, are you willing to take your valuable time away from other clients?

✔ If the friend is unpleasant to work with, can you terminate the business relationship?

✔ If your friend doesn't pay, how will you address it?

Consider the following ways to gracefully avoid the friendship trap:

✔ **Be too busy to take on the project.** Anytime someone calls and says, "Are you busy?" make a point of saying that you are. If you say you're not busy, you leave yourself open to requests. Saying you're busy will probably save you from being blindsided by a request.

✔ **Set a no-friends policy.** Say up front that you have a policy to not do business with friends.

✔ **Quote an exorbitant rate.** Explain that you must bill a certain number of hours at a certain rate and quote a rate that's so high you know they won't pay it.

If you're like me, you will probably ignore this advice and have to get burned a few times before you put some of these heartless rules in place. That's okay. One way or another, the lesson is going to happen.

Rating a Project's Potential

Even after you've considered the four desirability factors of a project (covered in the preceding section), you may still be undecided about whether it will be a good project to take. If a project's potential isn't obvious, try a slightly more objective means of deciding: Use a decision chart, which is discussed in the following sections.

Trying a logical approach

One fallback position I sometimes use in deciding on a job is the put-it-on-paper approach. Take the following steps, an example of which is in Table 12-1:

1. **Down the left side of a page, write the four potential benefits of any project: money, additional business, new or improved skills, or fun.**

2. **Read each one, and rank the project from 1 to 5 according to how much or how little it will provide the benefit.**

   Use 1 as the least favorable and 5 as the most favorable.

3. **Add up all the numbers.**

   If a project doesn't score at least 5, strongly consider turning it down.

Table 12-1	Sample Decision Chart
Desirability Factor	*Rating (1 Is Lowest; 5 Highest)*
Money:	3
Future work:	3
New skills:	2
Fun:	4
Total rating:	**12**
Maximum rating possible:	20
Minimum rating acceptable:	5
This project:	12

If a project scores a five in any category, it deserves attention. If it rates a two or below in any area, that's pretty unfavorable, so look carefully at other factors to make sure they outweigh the negative.

Listening to your gut

Suppose your otherwise objective rating system tells you to accept or to reject a project, but you still feel unsettled with the outcome. Wrangling with yourself over "let's do it," and "no, let's not" can drive you to distraction. Feeling unsettled over your decision may mean that your gut knows more than you do. Try the following:

✔ **Pretend that you've taken the job you're considering, and you're now living one month in the future.** Imagine all the possible results of your decision.

✔ **Pretend that you have not taken the job you're considering, and it's one month in the future.** Imagine all the possible results of your decision.

✔ **Pay close attention to how your body feels.** Do you have a sense of relief or do you feel you've made a decision you'll regret?

At times, I overrule my own logical thinking to follow my gut instinct. Sometimes I'm glad I did; sometimes I'm not. Regardless of the outcome, I always find that I learn something from the process!

Living within Realistic Time Frames

Suppose you look at all the factors and decide that this project is one you'd like to take on. You're only half way there, though, because you still must decide two things:

- ✔ Do you have time to do it?
- ✔ Do you have the time and resources to manage someone else doing it as a subcontractor?

To answer the first question, you must know enough about the project to estimate how much time it will take. This may take some thought because you can't rely on a client's brief description to figure out the scope of the project: Clients aren't usually good judges of how long a project will take because they don't understand all the elements that go into it. A prime example of this would be my trying to tell a building contractor how long it should take to build my house. No contractor in his right mind would depend on my estimate to develop a plan.

A client may say, "This is a quick-and-dirty project. We just need a brochure." It's up to you to figure out whether the project is actually quick or not.

Estimating your time

After a lot of years of freelancing, I can predict fairly accurately how long a job will take. I consider the client and how many changes they usually make, and then come fairly close to an accurate estimate. Then, like any good freelancer, I pad the time to make sure I don't go over the time I've predicted.

Always overestimate; most clients are impressed as long as you come in under budget and in advance of the deadline.

When you're just starting out, you may not be very good at figuring your time. That's natural, because you don't have any history with which to compare this project. Consider writing down each element of the project and projecting how much time it will take. For example, if you're a freelance decorator, include in your estimate taking meetings with the client, researching sources, collecting samples, pricing items, getting the names and numbers of subcontractors, and so on, guessing how much time each would take. Don't be surprised if, in the beginning, you underestimate. Most people do. Your *padding* (the extra time you build in) will protect you from big mistakes in this area.

Don't forget to let your client know that you include travel time in your estimates and to specify what that includes. That way, you can account for the time you spend driving from your office to the client's location and back. I have one client who is five minutes away, and that's convenient. But think how your time adds up if your drive to and from a client's office is 30 minutes or an hour. That time is time away from other work and it's time you must get paid for. Be sure to include your travel time in your work estimates. Some people, such as photographers, call this time charged *portal-to-portal,* meaning from their door to the client's and back.

Squeezing projects in

Your schedule is tight. The potential project is juicy. Can you possibly cram it into your timetable? Jobs always take longer than you expect, so before you squeeze one in, consider how this one extra project may affect you. Just how many hours a week are you willing to work? Do you still need to sleep? Can you give up eating? Sure, you can squeeze a lot into your schedule. The question is, what will you have to give up to do it?

Subcontracting to keep doors open

Turning down good projects is tough, but sometimes there's a way around it: You can subcontract work to other freelancers. In Chapter 8 you find out more about where to find people you can trust to help you get your job done.

Even if you're turning work over to someone else, you're still responsible for supervising and managing. Hiring others to do work for your clients means you're putting your reputation in someone else's hands. When you present the finished work to the client, what you deliver represents you, no matter who actually did it. Estimate your time to include checking the other person's work and re-doing some of it if necessary to bring it up to your standards.

When you subcontract, you pay people to have them do the work. You can handle this in different ways:

- ✔ **Hire someone who has a rate that's lower than yours.** Charge the client your hourly rate because you must supervise. You benefit from the difference in the lower rate and yours.

- ✔ **Hire someone whose rate is higher than yours and pass the higher rate along to the client.** If you plan to do this, remember to build the additional charge into your estimate. (If the client doesn't balk, you may need to increase your rate!)

- ✔ **Hire someone with a rate that's the same as yours, and take one of two previous options.** Either charge the client for the time the subcontractor spends plus the time you spend supervising the job, or just pass through the subcontractor's charge and consider this goodwill that allows you to avoid turning down a job.

✔ **Hire someone with a rate that's higher than yours, charge the client your rate and lose money!** This is not a desirable alternative.

You may or may not want to let your client know that someone else is doing the work. In any event, you should be the contact person so that you can maintain your excellent relationship with the client.

Considering the quick project

In addition to the substantial projects you wish you could take, you may encounter *quicky projects* that seem tempting because they're good money for little work or for a short time. Or are they?

Some projects — even those that pay your standard rate — can be more trouble than they're worth. These are projects that don't take a lot of your time, but also don't necessarily give you a good payback. I classify quickies into the three following groups:

✔ **Good fill-ins:** Even when I'm working on a major project, I may have an hour or so to work on something that can be done fast. Fill-ins are the projects I can practically do in my sleep. I get them done fast and bill for them immediately — no pain, no strain. Sometimes, I welcome a fill-in because I need a mental break from a bigger project. A fill-in can be a mental vacation.

✔ **Diverting projects:** Sometimes I can't afford to do a fill-in because it destroys my concentration. For example, a client may ask me to write a letter, which may take me only about an hour. I can charge the client for an hour of my time, and sure, money is money. But if I'm in a zone working on another project, a fill-in can steal my time away from

more profitable work. When my attention is diverted, however briefly, it usually takes me a little while to refocus back to the bigger job. Then again, if the client makes changes, even if they're small, that's another interruption that once again requires refocusing. Then I must take time to create an invoice. I can't charge the client for any of my refocusing or invoicing time. In these situations, diverting projects cost me too much.

✔ **Could-ya-just projects:** A client calls and asks "Could you just take a quick look at this and let me know what you think?" While they're requesting a quick look, you will undoubtedly discover the project takes considerably more time if you give it the attention it deserves.

Some quickies you must take; some you shouldn't. I have clients I never turn down because their overall business is too important to me. I don't want to risk having another freelancer slip in the door with the quicky project. If a good client asks me to do one of these, it's worth my effort to build the goodwill and keep my contact secure. But if an infrequent customer wants to nickel-and-dime my time away, I find I'm better served begging off because of a tight schedule.

Turning Clients Down

Feast and famine: That's how many freelancers describe their work flow. The more work they have, the more they get. I don't know why it works that way, it just does.

Because you may find it difficult to count on work throughout the year, you may be tempted to take every job that comes along. That's dangerous, because when you're overloaded, you risk doing a mediocre job. To protect your reputation, invest the right amount of time in every project to make sure it's the best product you can deliver. Unfortunately, that means sometimes turning work down.

Saying no

You can say no in nice ways. How you turn down work depends on the circumstances:

✔ **If you want the client back, say no tactfully.** Here's an example: "Thanks so much for asking me, and I really hope you'll call me again. I've wanted to work with you, and hate that I can't take this project." This clearly lets them know that you want their business.

✔ **If you don't want the client back, you can try one of the two following methods.**

   • Say you're sorry you can't take the business and refer them to another freelancer. This increases the likelihood that they'll develop a relationship with one of your competitors. At the same time, it keeps them feeling positively disposed to you because you've helped them get their project done.

   • Simply say no politely.

Saying something between yes and no

The client is on the phone, asking if you're available. In the next three seconds, you don't have time to create a decision chart (see the "Trying a logical approach" section earlier in this chapter). You must give the client an answer, but you don't want to commit one way or another impulsively.

Saying no can build your business

While turning down work may seem like a bad thing, it can actually help you build your business. Being too busy to accept a job tells your client the following:

✔ You're in demand with other clients who value what you do.

✔ You're worth your fee.

✔ You have an opinion worth listening to.

Saying no is a great way to get the message across that you're popular and that clients have to compete for your time by paying well, being

nice to work with, and treating you nicely. Those aren't bad things to cultivate in a client.

If the client is one you'd like to work with, keep open the possibility of future business. Make a reminder note to yourself to call the client later and ask how the project went. This makes a fabulous impression of your professionalism and interest. Best of all, it reminds the client that you're around, and if the project doesn't go well, it reminds them that they should hire you next time!

Consider the following answers that are somewhere between yes and no:

✔ "I'm on deadline and would like to give your project my full consideration. May I call you back in an hour?"

✔ "I would love to be involved and would be happy to explore this with you. Would it be okay for me to attend the planning meeting to find out more about it, and then we can go from there?" Most of the time you wouldn't expect to be able to charge for the planning meeting, so don't get involved unless you're seriously considering the project or think it's vital that you attend to get exposure and keep your relationship alive. I had a fortunate opportunity recently to get paid for an 8-hour brainstorming session without actually doing the project. Because I contributed my ideas to the planning of the project, it was considered a consulting job.

✔ "I certainly would like to be considered. Can you tell me more about the project, and then I can see how it fits with my schedule."

By giving these answers, you're collecting as much information as possible and buying time to make a decision. In the solitude of your office — off the phone — you can argue the pros and cons and choose a path that you can live with.

Negotiating to keep clients on the hook

Suppose someone offers you a particularly juicy job. You really want it, but you can't possibly fit it into your schedule. Can you avoid turning this job down? Try this:

- ✔ Tell the client you're very interested and ask if the client has any flexibility in the schedule. You may be surprised at how many times their burning issue can be temporarily doused until you're available.

- ✔ Ask if there is a portion of the job they feel you'd be particularly key to. Accept that portion of the job so that you can stay in the loop.

- ✔ Decide for yourself what piece of the job you'd like to do and offer to do that part only.

At worst, your effort to meet their needs demonstrates how interested you are in working for them and shows how willing you are to try to work something out to help. That kind of attitude won't go unnoticed.

Avoiding Projects That Spell H-e-a-d-a-c-h-e

Being a new freelancer can make you a desperate person who's inclined to take every job no matter what the cost in psychotherapy. Please believe me when I say that some jobs are absolutely not worth it. The following are some other danger signs that should warn you you're about to encounter a job from hell:

- ✔ The client complains that all the freelancers before you were really stupid. (Translation: All the freelancers before you tore their hair out.)

- ✔ The client complains that consultants are untrustworthy, and that you'll have to prove your value to them. (Translation: They won't let you do your job, but when their ideas fail, they blame you.)

- ✔ The client expects you to develop a free proposal that's so comprehensive you may as well do the whole job. (Translation: They won't hire you, but they will steal your ideas.)

- ✔ The client dumps tons of background information on you for you to decipher but won't spend time explaining the project. (Translation: They don't know what they want and can't organize their thinking enough to help you. This will be a case of trial and error, better known as "I'll know it when I see it.")

- ✔ The client insists on living within a budget that's completely unworkable. (Translation: The client will nickel and dime you to death and complain about cost no matter what miracle you perform.)

When you detect one or more of these signs, plead that you're too busy and give the project away.

Living with mistakes

No matter how careful you are, at some point you'll probably misjudge some projects or clients. Some wonderful projects will slip away, and some icky projects will slip undetected through your decision chart (see the "Trying a logical approach" section earlier in this chapter). More than once, I've been excited about a new client only to discover later that my primary contact had a secret personality flaw. On the flip side, I recently anticipated the worst and was ecstatic to discover a delightful new client.

When you misjudge, try the following:

- ✓ **Resign graciously.** Explain that you feel you're not a good match for the project and that you don't want to fall short of their expectations. Tell them you believe that someone else can better meet their needs. Pick your timing carefully when considering resigning. Leaving a client in the lurch mid-project can be a real reputation spoiler. You may, however, find appropriate stopping points along the way when you can bow out gracefully.

- ✓ **Do the best job you can, mitigating the negative aspects of the job and learning from the experience.** Every negative experience teaches you a little more about judging character and evaluating projects before they become nightmares.

Coping with difficult clients

I remember only two or three clients who have truly treated me unfairly. That doesn't mean more clients than that aren't difficult to deal with — many can be picky, indecisive, unenlightened, or otherwise difficult to work with. But really unfair people are few and far between. In my case, one quibbled over a bill after I had busted parts of my anatomy delivering what he needed. Another asked me to put together a proposal and wouldn't return my calls to tell me what he thought (and that he had decided not to hire me).

I wish I could've had the last word on those projects, but I didn't. It's never a good idea to force a client to do something uncomfortable (like admit you're not the one they hired). I make it a policy to not ever, ever, ever tell off a client. No matter how hard I have to bite my tongue, I try to leave things on a positive note. Sometimes, that's as good as it gets.

Chapter 13

Managing Client Relationships

*H*appy clients make for happy freelancers, so all you have to do is keep everyone satisfied, right? That's a juggling act! You may be a great juggler, but you won't be able to keep all the balls in the air all the time.

This chapter gives you tips and tricks for keeping most of your clients happy most of the time, as well as hints on what to do when you don't.

Cultivating Clients You Love

A certain ecstatic look comes over freelancers' faces when they talk of their dream clients. Dream clients trust your judgment, take your advice, respect your time, pay their bills, and call you back. And if you're truly blessed, they're also smart and fun.

The more you are your natural self, the more dream clients you attract. When you're being yourself, people see what they're getting right away; when they purchase your services, they get what they know and paid for. When I started in business I thought I had to act professional, which I interpreted to mean serious and boring. Unfortunately, that attracted staid and boring clients. Because I couldn't keep up the façade forever, we always ended up with a big gap between what they thought they were paying for and what I was delivering. Eventually, they didn't like me. And, frankly, the feeling was mutual. Our personalities didn't click.

One day, when I was in particularly bad pain over a non-clicking client, I realized that every freelancer has two choices in business:

- Find a lot of clients and try to be what you think they want you to be.
- Be yourself and find clients who appreciate you as you are.

The second option is a whole lot easier and more satisfying. Here's an example of how the theory works in my life.

- I give honest opinions in a straightforward way, and clients who want to hear the bottom line appreciate this approach.
- I prefer to take the bull by the horns. When I see a client struggling with decisions, I try to help by exerting more control.
- I don' take orders well. When I get an assignment, I try to see it from the big-picture perspective and frequently suggest changes to the project. I don't attract a lot of clients who just want a worker bee.
- I push myself and I push my clients hard, but I deliver results.

You can imagine that my style doesn't suit everyone. It usually attracts two types of clients: Those who are confident and direct and like to work with other strong-willed people, and those who prefer more hand-holding and guidance. My strengths are compatible with both types. At the same time, I don't work very well with people who just want me to go do what they say.

Spend some time examining your strengths. Live by them, and you'll attract the clients you feel comfortable with.

Following your contact from company to company

I have a hairdresser who has moved all over the city, and I've followed her everywhere she has gone. I do the same thing with clients I like. One client has been at four different companies. She has introduced me to clients in each of the other companies, allowing me to build my base of business. (Unfortunately, in a couple of cases, when she left the company, the company left me.)

Keeping good clients when they move is hard work because the pace of a new job can distract a client. In addition, you may now be sep-

arated geographically, and the client may be coerced into using the accepted freelancers at the new company. You may have to put forth extra effort to keep their business.

If you can't have lunch anymore, keep in touch with regular phone calls or e-mail messages. Send notes or find other ways to keep your name in front of your client's eyes. When clients move, visibility is more crucial than ever. Step up your efforts to be seen.

Keeping Clients Happy

Consider two critical marketing rules:

- ✔ Finding a new client costs five times more than keeping an existing one.

- ✔ Repeat business and positive word-of-mouth are the lifeblood of every business. In fact, most companies consider this their best and most effective form of advertising.

The moral of the story is to take care of the clients you have and with whom you enjoy working. The following tips help you keep your existing clients happy:

- ✔ **Never promise something you can't deliver.** Clients will respect you more for turning down a job than if you take on more than you can handle.

- ✔ **Always do your best work.** Even if the project is small, rushed, or the client says "quick and dirty" is good enough, don't let your quality slide. Later, no one will remember that the project was of secondary importance. They'll only see that it was second-rate and that you did it. (Every job you do is an advertisement for you, so maintain high standards under all circumstances.)

- ✔ **Make every client feel as if he or she is your only client.** Never interrupt a client call for call waiting, don't rush out of a meeting saying you have another engagement, don't be late to a meeting because you were with another client (give yourself buffer time in between meetings in case there are timing overruns), and try to accommodate your clients' sudden needs.

- ✔ **Never surprise a client with bad news at the last minute.** When people know in advance of a pending disaster, they can figure out options. No one wants to be backed into a corner with no way out.

Communicating for results

"Where do we stand?" is a question your clients should never have to ask. One of your most important responsibilities is to keep your clients informed about a job's progress, even before they want to know. With just a quick update, you can contribute to their ability to relax and sleep easily at night; that's a trait that will make you loved!

The following are some steps you can take to keep your clients up-to-date on your work:

1. **Ask your client how he or she prefers to receive updates: on paper, through e-mail, by phone, or in person.**

   Ask if a particular schedule, such as a Monday morning phone call or a Friday afternoon e-mail, will work best.

2. **Gather key information.**

   Consider information such as the following: where you stand, whether you're on time and within budget, whether you're experiencing any obstacles (and how you will overcome them), and whether you need any help from the client.

3. **Organize your thoughts into a brief, bulleted report.**

   Prepare a summary on paper that you can send to the client or that you can use when you make your call.

4. **Deliver the goods.**

   If you've agreed to a regular timetable, stick to it.

By anticipating questions, you can look well prepared and can keep your client feeling comfortable that you have everything under control. That feeling of trust is a must.

Holiday Inn hotels used to have a slogan, "The best surprise is no surprise." For clients, that slogan still holds. The worst thing you can do to a client is give them an unpleasant surprise, especially when it's too late for them to do anything about it.

The two pieces of bad news you may have to someday give a client are that you can't meet their deadline or that you've gone over budget. Here are some tips on how to handle giving a client bad news:

✓ **When you discover a problem, deal with it immediately.** Don't hesitate, hoping the problem will resolve itself. The sooner you let the client know, the better. It allows your client to prepare his or her boss for the news or to make other arrangements to handle the situation.

✓ **Know what caused the situation and be prepared to explain.** Don't blame others; ultimately, if you're managing the project, you should be able to anticipate and control most of the process. When something derails, take responsibility for it. Yes, you can explain what happened, but be sure you examine your conscience before you blame someone else. Wasn't there something you should have followed more carefully or managed more effectively?

> ✔ **Never go to a client and say, "Here's the problem," and stop there.** Before you take the bad news to them, have solutions to offer.
>
> ✔ **Give your client the options you believe are best for handling the situation.** Be prepared to outline what the solutions will cost and how long they will take.

I find that most clients are understanding and willing to help find solutions as long as you don't wait until the last minute when they're backed into a corner. Leave time to take another route. See the "Managing Projects That Go Wrong" section, later in this chapter, for more information.

For more information on communicating in the business world, check out *Communicating Effectively For Dummies* by Marty Brounstein (Hungry Minds, Inc.).

Avoiding conflicts of interests

When you have a *conflict of interest,* you're involved in two situations that could put your interests and your client's interests at odds. For example, suppose your main business is consulting, but you also own part of a market-research company. You're working on a consulting project for a client that will require research. The client, without knowing that you're involved with the research company, asks you to coordinate the project. She requests that you locate three research companies and ask them to submit bids. Naturally, you have a vested interest in having your market-research company get the contract. You must inform your client that you can't objectively evaluate the proposals because you have an interest in the benefit of one of the companies. Participating without letting your client know is a conflict of interest.

Here's another example of a potential conflict of interest. You work for a particular company that is vying for a government contract, and you're asked to write the proposal. You also work for another company that is competing for that same contract. Can you do your very best work for both? Perhaps, but it's still a conflict of interest for you to work on behalf of two companies that are competing directly for the same project.

Because your client isn't necessarily aware of the other clients for whom you do business and doesn't know all your business interests, you have an ethical responsibility to do one of two things: either make the client aware of any potential conflicts of interest or decline the business. In the second situation, you don't have to explain everything in detail.

Keeping it on the QT

A big part of how happy a client is with you rests on your ability to keep a secret. As a freelancer, you are, in some ways, a company employee. You have a legal and ethical responsibility to act in the company's best interest. Corporate information can be highly sensitive, and when you're in the information loop, you must treat what you know confidentially by doing the following:

- ✔ Guard important company information to keep it from competitors.

- ✔ Keep corporate dirty underwear under wraps so it doesn't damage the company's reputation as an employer or as a well-managed business.

- ✔ Don't share information among departments. Department managers don't want others to know all their business.

Some companies, before they do business with you, require you to sign a confidentiality agreement promising that you won't reveal their information to anyone. Even if they don't, you still have a professional reputation to uphold.

The Securities and Exchange Commission (SEC) has strict rules about companies releasing important information. Any significant news that may affect the price of the stock, such as acquiring a new division, replacing the president, and so on, has to be released to everybody at one time, in a certain way and at a certain time. If you happen to be privy to such information, you must keep it confidential. The SEC doesn't kid around about this; if word leaks out, you and the company risk serious fines and even imprisonment.

Avoiding becoming a political animal

Don't think that just because you have climbed out of the corporate shark tank that you're now playing in the meadow with a lot of cuddly little lambs. Clients bring political situations with them, and you can be sucked in before you even know it. You have to keep an eye open for potential political issues and, from outside a company, that can be tough. Without the advantage of the inside scoop, you may have to interpret information without all the facts.

Some of the most powerful and informative people in an organization are the administrative assistants. They know and understand the political landscape and can offer valuable insight into who's who and what's what. Take a genuine interest in the people who sit at the right hands of your clients. Chatting with an administrative assistant can be some of the most useful time you spend in client relations.

The following are some examples of situations in which you may find yourself:

- ✔ Your contact is unpopular in the organization. (You probably won't get business from coworkers, because you're only as accepted as your contact is, either because of his personality or his power.)

- ✔ Your client is new to an organization, and the existing staff resents (and undermines) new ways of doing things.

- ✔ Senior management protects sacred cow freelancers, and your contact doesn't have the power or the desire to unseat them.

- ✔ Your formerly powerful contact is defeated in a corporate coup.

- ✔ Another freelancer uses unethical tactics to steal your business.

Fortunately, with experience comes understanding. In time, predicting behavior will become more and more second nature to you, and your radar will pick up signals early in the game.

Can you avoid politics completely? Very few people can. I've certainly seen a handful of artful dodgers survive multiple corporate regimes. Long-term survival doesn't happen often and, when it does, it may be as much a result of luck as of skill.

Keep in mind that multiple clients mean multiple political parties. You have to stay on top of how each group maneuvers. Organizations each have their own brand of politics, and freelancers have to simultaneously play *Risk,* Go Fish, and *Monopoly.*

Here are some good rules to follow to stay in good graces with a broad spectrum of clients:

- ✔ Keep your opinions about the political climate to yourself.

- ✔ As your mother said, "If you don't have something nice to say, don't say anything at all." Good advice.

- ✔ Try to maintain a little emotional distance with clients so you can remain objective. I've watched friends get fired, and while I was personally affected, I couldn't allow myself to be up-in-arms at the risk of my income.

- ✔ Don't take sides. When political battles rage, stay neutral. You may be surprised who supports whom: Taking sides can backfire.

- ✔ Don't play favorites. Be helpful to everyone, and make it clear that your goal is to benefit the company.

- ✔ Express positive outlooks about situations and support win-win solutions.

Politics exist in every area of life. Your best armor against politics is to simply do an outstanding job.

Putting Every Project In Writing

Working without a contract is like walking on a tightrope without a net. I've done it for years and so far, I have had only a few close calls. A lot of business is done informally; however, having a contract makes things easier and more clear-cut.

Whether you create your own or sign your client's contract, make sure the following items are covered:

- ✔ The names of the companies involved (you and your client).
- ✔ The dates that the contract is effective.
- ✔ A description of the product or service to be delivered. In corporate jargon, these are sometimes called *deliverables.*
- ✔ The payment amount and terms: This includes how much and when you will be paid. It also includes information on how you will charge for expenses such as phone, copies, travel, and other out-of-pocket expenses — some people charge *mark-ups,* which are charges that are computed by taking a percentage of the price of the item. For example, advertising agencies typically mark up the cost of printing by about 20 percent. This is their fee for coordinating it. While mark-ups are common, some freelancers may forgo mark-ups and simply be reimbursed for the items they purchase on a client's behalf. You also want to include consequences if the client doesn't pay by a certain time.
- ✔ Deadline (sometimes called a *termination date*) for delivering what you've promised: For big projects, you may want to plan several progress deadlines. In writing a *For Dummies* book, for example, I have four deadlines and I get paid a portion of my fee at each deadline.
- ✔ What steps to take if either party wants out of the contract.
- ✔ The signatures of both parties, with date of signature.

You can write a simple template agreement that is legally enforceable, but the safest route to take is to hire an attorney to guide you. Ask for help in writing one generic contract that you can use for the majority of your clients. That way, you pay one legal fee for a contract that you can use over and over again, simply changing the names, dates, and so on. Check out the following sample contract: As simple as it is, it does constitute a contract.

Agreement between Freelance Associates and Big-Time Corporation

This contract is made and entered into as of (day, month, year) between (name of freelancer) and (name of client).

(Name of freelancer) agrees to provide (list services and specify quantity).

In return for said services, Big Time Corporation agrees to pay (amount of money) in equal installments of (amount of money) on April 1, 2001, May 1, 2001, and June 1, 2001.

This contract is effective from (date) until (date).

If either party chooses to cancel this agreement (describe what will happen, whether any fees are sacrificed or required to be paid, whether partial work is to be delivered, or other stipulation of penalties or consequences).

_____   _____

(Your signature and date; your client's signature and date)

When you do a job that falls outside the realm of your usual work or is more complex, you can always ask for counsel on writing a contract for that particular job.

If you decide to research Web sites for potential contract information, be cautious. Some generic contracts don't take into account state laws. Better to take a look at information or forms at law offices or law school libraries. Another good source is *Business Contracts Kit For Dummies* by Richard D. Harroch (Hungry Minds, Inc.).

Managing Projects That Go Wrong

In the course of your business, somehow, somewhere, someday, something will go wrong. Someone will be unhappy. Somebody will have to pay, and in all likelihood, that somebody is you. What can you do?

- ✔ If it's a client you want to keep, you must do whatever it takes to satisfy him or her.

- ✔ If it's a client you don't want to keep, you must still do whatever it takes to satisfy him or her because if you don't, your client will tell 15 people what a jerk you are.

But what if the mistake isn't your fault? It doesn't matter, even if you can prove it. In fact, here's what's likely to happen if you prove you're right:

- ✔ The client may accept responsibility and pay.
- ✔ The client may look bad and be embarrassed.
- ✔ The client may never call you again.

This is certainly a case of winning the battle and losing the war. The better approach is to accept responsibility (covered in the following sections) and do everything in your power to right the wrong. Your client will probably be grateful and remember only that you saved the day.

Taking the financial responsibility for mistakes

Unfortunately, you may someday make a mistake that costs money: Perhaps a print job went wrong and had to be redone, maybe you planted landscaping and the plants died within a week, the concrete you poured never set, or a box of goods was supposed to be delivered and it was lost in shipment. Things do go wrong, and when that happens, money talks. You may have to repay your client for a mistake, replace the defective product, or pay twice for a service in order to get it right. Although buying your way out of mistakes isn't necessarily the best way to solve a problem, it has two advantages:

- ✔ It's a visible way you can show that you're sorry for whatever has happened.
- ✔ It shows the client how much they mean to you and how concerned you are about keeping their business.

Consider paying under the following conditions:

- ✔ When the product you deliver is wrong. Suppose you have a brochure printed and you overlooked a misspelled word. Pay.
- ✔ When your service was below standard. You missed your deadline, failed to double check that a delivery was made, or otherwise dropped the ball. Pay.
- ✔ When there was a misunderstanding about what you would deliver, and neither party has anything in writing. (For the future, this is why you want to use written contracts, covered in the preceding section.) After the misunderstanding has occurred, you're better off to take the hit. Pay.

If you decide to pay the customer, you have three options:

- ✔ **Pay in cash.** When the project or product requires some out-of-pocket expense, put up the money to pay for it.

- ✔ **Pay in reduced charges.** If your client is unhappy with the level of service you've provided for the price, you may have to reduce or waive your fee.

- ✔ **Pay in services.** If your client is unhappy with a level of service you've provided for the cost, offer to give the company its next project at a reduced rate or for free. When you promise to do that, you increase the possibility that they will use your services again. You can redeem yourself by delivering outstanding service the next time.

It's tough to work for free or to have to shell out your own money to pay for something you can't use. Consider it an investment in your own future. No matter how much it costs you, it's worth maintaining a good reputation with your clients.

How much you should pay depends on several things. First, how important is this client to you? If the client is vital, and the mistake is small, eat the whole cost. (Of course, the term small is relative. If your client pays you $50,000 a year, even several thousand dollars may be small.)

If you can't afford to pay the whole amount, negotiate with the client for a payment schedule. If all else fails, you may ask the client to share the cost with you. I don't consider this ideal by any means, but it may be your only alternative if the cost far exceeds your means.

Turning complaints into compliments

Research shows that when something goes wrong in a client relationship and you fix it right away, the customer becomes more loyal. This means that you can retain your best clients by addressing their complaints promptly. Here's the best course to follow:

1. **Don't be defensive.**

   Listen. Keep your focus on the client's need, not on your culpability.

2. **Apologize.**

   Even if you didn't do anything wrong, say, "I'm sorry for your inconvenience."

3. **Look for solutions.**

   Ask, "What can I do to make this right?"

4. **Take action right away.**

   The sooner you fix the problem, the sooner people will stop spreading the word about your mistake.

5. **Follow up: Ask whether the client is happy with the solution.**

6. **Send a note telling the client how much you value his or her business and that you look forward to your next project.**

I've done a lot of work with customer-satisfaction surveys, and I've seen many letters from people who were unhappy and then had their problem fixed. Because so few companies really listen to people's problems, you can win undying loyalty by lending an ear and responding with a solution.

Getting fired

It's the moment every freelancer dreads, the business equivalent of being told, "I don't love you anymore." Unfortunately, if you stay in business long enough, you'll probably be fired at least one time. The most important thing to remember is: Don't take it personally. You may be fired for any of the following reasons:

✔ **Organizational and financial problems:**

- Your main contact leaves the organization, and you don't have other contacts to keep you in the game.

- The company reorganizes and your client is no longer in charge of the area.

- The budget is cut and your projects are eliminated.

- A larger agency takes over multiple accounts in the company and swallows up your piece of the pie.

- The company loses money, its stock takes a dive, and you're part of the fat they cut.

- Departmental cuts eliminate budgeted money for outside help. You're among the cuttees.

✔ Build a client base throughout an organization to protect yourself against one organizational change. Unless the company has a sweeping layoff or other event that wipes out an entire group, you can always pick up slack by working with other groups. Maintain multiple clients at different companies; don't put all your eggs in one basket.

- ✔ **Political problems:**

    - A new person comes in from outside the company and wants to work with his or her own trusted freelancers.

    - New management can't afford to be politically aligned with the old freelancers.

- ✔ Don't become too aligned with one client. If others perceive that your loyalty is too strong, you may be seen as a threat to a new regime.

- ✔ **Performance problems:** You could be fired simply because you didn't deliver according to your client's expectations.

- ✔ Always put forth your best effort. Check with clients regularly to make sure your work is meeting their high standards.

As a freelancer, you're probably not being fired from a position that's your only paycheck. Balance your client portfolio so that no one client represents a potentially devastating loss. In reality, too many freelancers become comfortable with a single huge account. With the mergers and acquisitions situation in business today, that's a dangerous game. Diversify.

Finding opportunities that arise from being fired

Losing a piece of business can be a great thing if you know how to play it. Here are some of the benefits you can enjoy from being fired:

- ✔ If you're fired for poor performance, it can be a necessary reminder to improve your work. Sometimes I find that I become complacent, and I need to remember that there are people who can easily replace me.

- ✔ If you're working on boring projects, it will give you the nudge you need to seek new challenges.

- ✔ If you're fired because your client goes to another organization, it can be a chance to explore some new opportunities. In sales, potential clients are sometimes called *diamond mines;* where you find one diamond, you're likely to find more. Having a client move to another company is like discovering a new diamond mine — a place to look carefully for more shiny new clients.

Knowing how to react

When you're fired, remember not to take it personally. Even if you've contributed to the situation, don't beat yourself up over a mistake. It's still just business. Learn a lesson and use it to build an even stronger business foundation. Although this may seem like a totally negative situation, it's just another opportunity to sell. Send the client a handwritten note, thanking him or her for the chance to work with them, mentioning something positive that he/she contributed to you or, if necessary, apologizing. Personal notes always make the receiver feel good and leave the person with a positive impression of you. Think how great it makes you look for letting bygones be bygones. And, believe it or not, it could make the client reconsider!

Do, however, keep the do's and don'ts of being fired (see Table 13-1) in mind:

Table 13-1	Do's and Don'ts of Getting Fired
Do	*Don't*
Accept responsibility for any mistakes you've made and apologize.	Become defensive or blame someone else.
Tell the client you've enjoyed working with him or her and you're sorry that at this point you're not a good fit.	Try to prove your client wrong.
Ask how you can rectify the situation.	Bad mouth your client to others in or outside the company.
Ask for another opportunity to serve the client.	Burn your bridges — you never know when that person may pop up in another area or at another company.
Continue to stay in touch regularly.	

Firing a client

Firing a client is a moment of truth for all freelancers, most of whom say that they went into business to be able to choose the clients they work for — or not.

Strangely enough, when people are sending you checks, you may be surprised at how much you can tolerate with a smile on your face. But at some point, you may decide that a client isn't for you. At those times, you really can fire a client, but be sure to do it only for the right reasons.

The following are the proper reasons to fire a client:

✔ **When the client makes you feel bad.** This may happen for a variety of reasons, and you may not be interested in knowing why. But if you get a bad feeling in your stomach when you work with someone, that's enough.

✔ **When the client insists that you produce work that doesn't meet your standards.** Producing sub-standard work can negatively affect your reputation. It may come back to haunt you.

✔ **When you don't enjoy a sufficient return on investment.** Some clients are so high maintenance that they're literally more trouble than they're worth. Weigh how much trouble they are against how much they pay you. If you can do without the money, jump ship.

✔ **When a client doesn't show you the respect you deserve.** Every freelancer deserves to be treated politely and respectfully. Some clients are repeatedly inconsiderate of a freelancer's time, expect free work, speak disrespectfully, don't pay on time, fail to return calls or e-mails, make unreasonable demands, scream, or act in other ways that show a lack of respect. You don't need this kind of abuse.

✔ **When a client doesn't pay your invoices.** Sure, sometimes your bill gets lost, the check's in the mail, or a client simply overlooks your invoice. An occasional late payment is no reason to abandon a good client; however, when late payment becomes the standard operating procedure, you may want to look elsewhere for work. And when a client doesn't respond to your second request for payment, seriously consider why. Is the client simply forgetful or disorganized or is something more serious going on, like financial problems?

Consider, however, the wrong times to fire a client:

✔ **When the client is your bread and butter.** Cultivate other business before you cut your primary client loose.

✔ **When they are generally a good client but are driving you crazy on one project.** Be patient: This, too, shall pass.

✔ **When you've just messed up a project for them and you're humiliated.** Redeem yourself first and then decide if you really want to leave.

The best way to fire a client is so that they don't know you've fired them. Being fired never feels good, and this is not a feeling you want to leave them with. You don't have to come out and say, "I don't want to work for you anymore." Instead, do the following:

✔ **Be unavailable.** Let them know that your schedule is really tight and you won't be able to start on their project until some future date.

✔ **Explain that you're focusing your efforts toward a different type of work.** "I'm investing most of my energy now specializing in doing people's taxes, and I don't do bookkeeping anymore."

✔ **Increase your fee past the point that the client is willing to pay.** You probably have some sense of just how high your client will go or what the budget is. Boost your rates above that and the client may simply not call you anymore. Of course, what sometimes happens is that you discover you were more valuable than you thought or that the client has more money than you knew. If this is the case and they still want you, perhaps you could consider doing the work for the higher price.

✔ **As a last resort, explain that you don't feel you're the best person to meet their needs and recommend someone else.** Be sure to warn the other freelancer first!

If you're suffering with an abusive client, you may think that telling him or her off would be the greatest feeling in the world. While some situations may warrant politely letting loose and taking the consequences, you'll probably regret the emotional outburst, feel compelled to call and apologize, and will not have enjoyed a moral victory. Instead, try to keep your cool. You don't have to resort to abusive client's tactics.

Chapter 14

Staying Current

*I*n my best business fantasy, I swoop into a dire situation and use my super-hero powers to save my clients from personal and corporate disaster. I am all knowing and use secret weapons that are unavailable to anyone else in the world. That's the fantasy. In reality, I have to work hard at staying current and using any newfound knowledge to my clients' advantage.

About three years ago, a client started using e-mail — a lot — and he expected me to do the same. I'm not known for being enthusiastic about faddish techno gimmicks (I still don't own a hand-held computer), so I rather reluctantly added e-mail to my tools as a necessary evil. Today, I rely on e-mail only slightly less than I rely on my aorta. Not only have I come to value its effectiveness, I've come to understand how much easier it makes my life. Without e-mail, I would be a dinosaur in the freelance world.

No profession stays the same from year to year. Even without major inventions like the Internet, you still experience constant change through scientific discoveries, lifestyle changes, economic factors, shifts in markets, and other factors. To be an expert in your field, you must stay up-to-date on the latest developments and trends in your industry, as well as the latest ways of doing business efficiently. This chapter gives you some examples of ways to stay current so that you're always at the top of your game.

Staying in the Know

Smart freelancers stay informed about the following types of information:

- ✔ **Current world events:** To be considered a knowledgeable person, you must be able to converse intelligently about what's going on in the world.

- ✔ **Local events:** What's happening in your community can be a good source of small talk with clients. (Steer clear of political chat, though; it can detonate strong feelings.)

- ✔ **Local business happenings:** Knowing who's doing what in business is the foundation for understanding your clients and the environment in which they operate. Besides, looking in your backyard (your town) is one of the best ways to find clients.

- ✔ **Business trends:** Be the first to tell your clients about the latest management trend or a hot new business book, and they'll see you as a true asset and an up-to-the-minute expert.

- ✔ **Your profession:** Of all the things you should know inside and out, your profession is at the top of the list. When you know your stuff, you're able to do your best work, serve your clients' interests, and to be seen as competitive.

Networking

If you want to be an expert, hang out with experts. People love to talk about their work, and what better way to find out the latest and greatest than from the people who are doing it every day.

I stay current by practicing my own form of *osmosis,* a usually highly scientific term that I use to mean soaking up a lot of good stuff from other people: I enjoy hearing about new ideas and techniques that others have tested and seeing what they think about how well they work. That saves a lot of time in figuring out what works and what doesn't.

One of the best places to find people to network with is in business associations. Business associations tend to keep members informed of the hot topics that affect their business. Join a professional association that has national affiliation, and you generally receive their newsletter or other method of communication that's chock full of information. Business organizations also bring in guest speakers who touch on topics that relate to the industry or discuss subjects that are of interest to the general population: an upcoming election or political referendum, a social situation, or a community concern.

A massage therapist with a business touch

Ann Webb Davis is an expert at therapeutic massage, but she combines her holistic approach to health with a healthy business savvy. When I met Ann, she was completing a special degree program that she designed with the help of a professor at the University of Memphis. After that, she worked to pass legislation that requires certification for therapeutic massage. She regularly takes classes to update her skills in such technical areas as infant massage, but she also participates in the Rotary Club, has learned how to create a non-profit organization, has taught herself to use desktop publishing software, has been tutored in writing skills and now edits a newsletter, and has become a certified quality assessor using the principles of the Malcolm Baldridge Award — who knows what's next?

Ann believes that the same principles apply to small businesses and corporations. Since she founded Memphis Massage and started hiring a handful of employees a short while ago, she has written a procedures manual, created a training program, and applied planning and quality control techniques to her business. One of her beliefs about business is, "If you're not growing, you're dying." Keeping up with Ann is an education in itself!

Joining an association can also pay off in the following ways:

- ✔ Providing networking opportunities
- ✔ Acquainting you with other professionals who can provide backup support or be a source of contacts
- ✔ Helping you meet people who may eventually become good buddies

In a general business association, you can find experts of all sorts. Tap their power. Association members tend to feel an obligation or loyalty to each other, and loyalty can be a big plus when you need assistance.

A great way to meet someone is to ask for his or her opinion about something that the person is an expert in. At an association meeting, learn people's areas of special skill or interest, and ask for their advice or insight. Most people will be flattered and will thoroughly enjoy taking you under their wings.

Association membership mailing lists are resources for marketing your own freelance business. You can target the particular groups that have a strong need for what you do. For example, if it's a group of small business people, you know they need accounting advice: That's a perfect match if you're in the accounting business.

Reading for fun and profit

Reading to keep up with current events is something you can do almost anywhere and anytime. By subscribing to certain news sources, you can easily and inexpensively keep up with everything you need to know. Unless you're a speed-reader, you may not be able to read every word of every publication; but even skimming headlines helps you be aware of important topics and sensitive issues.

Some of the most helpful media are as follows:

- ✔ Your local newspaper
- ✔ Newspaper Web sites, such as www.usatoday.com, www.nytimes.com, or Web browser news pages
- ✔ Your weekly business newspaper
- ✔ A general national news magazine or newspaper
- ✔ A trade publication that deals with your industry
- ✔ A trade publication (or publications) that is important to your largest clients
- ✔ Top-selling new business books

Don't focus just on business topics. You'll be well-rounded if you also read sports, science, and other non-business articles.

Professional newsletters often summarize the latest business books, which can save you time and allow you to pare down your list of must-reads. Subscribe to one of these and you'll come across as well-informed, without taking the time to read unnecessary information. Find a well-respected source you trust — reviews and critiques are slanted by design, and you want one that approximates your beliefs, likes, and dislikes.

Find these publications by checking the following sources:

- ✔ **Your professional trade association:** Most groups have regular publications.
- ✔ **Your local library listing of periodicals:** Bacon's directories, for example, list a host of magazines and newspapers by industry category, such as architecture or travel.
- ✔ **An Internet search engine:** Access a variety of publications on your subject. For instance, I type in **Public Relations Magazines,** and the Internet gives me a choice of many.

TRUE STORY

Keeping up with fads and fashions

Have you read *In Style* magazine lately? Been to the mall? Watched MTV? Scanned *My Generation* magazine? Been to a sporting event? These activities may seem like a stretch, but to be able to relate to clients of all ages and backgrounds, you must keep tabs on the hottest new stars, the biggest box office hits, the latest rage in cars, and the fashion sensations.

Developing rapport is vital to building any client relationship, and shared experiences are key. If you don't speak the same language or understand the same references, you'll have a tough time building a relationship. Using dated reference points or outmoded language shows clients you just haven't kept up.

Here are some ways to learn the latest hits among all ages:

✔ Check the bestseller list and *People* magazine reviews. Read one.

✔ Watch MTV or VH-1, the music TV stations.

✔ Visit a music store and ask to see the latest hit CDs.

✔ Read specialty magazines for young, hip readers like *Rolling Stone* and *Spin* for music or *Fast Company* for business.

✔ Go to a new movie.

✔ Check out a technology store or a Sharper Image catalog.

✔ Watch the top-rated sitcom, drama, or primetime soap on TV.

✔ Read the comics.

✔ Check the Internet news services. Most Internet service providers have home page links to news updates such as MSNBC or Looksmart.

✔ Talk to people, young and old.

Continuing Your Education

School days, school days. You probably thought your formal education was over, and it may be, but going back to school may be a necessary part of keeping up with your professional obligations. This section tells you about your educational options and how they not only make you a more effective freelancer, but also enhance your earning power and potentially lead to exciting new career possibilities.

Staying certified or accredited

Some professions, such as accounting or law, require that you earn a certain amount of credits in your profession to stay accredited or certified. These are called *continuing professional education* (or CPE) requirements. You must attend approved classes to qualify for these credits. Check with your local college or university to see what options you may have in your area.

Your professional association may also sponsor sessions, either locally or at national meetings and training sessions. Out-of-town seminars and workshops can be somewhat pricey, so build some money into your budget to accommodate a trip every year or however often your certification or accreditation requires.

Moving toward a new career path

One of the biggest advantages freelancing can offer is scheduling options. For anyone who wants to go back to school for an advanced degree, enhance skills through career development classes, or even switch careers, freelancing gives a distinct advantage. Unlike a 9-to-5 job that may restrict you to off-hours schooling, a freelance position lets you set your own timetable. If you choose, you can enroll in a daytime class or limit your workload temporarily so that you can study.

For example, you could go back for that Masters in Business Administration (MBA) you've always wanted or complete a teaching certification. A land-scaper may study to be a master gardener, or a programmer could become a systems engineer. Suppose you wanted to switch careers completely; free-lancing would let you do that and make money while you learn. I know a career counselor who freelanced while she kicked off a writing career, and a marketing consultant who started a publishing company. When you control your schedule, you can also control your career future.

Advanced degrees sometimes warrant an increase in fees, as well. By attaining special certification or a higher level of expertise, you can expect to pull in compensation that matches your greater professional designation. After you've gained your new distinction, be sure to check out the competition to see what type of increase is consistent with the market.

Certain types of education expenses may be tax deductible; however, there are a number of restrictions on what type of education you pursue and the expenses you incur, ranging from tuition to books to travel. Check with your tax advisor or the IRS to make sure your expenses qualify.

Improving your skills

Professional seminars not only inform you of new ways of doing business, they also revive your enthusiasm for your chosen work. Several types of sem-inars and workshops can boost your value to your clients and increase your effectiveness as a businessperson:

✔ Skills training that expands your knowledge of your profession or makes you more aware of current issues, such as a cost management seminar for a caterer.

✔ Skills training that makes you a specialist in your field. (In some cases, having this type of specialist status is grounds for increasing your rates.)

✔ Training in skills that help you be a better freelancer, such as improving communication skills or gaining familiarity with software programs.

✔ Sessions that enhance your knowledge of business in general, such as a seminar on trends in customer service.

Whether or not you go out of town to attend seminars, they should provide an opportunity for you to socialize with new acquaintances, renew your enthusiasm for your area of expertise, and revive your zest for freelancing. Out-of-town trips can also be fun, vacation-like tax deductions. Just be sure to check with your tax advisor to find out how you can combine work and play and follow guidelines for IRS requirements.

Part IV

Managing Your Money

In this part . . .

Personal fulfillment is one thing, but most freelancers also prefer financial success. Systematic approaches help pay your bill to Uncle Sam, manage your money day by day, and contribute to your future wealth and well-being. This part gives you the nitty-gritty of setting up a record-keeping system, knowing how and what to charge, protecting yourself and your company with insurance, and investing for the future.

Chapter 15

Budgeting and Accounting

In This Chapter

▶ Financing your business

▶ Getting credit

▶ Creating a budget

▶ Overcoming your fear of numbers

▶ Using accounting information as a management tool

*W*hile working for yourself is all about fulfillment and freedom, it's mostly about the big M word: money. Knowing how much money you can expect to take in and how much you will probably have to spend is important information to have each and every month. This chapter tells you how to figure out whether you're running the business or the business is running you.

Managing Your Finances

Unlike in *Monopoly,* where you deal in cash, your business requires a systematic approach to money coming in and money going out. You don't want to run your business using cash, because it's safer and easier to use checks and credit. The following sections help you manage both.

Opening a business checking account

Small-business people make the mistake of thinking that their money and their business money are one and the same. Although ultimately that's true, you still should keep your funds and your business funds separate. Here's why:

✔ You can keep better track of how much money your business is making.

✔ You can more easily figure your taxes.

✔ If the IRS audits you, your records will probably be easier to decipher.

Putting all your business money and your personal money together is called *co-mingling funds,* which just means all the money is mixed up in one pot and it's harder to separate what went where. You don't want to co-mingle funds because the accountants of the world will consider you a pariah (that's a big word for a goob).

One easy way to keep your finances separate is to open a checking account that's solely for your business. For convenience, you may prefer to open your business account at the same bank as your personal account; however, many banks offer different services for business accounts, and you'll want to check them out. And don't think that a bank is a bank is a bank. Compare the services and fees at several institutions to see the variety of options at each. Visit your bank, talk with a person who opens accounts, and ask which type of account will best fit your needs. Here are some benefits to consider:

- ✔ **Minimum balance:** Do you need to maintain a minimum balance? If so, how much?

- ✔ **Automatic teller services:** Can you have access to automatic teller machines?

- ✔ **Fees:** For some accounts, you must pay a monthly fee; others may charge by the transaction.

- ✔ **Check writing:** Does the account offer unlimited check writing, or are you limited to a certain number of checks you can write each month without being charged?

- ✔ **Overdraft protection:** In business, you certainly don't want any checks returned for insufficient funds. Some accounts offer *overdraft protection* so that if you miscalculate and accidentally write checks for more money than you have in your account, the bank processes the check without charging you an overdraft fee. This may require that you set aside funds in a savings account that the bank can access to cover the overdraft.

- ✔ **Interest bearing:** With a minimum balance, certain checking accounts pay interest. Even though the interest rate paid on checking accounts is generally lower than the rate you may expect through another type of investment, even a small amount of interest can add up to a little extra cash.

- ✔ **Accessibility:** What are the bank's daily hours, and are they open weekends? Is there a branch in your local grocery or other convenient location? Being able to combine a trip to the bank with dropping off your laundry is a real timesaver.

- ✔ **Other services:** What other benefits can your bank offer? My bank offers the following services: online banking, overdraft protection, investment services, bill payment, trust services, and advice about all sorts of small business issues such as benefits and retirement accounts.

You can likely find information about your local banking services on the Internet. Check it out; it could save you a trip to the bank.

Online banking gives you choices

Always interested in saving time, some free-lancers enjoy the convenience of banking on the Internet. Banking online allows you to take care of much of your banking business from the comfort of your home office — no waiting in a drive-though line or standing in line.

What can you do online? Services vary from one bank to another, but the following are some of the common services you can access online:

- ✔ **Banking transactions:** Pay bills, look at your financial statements, order checks, transfer funds, and pull up your banking information 'round the clock every day.

- ✔ **Credit services:** Get mortgage loan approval or apply for a credit card.

- ✔ **Investments:** Purchase Certificates of Deposit (CDs).

At one time, conducting financial transactions online was considered risky business, but today it's routine for many people. Naturally, you want to make sure the institution you select is approved by the Federal Deposit Insurance Corporation (FDIC).

You may choose to do your online banking with your current financial institution. If so, just go to their Web site and look for the online registration area. You may need software that's compatible with your bank's system.

Aside from using your traditional bank, you may also want to check out a bank that's an Internet-only service. Internet-only banks exist only online, with no physical branches as we know them. Because an Internet bank doesn't have branches, tellers, and other tangibles that cost money, they have a reputation for offering lower fees and higher interest rates than traditional institutions. That may or may not be true. Finding the right Internet bank can take some research, so do your homework and compare. I find the Web site www.fool.com to be a good source of general info, as is the Gomez Internet Banker Scorecard.

If you do decide to use an Internet bank, be sure to find out how long bills take to be processed and whether you have to mail in your deposits. These can be drawbacks. Of course, you'll need a password — be sure to guard your password so you don't give access to anyone you don't intend to have it.

When you open your business bank account, give some thought to who you want to have check-writing authority. Are you the only person who will write checks on your business account? That could make things a bit inconvenient, and even difficult. Consider the following reasons to authorize an additional person to write checks on your business account:

- ✔ In case of an accident or serious illness, you could be incapable of writing checks. Someone should be able to pay your bills or take care of business in your absence.

- ✔ If you travel, business may arise while you're out of town that requires someone else to write a check (with your permission, of course).

✔ If you're lucky enough to have a bookkeeper or assistant to pay your bills, this person can conveniently do that without your signature. Naturally, you must review everything they do to keep a system of checks and balances on what is spent. (While you may have the most trustworthy help in the world, it always pays to have two sets of eyes looking things over.)

If you don't have a bookkeeper or assistant, who should you assign to write checks? Your spouse, grown child, or trusted friend could stand in for you when necessary. Only you can decide who is the most trusted and competent person for the job.

Using a business credit card

Who needs a credit card in a freelancing situation? You do. I have a philosophy of not being in debt, especially in my business, but I also know that having a business credit card is not only a necessity but also an economic benefit. Even if you don't expect to charge anything to your business, you can benefit from having a separate business credit card for several reasons:

✔ **Convenience:** A credit card allows you to buy products and services without paying cash on the spot. Not only does this mean you don't have to carry cash, it means that in many cases you can order things over the phone or on the Internet without showing up in person to pay. I order printing and other services this way; I hate to spend my valuable (billable) time running around to suppliers just to write a check.

✔ **Expense tracking:** Using a credit card is a way of having a receipt for and tracking purchases you make that are related to your business. Major credit card companies offer small business services that include tracking your expenses for you.

✔ **Image:** When you take a client to lunch, it gives you a professional appearance.

✔ **Cash advances:** Some credit cards allow you to get cash advances at automatic teller machines. This can be especially convenient if you travel. Banks and credit card companies do charge fees for cash advances.

✔ **Conserving funds:** Suppose you have a business checking account that pays interest. You want to keep as much money in the account as you can to earn as much interest as possible. By using a credit card, you can leave your money in the bank until you have to pay the credit card bill, which means you're earning interest during that time.

Be sure you're earning more interest on your checking account than you're paying on your credit card, or you may actually be costing yourself money!

Like banks, credit cards differ in fees and services, and it pays to compare. What should you look for in a business credit card?

- ✔ **Monthly or annual fees:** Depending on what type of card you have, you may incur a flat annual fee that can range from about $45 to several hundred per year.

- ✔ **Interest:** If you don't pay your entire outstanding balance, the company charges you interest on your balance. The percentage varies from card to card, so shop around for a good interest rate.

- ✔ **Fees for purchases over your credit limit:** Spending beyond your limit can get expensive if your card charges for that. Pick a card that doesn't charge for this or keep close track of how much you're spending and back off when you get close to your limit.

- ✔ **Payment terms:** Does the balance have to be paid in total each month, or is there simply a required minimum payment?

- ✔ **Access to ATMs:** When you can't write a check and you need cash, a business credit card is a convenient solution as long as yours is accepted at the ATM locations you need. Because you'll pay a fee, weigh the convenience against the amount.

- ✔ **Additional services and benefits:** Credit card companies are competing like crazy for business, and extra added attractions help them lure customers. Look for special business services such as discounts on purchases, frequent flyer or hotel benefits, warranties or theft protection on purchases, legal referrals, and a host of other extras.

Managing your checking account

My former assistant, Tim, jokes about when he used to keep my personal checkbook for me. He always had money "hidden," that he didn't show on the check register. (I loved having this little buffer, knowing I had more money than I thought.) And even though the checkbook balance wasn't real, Tim knew exactly what the true balance was. Every month he reconciled my checkbook with the bank statement and scrutinized any discrepancy. He would investigate like Sherlock Holmes until he made the figures match to the penny.

You may not practice pinpoint accuracy when it comes to your personal finances, but you must keep up with your business finances. One aspect of that is in *reconciling* your bank statement each and every month. *Reconciling* means checking to see that you and the bank agree on what money has been deposited and what money has been withdrawn, so that you're certain your bank balance is correct. This is a time that you can check to see if either you or the bank have made any errors.

If worst comes to worst, take your records to the bank and they will help you find the error. When you have to file reports with the IRS and other agencies, a ballpark estimate won't do. Keep your records straight each month and you'll save yourself lot of grief trying to find mistakes in multiple months' records rather than one.

Watch out for credit traps!

Business credit cards have the same potential pitfalls as personal credit cards. Buyer beware: Read the fine print to find out the whole story. Credit card companies may offer you a low interest rate to transfer your balance from an existing credit card. If this is the case, check how long the new rate is effective. Often, the transfer amount may be at a low rate, but any new purchases you make incur extremely high interest charges. Likewise, when the introductory period runs out, whatever balance you have from the original transfer may escalate to the new, higher rate.

I've never believed there was such a thing as a free ride, and I tend to look for long-term gain versus short-term. I try to stay with a financial institution because I believe that my history with them will be an advantage if I ever need additional credit or other assistance. Besides, my time is worth money, and if I "spend" a lot of my time switching credit cards back and forth, I may as well just pay a slightly higher rate.

Another pitfall: If you pay the minimum payment each month, you may find that it takes years to pay off the card balance. Consider paying off the card each month.

Finding special loans

Many freelancers, especially those working from home, don't need a lot of money to get a business started. But if your work requires you to buy equipment, lease office space, or buy a lot of inventory, you may need financing assistance.

State and federal agencies, such as the Small Business Administration (SBA), loan money to small businesses. They have especially attractive programs to help women and minority business owners, too. Should you need financing for your business, check out your local economic development office or the SBA (at your local office or at their Web site) to see what's available at low interest rates. Getting loans this way can be a paperwork maze; you may want to get professional help from an accountant or financial professional to help you meet the requirements.

Establishing a line of credit

Establishing a line of credit is like taking out a loan. You fill out all the paperwork as if you were getting a loan, and when it's approved, you have the leeway to spend a certain amount of money for your business purpose whenever you prefer. A line of credit can be used for anything you want and isn't tied to the purchase of an item that's being used as collateral. (*Collateral* is the tangible item you put up as security for the loan, meaning that you agree to forfeit the item to the loan institution if you don't pay the loan off. For example, when you buy a car and get a loan, if you don't repay the loan, the lender will repossess the car. The car is the collateral.)

Suppose you establish a line of credit for $10,000. The bank gives you checks or a bank card that you can use to spend up to that amount. Until you spend it, you pay no fee. When you do spend a portion of the line of credit, you then receive monthly statements showing your balance and requiring you to pay a certain amount that's like a loan payment. If you have a $10,000 line of credit, and you spend $6,000, you still have $4,000 that you're pre-approved to spend. After you pay back what you owe, you still have $10,000 available to spend.

A line of credit is something you can have indefinitely. You may want to consider getting a line of credit while you're still employed by someone else, because you'll having an easier time getting approved.

A small business person will usually have to put up collateral to establish a line of credit. Collateral is something tangible that the bank can take possession of if you don't pay back your expenditures. For example, you may use your house as collateral to establish a line of credit. If you fail to meet your commitment, the bank can take possession of your home.

Beware of easy-to-get, high-interest loans. These can be a scam that could result in your losing money.

Preparing a Budget

A budget is a plan for managing your money; it helps you have more control over when and where you spend. Although you can live without a budget, it's like flying blind. Without a budget, you never really know what your financial situation is. That could mean you worry needlessly when you actually have plenty of money, or you could spend money you don't really have, approaching things with a more carefree attitude than you safely can. A budget gives you the information you need to make decisions about how you're charging for your services, whether you need to reduce your expenses, whether you can afford to buy new equipment, or how you need to enhance your business.

The foundation of every budget is money coming in and money going out. The following five sections show you some easy steps to preparing a budget.

Step 1: Determining your financial needs

Determine how much money you need or want to make each month. Add up all your business expenses, including the salary you plan to pay yourself. Don't forget to include money you need to set aside for income tax, retirement and savings, college funds, and so on. The total of your expenses is the

228 Part IV: Managing Your Money

absolute minimum amount of money you must earn to make ends meet. Use the following convenient checklist to help you:

- ✔ Your salary (and you know how much this should be based on your family's needs to pay a mortgage or rent, to eat, and so on)
- ✔ Employee salary (if any)
- ✔ Office rent (if any)
- ✔ Office equipment
- ✔ Payments on loans or lines of credit
- ✔ Office supplies (letterhead, copy paper, postage stamps, copier or printer ink cartridges, rubber bands, paper clips, and so on)
- ✔ Office expenses (phone, utilities, maintenance, cleaning)
- ✔ Payments to other providers (courier or delivery fees, subcontractors, attorney, accountant, bookkeeper)
- ✔ Taxes (see Chapter 17)
- ✔ Insurance (see Chapter 18)
- ✔ Travel and entertainment expenses (taking clients to lunch)

You may think that when you go into business for yourself you'll have more expenses, but here's a happy surprise: You may also reduce your expenses in some areas, including fewer lunches out, lower dry cleaning bills, and maybe even lower clothing and gasoline costs.

Step 2: Calculating income

Figure out how much money you're likely to make. Remember, you can't charge for every hour you work, because clients don't pay you to order office supplies, do your bookkeeping, clean your office, and so on.

Here's how to figure your potential monthly income, depending on how you charge for your services:

- ✔ **On an hourly-fee basis:** Assume that you can charge clients for about 60 percent of the hours you work. (Assume that the other 40 percent of your time will go toward performing tasks you can't charge for, such as selling, doing your bookkeeping, and so on.) Multiply your hourly rate times 60 percent of the hours you work each week. That's how much money you can expect to generate.

- ✔ **On a daily-fee basis:** If you work on a *daily-fee basis,* you get paid a certain amount per day that you work. Total up the number of days you plan to work for a client and multiply that times your daily fee (see Chapter 16 for information on setting your rates).

✔ **On a project basis:** Working on a project basis makes it a little easier to figure how much income you anticipate, because working on a *project basis* usually involves being paid a set amount at different times of the project. For example, if you have a project lined up that will pay you $1,000 on the front end, $1,000 midway through, and $1,000 at the end, you can predict exactly when that money will be paid. Just add up all the project money you can count on for the month.

✔ **Speculative work:** If you've chosen to work on something on a *speculative basis,* you get the fee only if you're selected from a group of companies, all of which are bidding on the same project. This is work you can't count on. Don't include speculative work income in your monthly income projections. If you end up getting a speculative project, it will feel like a bonus!

Step 3: Figuring the difference

The next step is to subtract your expenses (see Step 1) from your income (in Step 2).

Knowing that you can at least meet your expenses will probably give you a lot more peace of mind. If you see a potential shortfall, you can consider ways to generate more income or to reduce your expenses. If you see that there's excess money, consider taking yourself out for a steak dinner to celebrate!

Improving your cash flow

Cash flow has to do with timing: when money comes in and when it goes out. You have to always have enough money to pay your bills when they're due.

✔ Pay your bills on time, but not before they're due. (Many bills are due either on the first or the fifteenth of the month, so try paying bills at those times.) By keeping more of your money — even a small amount — in an interest-bearing checking account, you can earn a little extra cash.

✔ Set a time to pay yourself, either weekly, every other week, or once a month. This will help you develop discipline and not dip into your business account whenever you feel like it.

✔ Don't tie up all of your money in long-term investments (see Chapter 19). Keep some aside for unexpected needs.

✔ Use your line of credit to pay for larger ticket items, such as computers, so that you're not spending all your cash. Even though you pay interest, you may also be able to deduct it as a business expense.

Step 4: Estimating cash flow

Just because you're making money doesn't mean you're in the clear. The true question is: Will you have money when you need it? Imagine that it's January 15. You've just signed a contract for a big project that will pay you $5,000 when the project is complete, which is at the end of March. That sounds great, until you realize that until March you won't get paid anything else. Your rent is due, and your loan payment for your new computer comes in at the end of this month. The fact that there is money coming in later doesn't help you. You have a *cash-flow problem* — not enough cash when you need it.

To avoid cash-flow problems, make sure you have some money in the bank before you jump into your freelance enterprise (see Chapter 4). As you look at your income and expenses, consider timing as an important factor, and make sure you have enough cash flow to pay your bills. If your income and expenses fluctuate, so will your cash flow. Review your cash flow position each month to make sure you're continuing to be able to pay your bills, and, hopefully, set some money aside.

Step 5: Putting extra money to good use

What's left after you subtract your expenses from your income? If there is money to spare, consider the following:

- ✔ Paying yourself a bonus!
- ✔ Putting the extra money in an account that earns interest

Keeping Books and Accounting for Your Money

Do you love to concern yourself with the tiny details of business, revel in taking hours to pore over your expenses line by line, and adore typing up numbers by the hundreds? I thought not. Few freelancers enjoy the mundane aspects of minding the shop. Most tend to be more interested in thinking, troubleshooting, getting the job done, and experiencing the adventure of independent work. Unfortunately, someone has to get their hands dirty keeping track of your accounts, your money, your expenses, and all the less exciting aspects of your business.

This section explains the areas you must consider, and how to minimize the time you spend on it. Another great resource is *Accounting For Dummies* by John A. Tracy (Hungry Minds, Inc.). Needless to say, freelance bookkeepers and accountants can skip this chapter.

Appreciating the benefits of keeping records

Keeping accurate records each month can help you do the following:

- Track how much money you're making — now that's fun!
- Recognize which clients pay on time and which don't.
- Determine which of your products and services are most profitable.
- Know when to pay your bills.
- Make it easier to keep track of potential write-offs, special expenses, and other financial issues as they happen, rather than trying to collect all the receipts and remember or reconstruct events at the end of the year.

A number of agencies, including the IRS, your state government, and your local government want to know how much money you're making. Staying on top of your record keeping can make this information available when you need it.

It figures

When she was younger and single, Colleen Wells took a pretty casual approach to budgeting: If she had money, she spent it, and if she didn't have money, she didn't. Her desktop-publishing business generated plenty of income for her as an individual. It also gave her the freedom to do what she really wanted most. After going it solo for five or six years, she got married and started a family.

"In some ways, freelancing gave me the freedom to take time off to have children," says Colleen. "In other ways, it made things harder. When you're on your own, you don't get paid maternity leave, so taking that time off required considerable planning. I had to work a lot more before the baby was born to get ready for the time I'd be off, not making any money at all. Then, after the baby came, I had to get back to work pretty fast. Considering I had a cesarean section with both children, that was a feat.'"

Now that she has other people (namely her children, Gabriel and Faith) counting on her for their livelihood, Colleen takes a methodical approach to making and spending money. She asked a friend who is a financial consultant to help her develop a budget. "Information is power," she says. "I feel a lot more security and less worry now that I know what's what. Before, my financial situation seemed overwhelming. Today I realize it's all do-able. After I saw things on paper, I realized I could survive on a lot less than I thought I needed. I could save money by not eating out as much, eliminating cable television, clipping grocery coupons, and practicing small money-saving tips like buying office supplies at a discount store and getting a slightly lower quality of paper.

"With just a little extra effort, I can spend time with my kids without constantly thinking, 'I should be working.'"

If you take away only one thing from this entire book, it should be this: You must keep accurate records of your business finances. With accurate records, you can simplify your life. Without accurate records, you open yourself up for heartache with your clients, the tax authorities, your financial advisor, and with anyone else who tries to make heads or tails of your business. You absolutely cannot live without a system for tracking your finances.

You must record all payments you receive, even if they're paid in cash. You owe taxes on everything you earn, and the IRS has ways of finding out if the amount you report is different than the amount you take in. Remember that bank records are tracked by Social Security number or federal employment identification number (EIN), and so are quite a few other things. It's illegal to underreport your income. Don't take the chance.

Paying your expenses

As long as you're a one-person band, you probably don't need to do a lot of fancy financial calculations and projections with the information you collect. Knowing a few basics is enough to keep you on track. The following sections can help.

This cobbler has shoes

What happens when an accountant goes into the freelance business? He gets to practice what he preaches.

Phil Schaefgen, CPA, had successfully climbed the corporate ladder. He was working as a senior vice president of a subsidiary of a *Fortune* 100 company when he fell victim to corporate restructuring, Phil stepped out on his own to do what he loves: Use his CPA credentials to help clients by managing other people's taxes as well as consulting and teaching. "I found out that many people have dreams, but don't know how exactly to fulfill them," says Phil. "My experiences and knowledge allow me to assist them in realizing their dreams, which is fulfilling my own. It's the best of both worlds."

Phil dives into new business ventures with equal gusto, whether he's working on his clients' behalf or his own. An early riser, he uses the oldest trick of his trade: organization. He uses a computer, calendar of notes, and a creative filing system. "To look at my desk you'd think I have no clue what's what; however, there is a rational priority to the stacks of papers and files." Each file has a priority order and position: Today's files are on the desk, while tomorrow's are put away with notations of deadlines or when to check back with a client. He uses a database-management program to make sure nothing falls through the cracks.

By keeping his work in tip top order, Phil can juggle a teaching and lecture schedule at a local university and entertain entrepreneurial opportunities as they arise. He balances that with his family time, volunteer activities, and taking care of his elderly parents. Somehow, he finds time for it all. "I only wish I had left the corporate world earlier," he says.

When the money's not there

Horror of horrors: You've just added up your bills, and you don't have enough money to pay them all. Now what?

✔ Don't panic. Panic won't accomplish anything.

✔ Look at all the due dates, and see what can be paid later in the month.

✔ For any credit card bills, pay as much as you can, rather than the entire balance.

✔ If you can't pay someone, call and talk with them about it. Don't hide! If they're small business people, they probably understand. Try to work out a payment schedule.

✔ Take a close look at your finances and spending habits to better understand how you got in this fix. Is it a cash flow problem, meaning that you expect the money but it hasn't arrived yet? Are you sure your spending habits are in line with your ability to pay?

Paying bills

A simple filing system can help you know when to pay bills. Keep two files:

✔ Bills to pay on the 1st of the month

✔ Bills to pay on the 15th of the month

As you receive bills, stash them in whichever folder is appropriate depending on when the bill is due. Before the due date (allowing enough time to mail the checks), write checks for the bills, mark the bills as paid, record the date and check number used to pay each bill, and place the bills in your paid file.

By using a credit card or paying by check for all your expenses or bills, you can keep an indisputable record of your expenses. Of course, occasionally, you'll need to pay cash for small items. If you do pay for something in cash, keep the receipt for your records and be sure to record it in your expense file.

Using this simple system, you have a record of all your expenses. If a question arises later about whether you paid something, you can refer to your file and have all the information you need at your fingertips.

Paying yourself

How you pay yourself depends on what type of business organization you have set up. If you're a sole proprietor or an LLC (see Chapter 5), the process is simple, and you can decide how often to pay yourself.

Good record-keeping for more reasons than one

Keeping copies and accurate records of bills, expenses, and client project requests is not only essential for running a business profitably, it can also keep you out of hot water.

A freelancer told me of two legal hassles that arose when clients claimed that her company incurred expenses without approval. In both cases, the client refused to pay invoices for expensive equipment rental and subcontracting. Both matters went all the way to court.

The results, however, were quite different. In the first case, business was done on a handshake, but trust wasn't enough. In court, my friend wasn't able to provide enough backup to substantiate that the client had asked for the work to be done.

The second situation had a happier ending. Having learned from the first court battle, she kept meticulous records of every transaction, every request, every expense, and every phone message and e-mail request. It was all in writing. When her second day in court came around, she was armed with detailed, dated information that proved what she said. The judge awarded the money to her, and she became a fanatic subscriber to the school of record keeping.

If your business is a corporation (also discussed in Chapter 5), you are literally an employee, and the process becomes more complicated. Corporations must pay monthly withholding and payroll taxes on employees, including you. Your monthly deposit will vary according to how much money you make. The more you make, the more you must deposit. This means you must have enough money not only to pay your salary, but also to cover the payroll tax deposit. Talk to a tax advisor about the best approach.

Making payroll

Employing other people complicates your accounting, because payroll tax laws are tricky, and you must compute employees' withholding tax, make tax deposits monthly, and deal with details that you don't have to do for yourself.

If you have employees, consider hiring an expert to handle your payroll. If you choose not to do that, check out payroll accounting software that can simplify the process.

Overcoming accounting phobia

To the numerically challenged, accounting can be overwhelming. But in the long run, accounting is just a way of writing everything down. That's all. Accounting simply tells you where your money came from and where it has gone. You don't have to use an elaborate financial system. All you have to do is keep track of what you make and what you spend.

Keeping records simple

When I started my business, the computer age was just dawning for small business people. To keep my records, I used a simple system. Here's how I did it:

- ✔ I kept copies of all the invoices I sent out. When I got a check, I attached the stub to the invoice, marked it paid, dated it, and stuck it in my *accounts due* file.

- ✔ When I spent money, I put a copy of the invoice in my *expenses file.*

- ✔ I kept an ongoing list of how much I made and spent so that it was up-to-date and I didn't have to add it all up at tax time.

- ✔ At the end of the year, I could see the total I took in and the total of how much I spent. Lucky for me, that was pretty exciting!

That was my original bookkeeping system. You're not running a multimillion dollar corporation (yet). You can exist quit nicely with a simple method like the one I used.

Using tools

My pencil and paper work great, and they still would for me, except that I have an even better system today. The technological age has come to the amateur accounting world. Shop your local computer store and you'll find all kinds of simple software packages that make accounting a quick and easy process. But remember, no matter what features the accounting software has, it still is just a system of tracking how much you take in and how much you spend.

Using accounting to make business decisions

The information you collect is vital to any analysis you make of your business. Are you making money? If so, from where? If not, why not? Should you grow? Where should you cut back? Do you work with clients who aren't profitable?

When you're faced with these questions, you can't make decisions based just on your own guesses or on gut instinct. Solid businesses are built on solid decisions. Solid decisions are based on facts and figures. Where will you get the facts and figures? From your own records.

The only way you'll know how to effectively manage your business is to be able to easily access the information that's in your files. Computer software now allows you to print out reports that analyze your business from a number of aspects. Learn to use the simple software, and you'll be a leg up in growing your freelance business!

Chapter 16

Setting Rates and Collecting Fees

. . . .

In This Chapter

▶ Putting a price tag on your services

▶ Giving yourself a raise

▶ Sending bills and getting paid on time

▶ Dealing with slow-pays and no pays

. . . .

*H*ave you ever cringed at the outrageous fees you pay your plumber or your electrician? Ever just about fainted at a lawyer's hourly charge or a doctor's bill? And what about those overpriced consultants, who make a killing at the company's expense? Guess what: You've just joined the club. You're about to find out why those people charge you so much to provide a service. This chapter shows you how to figure out what people will pay for your work and how to go about invoicing.

No matter what you charge or how you agree to be paid, consider putting your agreement on paper, in contract. See Chapter 13 for details.

Of course, one of the best parts of working for yourself is getting paid, but getting money from clients doesn't happen automatically. You have to follow a methodical approach to track who owes what, to actually ask for the money, and to keep a clear record of all the money that changes hands. This chapter shows you how.

Setting Your Rates

What should you charge for what you do? Deciding takes some research. Look at several things, including the following:

✔ Does anyone else in your area do exactly what you do? If so, what do they charge?

✔ Do you offer unique services, such as a special approach, better credentials, or faster service? What is that worth?

    ✔ How do you want to be seen: as the high priced brand, the middle of the road, or the bargain brand?

If you price yourself too high, clients won't come back. If you price yourself too low, clients may think you don't offer a quality product. As a freelancer, you don't want to be seen as the bargain-basement provider.

As you set your rates, consider factors such as what the competition is charging and what the market will bear, but also keep in mind the need to set a price that you feel good about; a price that you believe gives your clients a good value for their money. I have a variety of clients. Some have more money than others. Naturally, I control my rates, so I choose what to charge each of them. But should I charge one client more than another? I don't think so. Oh, sure, I sometimes reduce my fee for a worthy cause (see the following section). But for the most part, if one client must pay me a certain rate, so must another.

Which is true? You're worth what you charge, or you charge what you're worth? Often, a client's perception of your value can be a direct result of how much you charge. If you charge a low fee, your clients may think you're not as good as your high-priced competitor. If you charge a high fee, they may think, "Hey, she must be good to be able to charge that much." On the other hand, even if you can command outrageous fees initially, eventually your clients will know that you're gouging them. When they realize this, they won't come back.

You may be amazed at how often I've heard freelancers say, "I have a hard time setting a premium on my work." One of my friends, in fact, had to leave freelancing because she couldn't survive on what she was charging and was uncomfortable raising her rates. Believe in what you do. Believe it's worth the same as or more than what your competitors charge. Charge that amount and don't look back.

Discounting your fees

After you set a rate, stick to it. You've decided that you're worth a certain amount, so don't let your lack of confidence or fear drive you to take less.

You may think that you should cut your price (called *discounting your fees*) to get a certain job. Remember, though, that you're setting a precedent. After you've worked for a client cheap, you will have a hard time increasing your rate. And if your clients are in the same company, word travels fast, so don't think you can get away with discounting every so often.

Discounting fees can have several negative results:

- ✓ Clients who are paying full price may find out and feel gouged.
- ✓ If clients know that you commonly cut your rate, you may soon have nothing but cut-rate clients.
- ✓ Discounting creates the impression that you're hungry; that is, that you don't have enough clients.
- ✓ You may earn a reputation for having rates that are unrealistically high.
- ✓ Cutting rates engenders resentment on your part.

Charging cancellation fees

What happens when a project is going along as scheduled and the client suddenly cancels (sometimes referred to as *kills*) the project? When you've set aside time to work on something, you've probably turned down work from other sources to accommodate that project. Having a sudden cancellation can leave you without income to replace the project that's been killed.

To combat this, some freelancers charge cancellation fees, such as 30 to 50 percent of the job. If you do this, you must let the client know at the start of the job that this is your policy. No client wants to be surprised with having to pay for a project that doesn't get done.

Establishing a minimum fee

Assume that you charge an hourly fee, and a client asks you to do something that takes only ten minutes. When you consider the additional time it takes you to process that ten-minute job, that is, send an invoice, record the payment, take the check to the bank, and so on, the job may not even be worth your time. What are your alternatives? One is to just chalk it up to good will and not charge the client at all. The downside to that approach is that these small jobs add up, and eventually taking on too many non-paying jobs affects your income. Second, when you don't bill, clients quickly forget that you've done them this favor. You want credit for all your hard work — and you want money!

To protect yourself against these nickel-and-dime projects, you may want to consider establishing a minimum fee. A *minimum fee* lets a client know that you will charge at least a certain amount for any work you do under a certain time. I have a minimum one-hour fee, so I charge clients the cost for one hour's work no matter how brief the job.

Establishing a minimum fee does several things:

✔ A minimum fee weeds out clients who are fishing for information and aren't serious about doing a project. I've known clients who called repeatedly about a sequence of potential jobs that never quite got going. By having a minimum fee, I make it worth my while to participate in these excursions or I discourage such flights of fancy.

✔ A minimum fee assures that your administrative costs are covered when a project doesn't get off the ground. For example, I must do a bit of research and brainstorming before a project even begins. I routinely spend an hour or so thinking about it in advance of a client meeting. When a client explores a project and then cancels before we even begin, I would feel guilty about charging them for no product. But having a minimum fee allows me to let them know in advance that they'll pay for my thinking, even if there's no product to show for it.

✔ A minimum fee places a value on your time.

The actual project work is only part of the equation. I have regular clients who call me to do small projects that take me only half an hour, but the reason I can do them so quickly is because of my experience and my knowledge of the client. It would take a new freelancer much longer, so I charge a minimum fee: I feel that my intimate knowledge of the client is worth paying for.

Considering an irritation fee

Face it: Some clients are no fun to work with. You take a project, and the client makes your life miserable: phone calls in the middle of the night, unreasonable demands to meet deadlines, or changing the rules halfway through. The final blow is when they don't treat you with respect.

You don't ever want to work with them again, but you have to complete the project you're working on and you have to maintain your calm and professional demeanor. An irritation fee may be in order. Charging a client a little extra for being obnoxious is one small way freelancers have of making a terrible job worth their while. It's the freelancer's way of saying, "Go ahead. Make my day." Of course, you have to let them know in advance of special charges.

Naturally, you can't send a bill with a line that says, "Irritation fee." And if you've given an estimate at the beginning of the project, you have to live within that at the end. But once you see that the job is becoming your worst nightmare, you can use some appropriate ways to charge what you feel is a fair price for the job:

✔ Inform the client that you charge an *express fee* for work that's expected in an unreasonable time.

✔ Explain that you charge a fee for work that's required on nights or weekends. If I choose to work nights or weekends for my own convenience, that's one thing. If the client gives me work on Friday afternoon and expects it to be done over the weekend and ready Monday morning, that's different.

✔ Charge extra for phone calls after hours. For example, suppose the client is traveling in a different time zone, and you have to make yourself available before or after normal work hours because of the time difference. With a steady, reasonable client, I wouldn't charge them additional fees for those off hours. With an unreasonable client, those minutes count.

✔ Track your time meticulously and charge for incidentals that you normally would not bill a reasonable client for. I wouldn't normally charge a client for a couple of copies, but when a client is very unpleasant, they get charged a five-cent-per-copy fee. It's not much, but it makes me feel powerful!

Working on retainer

The word *retainer* refers to a fee paid because you've set aside your time to be available to do work for a client. Clients pay retainers to keep valued freelancers around whenever they need them and to assure that a certain amount of the freelancer's time is devoted to the client's needs.

A retainer has a number of advantages and disadvantages from the client's and the freelancer's perspectives:

✔ **Advantages:**

- **To the client:** Guaranteed freelance availability
- **To the freelancer:** Predictable income; financial security for the period of the contract

✔ **Disadvantages:**

- **To the client:** Paying regardless of whether the freelancer is working
- **To the freelancer:** Risk of being treated like an employee; less flexibility to accept other assignments

In some cases, freelancers and clients agree that unused hours from the retainer can be carried over to the next month. To my mind, this can be dangerous for the freelancer because you can unexpectedly become burdened with so much work from that client that you can't accept other projects.

To establish a retainer, you need a contract that specifies exactly what you will do, what the payment will be, what will happen if you work more hours than the retainer states, and what will happen if you work fewer hours in a month than the retainer specifies.

A retainer agreement should include the following items:

- Your company name
- Your client's company name
- The date the agreement is signed
- The period of time it covers
- The amount of the fee to be paid
- Specific dates when the fee is to be paid
- Specific services you will provide for the fee
- Cost of additional services you may provide over and above the ones named in the contract
- Whether any extra expenses will be paid separately (such as costs for long distance calls, copies, faxes, or other expenses you may need to be reimbursed for)
- What must be done to cancel the agreement and how long in advance the notification must be made
- What happens if you don't deliver the services or the client doesn't pay: How will the agreement be arbitrated and who will pay for it?
- Original signatures of both parties and the date signed

If this seems like a very detailed way to do business, it is. While you may assume that normally upstanding business people can come to an agreement on a handshake, this is business. What would happen if your client left the company and the person's successor didn't want you to continue? You would need financial protection for a period of time to cover replacing that business. And, after all, simple misunderstandings do occur, and you need to protect yourself from unforeseen problems.

Working on spec

Speculative work (also called *working on spec*) is work that you do in hopes of the client approving the project. With spec work, you have no guarantee of being paid. An example of speculative work is a graphic designer being asked by a corporation to develop a logo for them, to be considered with several other designers' logos. The designer does the work and is paid only if the company chooses the design.

Experienced freelancers seldom do work on spec because they feel their time is too valuable and they don't need the work. Several factors could entice you to accept speculative work, however, despite the risky financial aspect:

- ✔ If you're new to a business, spec work is good practice, and you can get your foot in the door.

- ✔ If the project offers high prestige or visibility, you could build your reputation.

- ✔ If the project is for a high-profile client, spec work may earn you a chance to add a project of great value to your portfolio.

- ✔ If the project is potentially highly profitable, you may believe it's worth the risk.

- ✔ If the project is fun, you may just want to take the chance!

Writing proposals for books is speculative work, but one that I consider worth the risk. You have to decide which projects are worth your investment.

Marking up

Retailers make money *marking up:* They buy an item for one price and sell it for a higher price. Some freelancers do this, too. Should you mark up the products and services you sell a client? It's up to you.

Consider the two following ways to be paid for the subcontracted work or products that you sell a client:

- ✔ **Mark ups:** For example, suppose you're an event planner. You subcontract with a T-shirt manufacturer to produce specialty shirts for a client's employee party. The shirts cost you $3 each. You could mark up the price 20 percent, and charge the client $3.60 for each (plus tax). The extra 60 cents per shirt would be your "fee" for handling the T-shirt part of the event.

- ✔ **Project-supervision fees:** You can charge the client your hourly fee to supervise all the elements of a subcontracted job and pass the cost through to the client. Here's how that works: You sell the T-shirts to the client for the $3 you pay, but you also charge an hourly fee for the time you spend finding them, dealing with getting them imprinted, having them delivered, and so on.

In the first example, the more shirts the client buys, the more money you make. In the second, you're paid only for your time, so you make the same amount no matter how many shirts are involved.

This process works the same way when you're subcontracting a service. If you hired a researcher, for example, you can mark up the researcher's fee to you, or you can charge an hourly rate for managing that researcher's work.

You must decide what your philosophy of doing business is and whether you feel it's appropriate to mark up or to charge project fees. Your accountant can help you determine the most financially feasible route for you.

Educating clients about fees

Unless your client is in the same business you are, he or she won't know exactly what you do, how you're paid, or why you cost as much as you do. If you're in a service business, your fees can be difficult to explain, because so many of the things that go into your work are invisible to the client. For example, ten hours of research and brainstorming may result in a two-page project proposal, which looks deceptively simple. In addition, clients are often skeptical of freelancers' fees for the following reasons:

- ✔ Clients have heard of others being burned by freelancers who charge exorbitant rates or who focus more on creating additional work for themselves than they do on accomplishing the client's goals. (See the "Winning over clients who've been burned" sidebar.)

- ✔ Clients have been burned by freelancers who never delivered the promised product or results.

- ✔ Clients don't understand what the freelancer does, so they can't figure out why it costs so much.

- ✔ Clients aren't familiar with technical processes associated with the free-lancer's job, so they don't know how complicated the job is.

Winning over clients who've been burned

You're going to have to build up trust slowly, over time, with clients who've been burned by other freelancers. Explain every portion of what you do, teaching the client as you go. In addition, try the following tips:

- ✔ Deliver what's promised on time and on budget.

- ✔ Keep the client informed of progress and problems.

- ✔ Look for ways to add value to the project without charging more.

- ✔ At least meet (if not exceed) the client's expectations.

I do some video production, and clients sometimes request what they think is a simple change such as, "Can we cut out that sentence?" Because the client doesn't know the technical side of video production, they don't realize how tedious and complicated the process is. It may take five hours to do what looks like a ten-minute job. The only way I know to help a client understand such technical processes is to take him or her with me to an editing session.

You must help your client understand what you do to some degree. That may mean a trip to a printer or a manufacturing facility to show him or her a process, it may mean showing comparisons of how processes work, or it may mean telling your client how your rates compare with those of other freelancers.

Don't overwhelm your clients with too much information, but do give them enough data to see how important your role is.

Knowing When to Raise Rates

A good friend of mine has a therapeutic massage center. She hasn't raised her rates in five years. I asked her recently why she didn't ever give herself a raise. "Because I'm already in the top range of people in the city, and I don't want to be responsible for pushing this service out of sight for the average person."

When is it wise to raise your rates? Should you have an automatic annual rate increase? Yes, if the following applies to you:

- ✔ **When the demand for your work exceeds your available time:** If people are constantly calling you and you have to turn them away, it's time to raise your rates.

- ✔ **When your rates fall behind the going rate for your services:** If everyone else in your market is charging $500 and you're charging $300, you need to look at an increase.

- ✔ **When your expertise demands it:** I happen to be one of the most experienced (and, unfortunately, oldest) people in my field in the city in which I operate. My expertise commands a premium rate. What this means is that I can probably do the work faster and with higher quality than someone who is less experienced.

Someone I know well was recently told, "Oh, we couldn't possibly get anyone to do this as cheaply as you." Definitely time to raise rates!

A prescription for loyal clients

Scott Drake, a freelancer who happens to be my husband, is a medical transcriber. That means he listens to the notes doctors dictate about their patients and types them up. (He knows words like *craniopharyngioma* and *choreoathetosis,* which makes him a brilliant conversationalist.)

Dictation services typically charge a certain number of cents per line that they type. Scott started freelancing when he was in school in California, and he charged a healthy rate of 13 cents a line. When he moved to Memphis, he discovered that fee was out of range in this economy. To be competitive, he charged a

lower rate to get his foot in the door. After a number of years, he's well established with several doctors' practices, one of which has been his client for nine years.

For his loyal clients, Scott shows his appreciation by freezing rates for two years at a time. At the end of two years, he considers what the going rate is, and determines if it's appropriate to increase fees. "I know I do a great job, and I do everything I can to make things easy for my customers. I'm also reasonably priced. Even so, I hate the process of raising rates. There's always apprehension about whether they'll take their business to someone else."

Sending Invoices

You can be certain that no one is going to voluntarily send you money without your asking for it. The way you ask for money is by sending out an invoice (a bill) for services. Even though billing is another somewhat tedious administrative task, it can be extremely gratifying to see how much money you can soon deposit in your bank account.

Determining how to bill for your services

Freelancers bill for their services in one of four ways:

- ✔ **By the hour:** To charge by the hour, you establish an hourly rate that you will charge for your service, and you track how many hours you spend on a client's project. This is how I charge for my services.

- ✔ **By the day:** Certain types of freelance work are best defined by the number of days that are required to carry the assignments out. This is especially true in two situations:

- Where the job demands include diverse duties that may be hard to delineate in the course of a day. I could spend a whole day making multiple phone calls lasting a minute or two apiece, combined with a trip to scout a site, a meeting with the client, writing a one-paragraph letter, and compiling a job report. In this case, my entire day could be spent on one client, but it would be difficult (and inefficient) to split out the individual activities.

- Where your entire day is devoted to one client. When I do meeting production on-site, for example, I spend my whole day doing a range of things for the client. The day may last 8 hours or 12; regardless, I'm dedicated to their project.

✔ **By the project:** To charge by the project, you determine a flat fee for the project in advance, no matter how long it takes you to complete it. This can be a dangerous practice unless you have a lot of control over how long the project will take. How difficult or how easy is your client to work with? You need to able to answer that question before you agree to bill by the project.

✔ **Fee for services:** To charge this way, you set a standard fee for each service you provide. For example, if you offer housekeeping services, you may establish that you charge a certain amount for cleaning windows, a certain amount for spring cleaning, and a certain amount for light housework.

Understanding how often to bill

When do you want to be paid? Right away, of course! If you're providing services to individuals the way an interior designer, gardener, or seamstress may, you could, indeed, be receiving payment at the time the service is performed. In other types of work, that may not always be possible. The following list shows you some common payment schedules in the freelance world:

✔ **Job completion:** To simplify things for your client, you may choose to bill only one time, when a job is finished. That way, the project is wrapped up in a neat package, and the client can see exactly how much all the elements of the job cost. For jobs that drag on for more than a month, this method of billing may not be feasible.

✔ **Progress billing:** Jobs that go on for some time or are expensive may require progress billing. This means that you expect a certain amount of money at the beginning of the project, percentages at various predetermined points along the way when certain key assignments are completed, and a final payment at the end.

✔ **Timed billing:** You may be accustomed to receiving bills once a month from your creditors. That's a standard timing for bills. As a freelancer, however, you may have to bill more often to maintain a good cash flow. A friend of mine sets a goal to bill a certain amount each week. After your business is established and you don't have to worry as much about generating income as frequently, consider moving to a monthly billing cycle. Monthly billing makes you appear more professional.

Define your payment expectations at the beginning of each job so that neither you nor the client is unpleasantly surprised.

When you decide how you want to bill for projects, consider your cash flow (see Chapter 15 for further details). *Cash flow* is a term used to mean how much cash you have on hand. How you bill affects your cash flow. Say you accept a three-month job for a $5,000 fee, but you won't receive any payment until you complete the work. That means your time is tied up for three months, yet you have no income. You could have a cash flow problem, meaning that even though you were expecting a nice paycheck long-term, you wouldn't have any cash in the meantime. If you have no other money coming in, this can present a problem.

Keep a few more considerations in mind when you send invoices:

✔ **Be honest about the time you spend.** No one is standing over your shoulder, and you could pad your hours, but it isn't ethical or legal.

✔ **Don't take advantage of clients who are less educated about the process.** Clients generally trust what I tell them about how long a project will take and how much it is likely to cost. You can fool people who don't know any better, but you can't fool yourself.

Anticipating invoices due at the end of the year

Christmas and New Year's holidays make year end a busy time. Sure, you want to be fighting the shopping crowds and running up your credit card bills like the rest of the world, but be sure to plan your season to include some last-minute billing. As the year draws to an end, clients may want to close out their books, accounting for all of their expenses and paying remaining bills.

At this time of year, most of my clients ask me to submit invoices for all my outstanding charges, even for projects that aren't finished. Their accounting departments have a certain cutoff date, usually at least a week before January 1, so they have time to process all bills. Clients like to use as much of their budget money as possible in the current fiscal year so they have more money next year for next year's projects. Not only can you expect requests for billing, you can also expect a last-minute flurry of project activity, too.

Not all clients operate on a calendar year — some have a fiscal year that ends in June or September. You can expect the same type of crunch from them at these times.

What's a purchase order?

A purchase order is a form that some companies use to authorize a freelancer to do work on a project. Usually, the form briefly describes what work you've been hired to do. The client gives you one copy and keeps a copy for the company's file. Every purchase order has a number on it that allows the company to track the costs associated with a particular job. Use this number on your invoice so the company's accounting representative can confirm that you were contracted to do the work and can maintain their records of expenses and payments.

Not every company uses purchase orders. After you discover that a company uses them, be sure you get one at the beginning of every job. You won't be able to submit your invoice without one.

Signing off on a bill for a large amount of money without explanation can be hard for a client to swallow. Breaking down your services into specifics can help your client understand where your time goes and what efforts are required to do a particular type of project. Define the time you spend on areas such as meetings, proposal writing, research, gaining approvals, making revisions, and so on, with each of the major tasks you do. As time goes on, the client will understand how much to expect for certain types of jobs, and will trust you to be a good guardian of his or her money.

Scheduling time to send invoices

Set aside a time each week or month to create invoices and send them out. When you're busy with work, you may not have much time for this activity, but keep in mind that getting paid is why you're doing what you do.

Clients don't appreciate receiving a bill long after the work was done. They have monthly and quarterly budget projections, and staying on track with your expenses is one important element of that. Delayed billing makes it hard for you and the client to remember details, which can lead to misunderstandings.

Collecting your money involves knowing who owes what. In Chapter 15 you can read more about how to track how much clients owe you. Your records must be accurate and up to date. Whenever a client asks, you must be able to provide documentation of the work you've done and the charges you've billed for. If you're in business for yourself long enough, someone, somewhere, sometime, will question a bill, lose a bill, forget what work you've done, underpay, overpay, or somehow mess up your getting your money. Let it be their mistake, not yours. Keeping sloppy records is asking for trouble.

Hounding clients for money

I've known freelancers who live check-to-check and who become quite adamant about wanting their money right now. When I see this happen, I wonder about the person's ability to generate enough business and to effectively manage the business he or she has. (This is why you need a certain amount of cash reserves when you start out, so you don't have to scrimp and scrape to get by — see Chapter 4.)

Try to avoid hounding your clients for payment because they could assume you either don't have enough business or that you don't manage your money well. They may conclude that if you can't manage the money side of your own business, you can't manage any aspect of theirs.

Drafting an invoice

Use a standard invoice format to keep your billing consistent and contribute to your professional image. Be sure that your invoices include the following basic elements:

- ✔ Your company's name, mailing address, phone and fax numbers, and e-mail address
- ✔ The name of the client's company, the name of the client, and the address
- ✔ Date of the invoice (detailing when the invoice was drafted)
- ✔ Description of the work (describing what you did for the client)
- ✔ Amount due (the actual dollar amount you expect the client to send you)
- ✔ Terms (how soon the payment is expected): Terms may say, for example, "Net 30 days," which means that payment is due 30 days from the date of the invoice. If you assign any penalties for payment after that time, indicate that, too. For example, "Payment received after 30 days will be subject to a 1½ percent penalty."

What if your business isn't that complicated? Perhaps you prefer to go to your local office supply store and buy ready-made invoices that you fill in by hand. Fine — that works, too. You still need a numbering system to keep track of the amount you bill and the amount you receive. And be sure to have an invoice book that allows you to give the client a receipt and keep one for yourself.

Including an expression of your appreciation for your client's business is always a good idea.

For your own record-keeping purposes, consider using a numbering system for your invoices to easily track and look up information. This isn't rocket science: Devise something you can understand. If you really want to do it the easy way, just number your bills 1, 2, 3, and so on. (I would start with a higher number, like 100, because no one wants to think he or she is your first client and, therefore, your guinea pig!) You can also try the following numbering systems:

- ✔ **Company ID:** I started with a system that included the company name and a sequential number and the two-digit code for the year. For example, PHC-01-99 translates to PHC (initials for Promus Hotel Corporation), 01 (the first bill I sent to that client), and 99 (the year 1999). When I sent them a second bill, it was numbered PHC-02-99. You can pick any variation you like, just make sure the bills follow some sort of sequence.

- ✔ **Client ID:** As I began to work for more than one client in a company, I had to add the client's initials so I could keep projects for different people separate.

- ✔ **Project ID:** As you create your system, keep in mind that your clients may want you to look up bills for an entire project or for a group of projects you've done. You must be able to separate your invoices by project to do this. For example, I have a corporation that I do a lot of business with, and a lot of clients within that corporation. One client in particular has called me to say, "We're budgeting for next year. How much did we spend on the marketing plan last year?" To give him the answer he needed, I had to separate all his invoices from all the other invoices in that corporation. This can be a pain if you don't have a good ID system. Just having a code for the corporation isn't sufficient. I need more detail to be able to identify each client and each client's projects.

Please send checks and money orders to . . .

"Be the most enthusiastic person you know." That's how Elise Mitchell signs her e-mail, and I can't imagine anyone who practices what she preaches more than Elise. She tackles everything she does as the most important, fantastic project she has ever had. That includes bill collecting.

"I track my hours faithfully every day — I track by the quarter hour. You'll never remember what you did today unless you write it down. Rule number one for billing: If you don't track it, you can't bill it. Rule #2: If you don't bill it, you can't collect it!"

Elise views billing as her most important communication with her client, and she uses it as an opportunity to sell. "I insert a handwritten note to my client with each bill, thanking them for the opportunity to work with them or referring to a project that has recently been completed that was successful."

Talk about juggling: She handles a husband and two small kids, a successful marketing and communications company, a virtual staff, a fitness routine, and community involvement. And she makes it all look like a walk in the park. She truly is the most enthusiastic person I know.

If you use a software program to track your invoices, you can easily look invoices up by number or by project. Check out the following sample invoice, which includes an invoice number that's easy to track by client initials.

September 10, 2001

Mr. Bill Brown, Vice President

Human Resources

Jones Companies

1492 Columbus St.

Madrid, Tennessee 00000

INVOICE # JC-BB-100

Project Description

Employee Relations Brochure

Writing and editing (4 hours)..$320

Production coordination (6 hours)... 480

Total due: **$800**

Thank you for your business!

Terms: Net 30 days

Collecting Your Money

You pay your bills on time, right? So, surely your clients will pay theirs. Well, maybe — and maybe not.

You can pretty much depend on larger companies to pay their bills, because you have easy legal recourse if they don't. But what about individuals? What are the dangers of doing business with them? Suppose Ms. Smith hires you to do her clothing alterations, and when you deliver them, she gives you a check that bounces? Can you guard against such a problem?

One alternative is to require a deposit before you undertake the job, with the remainder due at completion. That way you find out ahead of time whether the person is sincere in hiring you in the first place. Another possibility is not to accept checks, but to take only cash. This can create an inconvenience for the client and can also result in your not being paid immediately. For the person to say, "Oh, dear, I don't have cash, I'll have to go to the bank and cash a check," is a definite possibility. Then what? Clearly, it's a good idea to know who you're doing business with before you agree to let people coast on credit even for a short time.

In the case of corporations, you have some other options if people try to stiff you. This section explains what to do if your sincerest requests for payment fail.

Getting your clients to pay

In a perfect world, the minute you delivered your project, the client would hand you a check. When your clients are individuals such as homeowners, that's usually the way it happens. You paint someone's house, give them a bill, and they write you a check. You rake their leaves, and when the bags are neatly piled in front of the house, you hand them a hand-written invoice and they write you a check.

In larger businesses, of course, it doesn't happen that way. First, you have to bill the client. Then you have to wait until the client's bill-paying process runs its cycle.

As you work with clients regularly, you'll probably discover patterns; some people are usually quick to pay and others routinely take a long time. The patterns tell you clearly which clients require you to follow up.

Slow paying can be a simple matter of a company's bureaucratic process. It can also be a sign of cash flow problems. Small companies sometimes rob Peter to pay Paul, trying to buy time, waiting to get in a payment from their clients before they can pay their bills. When red tape is the problem, you just have to be patient. When consistently slow pay is the issue with a smaller client, you may have reason to be concerned. At that point, think about what route you will take if the payment never arrives. And you should also reconsider if they're a good long-term client.

Keeping an aging report

The bookkeeping and accounting arenas use a technique known as an *aging report* that helps you keep up with how long a bill has gone unpaid. Accounting software can generate this report easily, or you can simply make a practice of checking your list of accounts once a month to see how much time has passed since you sent out an invoice. The aging report lets you know when to send out a second bill or a reminder notice.

Assessing late charges

Some corporations have a standard practice of waiting until the very last minute to pay their bills. (While the cash is in their pockets, they can earn interest on it.) Unfortunately, some companies are chronic late payers. As a deterrent to this bad habit, you can charge a late fee for bills that are paid after a certain time. You have the freedom to decide how much the late fee will be, and when a payment is technically late.

Let your clients know that you charge a late fee by putting a note at the bottom of your invoice. It may say: Bills not paid within 45 days are subject to a late fee of 2 percent per month.

For a bill of $500, this would amount to a $10 charge. A late fee (even a small one like this) may not guarantee that you receive your money on time, but it may contribute to greater awareness. Your client probably won't pay one bit of attention to this, but the accounts-payable department may.

Making the right connections

In a larger corporation, after your client approves and passes a bill along to the accounts payable department, for all intents and purposes, their involve-ment ends. Save your client headaches by getting to know someone in the accounting department. That way, when a bill is late being paid, you can check with your contact person and ask that they look into the situation and let you know when to expect payment.

Don't be timid about checking on payments that are overdue. Clients under-stand that you're in this business for money, not simply to help them out.

Cheerfully following up

Suppose you bill twice and still get no response. It's time to make a call. Bills do get lost in the mail, in people's in-boxes and, accidentally, in the trash. When you haven't received a payment in a reasonable time, give people the benefit of the doubt. Express your concern that something could have hap-pened to your bill or to their check. Give them time to research the problem. Always remember that although this issue is something you've been thinking about for a while, the person on the other end of the phone has other things on his or her plate and probably needs time to look up your records. Let your client know that your goal is to resolve the problem for both sides. Table 16-1 offers some ways to keep your interaction with accounting people a win-win situation.

Table 16-1	Dos and Don'ts of Follow-Up Calls
Do	**Don't**
Be polite and give your client the benefit of the doubt.	Expect immediate answers; it takes time toresearch invoices.
Be prepared with information about the bill number, date, and amount.	Be rude or pushy.
Follow up with a phone call.	Threaten legal action.
Thank them for their help in tracking down the problem.	

Taking action

As hard as this may be to believe, you may encounter a client who doesn't pay at all. When that happens, let the following sections guide you to your best course of action, even legal action.

Protecting your reputation

Unfortunately, being associated with a negative situation like a lawsuit can damage your reputation, even if you're justified in your claims. That's the first thing I consider: not money, not justice, but my reputation. My reputation is my most valuable asset, and in the process of collecting my money I don't want to do anything to damage it. It's true that I have a legal right to be paid for work I've done; but I have to weigh the importance of the money with the potential harm I may experience from being involved in a potentially ugly battle. How much is my reputation worth to me? A lot more than a few hundred dollars.

Looking for alternatives

When you're having trouble collecting from a client, consider the following to guide your efforts in pursuing them:

- **Is the client receptive to discussing the issue with you?** I find that many people fear confrontation and avoid phone calls like the plague if they know you want to discuss a payment dispute. Leave a non-threatening message that will defuse the situation. Say something like, "My relationship with you is important, and I'd like to find a solution that will help us both."

✔ **Is the client unhappy with your work?** I've had clients who didn't want to hurt my feelings or were intimidated to tell me they weren't satisfied. Try to explore with the client whether they are satisfied with what you've done, expressing your concern that you may not have fulfilled their needs. If that's why they're not paying, perhaps there's a way you can re-do the project to make them happy. See Chapter 13 for more information on working with a dissatisfied client.

✔ **Does the client dispute the amount owed?** By providing clear-cut project estimates and payment terms up front, you can generally avoid such disputes. If you haven't provided that type of explanation, the client may have had unrealistic expectations. Find out. You can then either re-do the project to meet the requirements or you can come to a compromise on the amount owed.

✔ **Does the client have financial problems that prevent payment?** When companies or individuals are having financial trouble, they don't generally want to broadcast that information. You have to be tactful in how you approach late payments, but you can suggest that you're open to accepting partial payments over time. This allows the client a graceful way out, without having to admit to financial problems.

Finding an arbitrator

In most cities you can find an arbitrator to help resolve disputes without going the legal route. Although arbitration is still a contentious situation, the dispute may be resolved more amicably than if you take a client to court. There's just nothing that damages a relationship quite like being sued! To find an arbitrator, call your local mayor's information line, library, Small Business Association (SBA) chapter, Better Business Bureau (BBB), or lawyer. Regardless of how amicably the issue is settled, I wouldn't count on working with that client again!

Considering collection agencies

You can hire a collection agency to hound your client for payment. Unless the client owes you a lot of money, I wouldn't consider this a good alternative. Here's why:

✔ **Collection agencies charge a high fee for their services.** If the agency is successful in collecting the money, you still collect only a portion of the entire amount owed. Decide whether this smaller amount is better than none.

✔ **When you hire a collection agency, you can be certain your relationship with the client is permanently over.** (Of course, you don't want a client who doesn't pay anyway, but if you later run into him or her at a cocktail party, having had a collection battle can make for a tense situation.)

✔ **People who feel guilty sometimes lash out and try to blame others.**
  Having a collection agency call can humiliate the person and stoke the
  fires of their guilt. Have you ever heard the saying, "The best defense is a
  good offense"? Your client could try to counter your attack by speaking
  ill of you to people who won't know the truth of who's at fault.

Going to small-claims court

If you've decided to go to court, consider small-claims court if the amount of
money you're owed is small. *Small-claims court* is a relatively informal and inexpensive way to seek restitution for non-payment of bills. The amount eligible
for small claims is determined by the state: In one state the amount covered by
small-claims court may be $3,000; in another, it may be as high as $10,000. If the
amount you're owed is higher than the court allows for small claims, you can
either go to small-claims court and request just a portion of the amount owed
or to a higher court, which means a lot more cost and time involved.

It doesn't cost much to file a small claim. You'll probably have to pay a fee for
serving the notification on the defendant and, perhaps, a fee for serving sub-
poenas to witnesses asking them to appear.

To pursue a small-claims complaint, follow these steps:

1. **Call your mayor's hotline or city information number and ask for the
   number for small-claims court.**

   I spent ten minutes looking in the government pages (blue pages) of my
   phone book under law, legal, court, judicial, small claims, and assorted
   other titles trying to find a listing that was specifically small-claims
   court. I suggest you save time and call to ask for the number.

2. **Call the court and find out the filing requirements.**

3. **File your complaint.**

   Include the name, address, and phone number of the person against
   whom you're filing the complaint. The court will notify the person by
   certified letter, ordinary mail, or in person, so be sure the address is
   up-to-date.

4. **If you want to call witnesses, provide the court with their names,
   addresses, and phone numbers so the court can serve them with
   papers that ask them to appear.**

5. **Plan to attend the hearing and remind your witnesses, too.**

   In most cases, the court date is set within a few weeks. Keep in mind
   that many people are intimidated by (or just hate) the prospect of
   appearing in court. You'd be surprised how many friends forget the date
   or don't answer the phone when they're asked to appear in court.

6. **On the date, arrive with your paperwork in order.**

   It's up to you to prove that what you claim happened, actually happened. Provide the facts:

   • What product or service you provided

   • The contract stipulating the service and fee

   • What amount of money is owed

   • Who was involved

   • How long overdue the payment is

You could win the case but the client still may not pay. In that instance, you'd have to return to court to file an action to enforce the judgment.

Taking people to court takes time and money. When I'm looking at the loss of a small amount of money, I can't usually justify the time or trouble of taking formal action against the client. Here's what I do:

✔ **Chalk it up to experience.** I try to understand ways I could've foreseen the problem, planned better, guarded against such an event, and so on.

✔ **Be more careful in selecting clients in the future.**

Going to big-claims court

If the amount of money you have at stake is larger than your local small-claims court handles, you can seek restitution in grown-up court. That means you have to bring out the big gun: a real-life attorney. In court, you want professional representation — only someone who studies the ins and outs of law can adequately and effectively plead your case and protect your interest. Before you decide whether you want to pursue a lawsuit in court, consider all the factors and how they will affect your business, and your personal life.

No matter how airtight your case may seem, you can't ever predict what will happen in court. For that reason, weigh the potential outcomes before you jump into a lawsuit. The first step to take is to consult an attorney and pay for a one-hour consultation. Bring your documentation and explain the situation so that the attorney can advise you about your most desirable options. In many cases, claims for debt collection are settled out of court. (In fact, simply receiving a letter from an attorney is sometimes sufficient to get people to pay!)

Be sure to ask the attorney about the following issues:

✔ **Time:** Pursuing a lawsuit can be a time-consuming endeavor. While issues in front of small-claims court are usually resolved fairly quickly, lawsuits for bigger claims can drag on for years. Add in the fact that it could be extended even further for appeals, and you're looking at a fairly substantial chunk of your life devoted to getting your money back. For a significant amount of money, you have to weigh the potential costs against the potential gain. The time you invest in the case is time taken away from your business, so be sure to account for what you'll lose in income preparing for and being in court.

✔ **Costs:** It may seem unfair that you have to pay to recover money that was supposed to be yours in the first place, but that may be the way it is. Consider the following fees involved:

- **Court costs:** Courts charge you for the privilege of being heard. Fees may be paid in one of two ways: you pay your court costs or, if you win, the judge may decide that the other party pays the court costs.

- **Attorney fees:** Paying an attorney can be a daunting thought, because legal fees add up fast at a rate of $175 an hour plus expenses. Consider several payment options. First, you can pay the attorney's hourly fee, recognizing that if you lose, you will pay. It's possible that if you win, the judge will direct the other party to pay your attorney's fees. Second, and not altogether likely, you may be able to get an attorney to accept your case on a contingency basis, agreeing to be paid a percentage of the money recovered if you win. If you lose, the attorney takes nothing. In order to take a case like this, the attorney will want to be fairly certain that you have an airtight case.

Chapter 17

Paying Taxes

. . . .

In This Chapter

▶ Hiring a tax advisor

▶ Reporting and filing

▶ Submitting employees' income information

▶ Dealing with sales tax

. . . .

*N*o doubt about it: Being self-employed is a taxing situation. Whereas once you relied on your employer to handle all the deductions from your paycheck, now you are responsible for setting aside money and sending it to an assortment of agencies for everything from self-employment tax to sales tax — all by the right date! To cope with the requirements, you need a systematic approach. Read this chapter to begin to find out how much to send to whom (and when) and how much you get to keep.

This book is not the be-all and end-all of tax information. My goal is to help you become aware of the issues and to direct you to sources that can help. Tax laws are complicated, and each one has many facets. I couldn't possibly include all of them in this book, mainly because it would put us both to sleep. My advice: Get advice from experts.

Getting the Lowdown on Taxes

Before you do anything else, you may want to browse the Internal Revenue Service publications for information about small business/self-employment. Their information, available at most libraries, can help you get a feel for the magnitude of knowledge you need to handle your taxes. It's perfectly possible for you to do your taxes yourself; it all depends on how much time and energy you're willing to invest in the process.

The IRS publishes printed materials on all the subjects you'll need to know about. You can also get the information online at the IRS Web site, www.irs.gov. Some publications you'll probably want to check out include

- ✔ What's included in income
- ✔ Estimated tax payments
- ✔ Business expenses and deductions
    - • Start-up costs
    - • Depreciation
    - • Normal business expenses
    - • Home-office deduction
    - • Travel and entertainment expenses
    - • Auto or truck expenses
- ✔ Self-employment taxes
- ✔ Payroll taxes and withholding

In addition, check with your state and local governments to find out about the following taxes:

- ✔ **State:** Franchise tax, income tax, unemployment tax, sales and use tax
- ✔ **Local:** Property tax, business use (or license) tax, sales tax

Often, the taxes you're required to pay depend on how your company is organized. Be sure to read Chapter 5 for more information about types of business organizations.

Selecting an Advisor

My upbringing leads me to have a healthy respect for authority and a desire to do things the way the people in charge say they should be done. In the tax area, I feel more comfortable asking for help than trying to decipher my obligations myself. Luckily, people (freelancers, even) specialize in giving tax advice.

I see three reasons for getting a tax advisor:

- ✔ They can make sure I'm aware of any rules and regulations that affect me.
- ✔ They stay abreast of changes, which happen yearly, so I don't have to worry about constantly updating myself.
- ✔ They can help me identify ways to save money because they're aware of potential deductions that I may never know about.

Looking for the right kind of advice

A number of people specialize in tax services, and I prefer an attorney or certified public accountant (CPA) who specializes in tax advice. To find an advisor, try these approaches:

- Ask friends in similar businesses to yours who they use.
- Ask your attorney to recommend someone.
- Contact your State Board or local CPA society and ask it to recommend a tax specialist.

Interviewing a candidate

Before you hire an advisor, be certain they offer what you need. Interview a potential advisor and be sure to ask these questions:

- What are your professional qualifications and where did you earn them?
- How long have you been in practice?
- Is a large part of your business with small businesses or self-employed people?
- How many clients do you have? Can you handle another client?
- What is the typical turnaround time; that is, how long in advance of taxes being due should I submit my information to you?
- Should I expect to have my return extended? (This is a perfectly routine occurrence.)
- What type of information will you require of me?
- How do you charge, by the hour or by the return?

After the interview, ask yourself some questions to decide if this person is the right advisor for you.

- What does my gut tell me about this person?
- Do I like him or her?
- Is this a person I can trust with my personal information?
- Does the price seem fair?

(If you're in doubt, try the project rating scale in Chapter 12 that helps you determine which projects to take.)

Try a little test. Call at a time when the person is unlikely to be in the office and leave a message. What's the response time? I find that if people don't respond quickly to my phone calls, they probably won't respond to my business needs, either. (When the person calls back, be sure to have a question ready to ask!)

Getting an ID Number and Finding the Proper Forms

Who would suspect that just going out on your own would suddenly make your business everyone else's business? Yet you're responsible for telling a host of agencies what you're doing, by keeping them informed quarterly and annually of how much money you're making and how much you're spending.

No matter what else you do, you must file tax returns. Even if you can't pay the tax, you must file or ask for an extension. By not filing, you create problems for yourself that may later be insurmountable. Bite the bullet.

Making your identity known with a tax I.D. number

As an individual taxpayer, the government tracks your income information through your Social Security number (SSN). When you start freelancing, you become a business, and the government tracks your business as an entity, too. (See Chapter 5 for the lowdown on forming your company.)

- ✔ As a sole proprietor, you can use your SSN as your tax identification number; however, it's better to get a separate employer identification number (EIN) by completing Form SS-4. This makes you appear more professional than if you just use your SSN.

- ✔ As a corporation or limited liability corporation (LLC), you must get an EIN. To get an EIN, complete form SS-4 at the IRS Web site, through tax software, or through your tax advisor. Use this same EIN on your state returns or any other documents that ask for your employer identification number.

Figuring out what you'll need to pay

Table 17-1 shows you all the taxes you may need to pay, when to pay them, what form to file, and who to send them to.

Table 17-1	What You May Owe		
How You're Organized	*Tax Liability*	*Paid To*	*Date Due*
Sole proprietorships and LLCs that elect to be taxed as partnerships	Federal income taxes (personal) and estimated tax payments	IRS	Quarterly
	State income taxes (personal) and estimated tax payments	State treasury or state depart- ment of revenue	Quarterly or annually
	Self-employment taxes (included in estimated tax payments and on the federal income tax form)	IRS	Quarterly
	Property taxes	City or county clerk	Annually or semi-annually
	Business use taxes (licenses)	Your city or county clerk	Annually
	State and local sales and use taxes	State treasury or state depart ment of revenue	Monthly
	Payroll taxes (FICA, Medicare, FUTA, SUTA — only if you have employees)	IRS and state	Quarterly
	Withholding taxes (only if you have employees)	IRS	Monthly
C corporations, S corporations, and LLCs that elect to be taxed as corporations	Federal income taxes and estimated tax payments	IRS	Quarterly
	State income taxes and estimated tax payments	State treasury or state depart- ment of revenue	Check for info
	State franchise taxes	State treasury or department of revenue	Annually

(continued)

Table 17-1 *(continued)*

How You're Organized	Tax Liability	Paid To	Date Due
	State and local sales and use taxes	State treasury or state department of revenue	Monthly
	Payroll taxes (FICA, Medicare, FUTA, SUTA)	Federal Reserve Bank	Monthly
	Withholding taxes (only if you have employees)	IRS	Monthly
	Property taxes	City or county clerk	Annually or semi-annually
	Business use taxes (licenses)	City or county clerk	Annually

This list gives you a good start, but check with your state and local tax authorities to make sure you pay everything you owe. Every state is different, so you may have additional regulations for your business.

Using online resources

The Electronic Federal Tax Paying System (EFTPS) has made tax preparation and submission much easier. You can now submit your tax documents over the Internet and save yourself the trouble of getting forms and mailing them. You owe it to yourself to check out the IRS resources online, not only for filing purposes, but also for general information.

Paying Income Taxes

You may be required to pay two types of income taxes:

- ✔ Federal income tax (everybody pays either personal or corporate or both)
- ✔ State income tax (if your state has one)

The following sections help you decipher how much in taxes you need to pay, when you need to pay them, and what deductions you're eligible for.

Deciding what is income and what isn't

What is considered income? Anything you take in from fees for your services. It may be in the form of checks, cash, or even bartered goods or services. You must report it all.

In addition to money you receive as a fee for services, you may also have other income that's subject to tax. This may include interest income from investments, income from the sale of property, income from selling a product, and so on. To make sure you've included all your income on your tax return, check out the IRS publication called Net Earnings from Self-Employment. This lists the specific types of income you must report.

Taking deductions

Everyone seems to think that being self-employed allows you to deduct all kinds of cool stuff, like vacations and cars, from your income. This is true only to a certain extent and within very strict guidelines. The IRS has clear-cut laws about what you can — and can't — deduct.

Self-employed persons may be able to take the following deductions:

- ✓ **Start-up costs:** To get your business going, you may have expenses such as advertising or other expenditures. These start-up costs are deductible.

- ✓ **Organization costs:** If you actually form a legal entity such as an LLC or S corporation, the costs of creating that organization are deductible. These include attorney's fees, state fees, and so on. A sole proprietor doesn't have these fees.

- ✓ **Depreciation:** When you spend money on something for your business that has "a useful life longer than one year," you're required to depreciate it, which means that you deduct it over a period of time. Primarily, this includes larger items such as equipment, machinery, furniture, and buildings. The IRS gives prescribed percentages to use in deducting costs — you can use these (20 percent, 32 percent, 19.2 percent, 11.52 percent, 11.52 percent, and 5.26 percent for five years, beginning with half of the 40 percent deduction in the current tax year and what's left in the sixth year) or you can do equal installments (again, half of the 20 percent, which is 10 percent, the first year, with 20 percent, 20 percent, 20 percent, 20 percent, and 10 percent in years two through six). The IRS way gives you a greater deduction in the early years than do equal installments.

You can also deduct up to $24,000 through what's known as a *Section 179 expense.* This means you can elect to deduct up to $24,000 of newly purchased fixed assets per year. If there is any remaining cost of the asset (say you purchase something for $50,000), you depreciate the remainder ($26,000) over five years. But for purchases up to $24,000, why depreciate when you can take up to 24,000 of the value in one year?

Find out more by searching the IRS Web site for MACRS (Modified Accelerated Cost Recovery System), which is the IRS term for depreciation.

✔ **Normal business expenses:** What expenses do you need to run your business? A telephone, office supplies, books, copy paper, and many other expenses are all considered normal business expenses and are deductible.

✔ **Home-office expense:** Using your home as an office can also entitle you to a tax deduction if you meet certain requirements. This doesn't mean you can simply stick a computer in a guest room and call it an office. You must regularly and exclusively use the area for your business, and your home office must meet one of the two following tests:

- You use it as your principal place of business
- You meet clients there

Assuming you meet the IRS criteria (and please check with your advisor or the IRS publications — the home-office deduction can be tricky!), you may be able to deduct a portion of the cost of your utilities, phone, maintenance, and other expenses. The amount you can deduct is calculated by figuring out what percentage of your home the office represents, and then figuring out the expenses according to that percentage.

✔ **Travel and entertainment expenses:** One of the most interesting deductions a self-employed person may get is the chance to deduct travel expenses as long as they relate to business. Suppose you have a client in another city and you must go see him or her. Your airfare, taxi fare, meals, lodging, and even your dry cleaning while you're there are legitimate deductible business expenses. This is true for travel you take for educational purposes, too, as long as the seminar, workshop, or other educational session is directly related to your business.

Don't think that you can take a business trip to Puerto Vallarta, extend your stay another week to lounge on the beach, and deduct the whole episode. To qualify for a deduction, you must spend a large majority of the trip doing business. (You may find a few exceptions, like if you extend the trip over a Saturday in order to get a lower airfare.) Be prepared to prove the purpose of the trip and be sure to keep your receipts, just like you would at home.

✔ **Auto or truck expenses:** Using your car or truck for your business can also give you the right to deduct all or part of those expenses for tax purposes. Deductions come in two forms:

- **Standard mileage:** The simplest way to deduct auto expenses is to check the IRS charts for standard mileage, which is expressed in cents per mile (and changes nearly every year). You track how many miles you drive for business purposes and multiply those miles by the standard mileage rate. For example, if you drive 10,000 miles for business and the mileage rate is 32½ cents per mile, you could deduct $3,250 in auto expenses.

- **Actual expenses:** This category includes gas, maintenance, repairs, insurance, depreciation or lease expenses (for luxury cars), and car washes. Check with a tax advisor to be sure you're covered.

To track your expenses or mileage, keep a small notebook in your glove box or attach it to your car or truck visor. Each time you make a business visit, jot down the client, location, and how many miles you drive. You can also keep a notebook log of auto repair maintenance, repair, and gas expenses. This record can be helpful when you sell your vehicle, because a new owner would certainly appreciate seeing just how carefully you've maintained the vehicle.

No matter which type of deduction you take, you must document your mileage or expenses. If you're audited, the IRS wants to see exactly how you came up with the figures you reported.

Submitting estimated tax payments

Typically, individuals pay their income taxes once a year on or before the infamous April 15 deadline. But freelancers have to pay a portion of their taxes — both to the federal government and to the state (if your state has an income tax) throughout the year. These are called *estimated tax payments* because they're literally figured on how much you estimate you will probably make.

To file estimated taxes, you must do the following:

✔ Estimate how much income you believe you'll have for the year.

✔ Figure how much tax would be due on that total income.

✔ Follow the IRS instructions, which specify that you pay 90 percent of the actual current year tax due (what you'll show on your tax return) or 100 percent of last year's taxes due. Pay your estimated taxes on April 15, June 15, September 15, and January 15.

When the 15th of the month falls on a weekend day, the tax is due by the following business day.

Review your income projections each quarter with how much money you actually made. If you see that you've made more than you expected, you have to adjust your estimated tax payment to cover that additional income.

If you end up making less money than you anticipated, you can choose to get money back or you can adjust your January payment to reflect the lower income. If you make more money than you anticipated, hurray! You'll have to pay more in taxes, but you'll also have more left over than you expected.

Although paying estimated taxes may seem like a shot in the dark, it can actually be very helpful in two ways:

- ✔ You won't end up with a huge tax burden at the end of the year (with no money set aside to pay it).
- ✔ It will force you to regularly look at your earnings and expenses, so you'll know if you're making money or not.

Filing an annual tax return

Yes, it's that time of year — time to send in your report to the IRS of your incredibly successful freelance year. You're probably accustomed to this being April 15, which is when regular, individual taxpayers' returns are due. Is it the same for you now that you're in business? A few things are the same, and a few may be different — see Table 17-2.

Table 17-2	Tax Filing Information	
Type of Organization	*What to File*	*When to File*
Sole proprietorship	Schedule C or C-EZ	April 15
S corporation	K-1	April 15
LLC that elects to file as a partnership	K-1	April 15
C Corporation	Corporate return	March 15

If your state has an income tax, you need to file that, too!

Filing tax extensions

A request for a tax extension is a notification to the tax authorities that you expect to file your return later than the normal deadline. Asking for an extension isn't out of the ordinary, and you aren't penalized for it, as long as the amount you owe is paid on time. See a tax consultant for details.

Owing Self-Employment Taxes

When you're employed by someone else, you pay half and they pay half of your Social Security taxes (FICA) and Medicare taxes (the half your employer pays is known as *payroll tax*). As a self-employed person, you have to pay your own way — both your half and your employer's half.

You pay self-employment taxes with the Federal estimated income tax payments and on the personal tax return (Form 1040).

Hiring (And Being) an Independent Contractor

You may need to hire people to help you in your work. They can be classified as

- ✔ Independent contractors
- ✔ Employees
- ✔ Corporations or companies

For tax purposes, the IRS is strict in defining who's who, because you're required to file different types of information depending on whom you hire. The IRS defines what it calls Common Law Rules that describe who's an employee and who's an independent contractor. Look for three areas of importance: behavioral control, financial control, and the relationship of the parties.

- Behavioral control relates to how the business trains and directs the employee to do the work. It encompasses such questions as when and where the employee works, what tools they use, where they buy supplies, and whether the training is specific.

- Financial control deals with whether the employee gets reimbursed for expenses, how much the worker must invest, how the business pays the worker, and so on.

- Relationship of the parties relates to whether contracts exist, benefits are paid, whether the relationship is permanent, and whether the work is a key part of the company's business.

These are not the complete descriptions: Review the IRS's detailed rules and examples to determine who is and isn't an independent contractor (including you).

Filing 1099s

When you hire others to do work, you must keep track of how much you pay them and report their income to them as well as to the IRS.

If you pay a company or an individual at least $600 in a calendar year, you must send them an IRS form (1099) showing the total amount you paid. You must also send to the IRS a Form 1098, a compilation of all the people to whom you sent a Form 1099. What this does is allow the IRS to compare your numbers and the subcontractor's numbers to make sure the numbers agree. If they don't agree, an IRS audit may follow to determine whose numbers are correct. (Oh, joy, an audit — the most wonderful words a freelancer can hear.)

To file a Form 1099, you must have the following information about the contractor:

- Social Security number (SSN) or federal employer identification number (EIN)
- Address
- Total amount you paid them

Get a Form 1099 free at your local library or from the IRS, or pay for a packet of the forms at your office supply store. You must send out your Forms 1099 by January 31 of the year following the year in which the person did work for you. The Form 1098 is due to the IRS by February 28.

The IRS is specific about the people you have to send a 1099 to. They include:

- ✔ Individuals
- ✔ Companies (but not corporations)
- ✔ Associates
- ✔ Limited liability corporations (LLCs)
- ✔ Limited liability partnerships
- ✔ Professional corporations that are legal or medical vendors
- ✔ Foreign limited partnerships

Notice that these are not just independent contractors.

Receiving 1099s

As a self-employed person, when you work for someone, you may be considered an outside supplier, too, and the company will send you a 1099 form if you're one of the types of companies listed in the preceding section. The total amount your employer reports having paid you and the amount you report having received must agree.

If your business is incorporated, you shouldn't receive a 1099. Make this clear to the companies with which you do business. I've had companies insist that they were going to send me a Form 1099, even though my letterhead clearly says "Spellbinder, Inc."

Paying Payroll Taxes

Payroll taxes include the employer's portion of Social Security taxes (FICA) and Medicare taxes that result in benefits after retirement. They also include an unemployment tax that gives benefits to people, should they become unemployed. Here's a breakdown of what you need to pay:

- ✔ **Social Security tax (FICA):** You must withhold a percentage of income for Social Security tax. There is a limit on the amount of salary you must pay tax on: At this time, the limit is $76,200 in a year. If you make more than that, you don't pay FICA on the amount over $76,200.

- ✔ **Medicare tax:** Medicare tax doesn't have a limit and is paid at a rate of 2.9 percent of total earnings.

✔ **Federal unemployment tax (FUTA):** You're required to pay FUTA if you pay at least a certain amount of wages to employees in one quarter or if you have an employee (any employee, not necessarily the same one) for 20 weeks of the year. There's a cap on the amount of wages that are subject to FUTA. Check Circular E, an IRS publication that you can order or download from the IRS or obtain from your tax advisor.

✔ **State unemployment tax (SUTA):** If you pay FUTA, you have to also pay SUTA. Each state has a specified rate for SUTA. To find out how much you must pay, multiply an employee's wages by the SUTA rate. There is a ceiling on the amount of wages that are subject to this tax, so after you've paid an employee a certain amount of money, you no longer have to pay SUTA. Check with your state Department of Revenue or consult your tax advisor.

Dealing with Withholding Taxes

Every employer (who has employees) has to pay *withholding taxes*. If your business is taxed as a corporation, you pay withholding tax on your own salary and on the salaries of any employees you may have. (If you haven't formed your company as a corporation, you pay self-employment tax on yourself, but you pay withholding on your employees.)

The IRS Circular C can help you understand what you have to do. Basically, this is how withholding works:

1. **You figure the amount of withholding required for each employee.**
2. **You figure the amount of payroll taxes required.**
3. **You add the two and make out a check from your business account.**
4. **You deposit the check for the employee's withholding and the payroll taxes in a Federal Reserve Bank on the correct due date.**

   The date depends on how much payroll you have and how often people are paid.

My accountant friend says small business owners get in trouble with the IRS over employee withholding taxes more than almost any other issue. When money gets tight, the employers hold off making their withholding deposits, using the money to tide them over until more money comes in from clients. This is an extremely unwise and illegal practice. The IRS is serious about how you handle employees' withholding taxes, because the money you're dealing with doesn't belong to you; it belongs to your employees. Don't miss the monthly deadline for making your withholding deposit — you will face severe penalties, including jail time, for failure to pay.

Paying Franchise Taxes

A *franchise tax* is a tax that allows your business the privilege of doing business in your state. It's computed in different ways for each state, and sometimes it's a flat rate. Most states base it on net real and tangible assets, net owner value, and net receipts. If you're paying this tax to more than one state, you can *apportion* it, which means you pay a portion to each state so you aren't taxed twice. The apportionment percentage, however, varies from state to state.

Paying Sales and Use Taxes

Are things complicated enough for you yet? Well, buckle your seatbelt, because sales and use tax computations are complicated and difficult to understand. If you do business in more than one state, you're really in for a ride. My advice is to meet with a specialist in this tax area.

In general, this is how it works: If you sell a tangible product and if your state has sales and use tax, you must pay the state a percentage of the total amount you sell. The rules and the amount of tax due vary from state to state. In fact, some states don't charge sales tax at all.

The tax man cometh

Taxes are a taxing subject for David Rawlinson. A graphic designer, David has been in business since 1987. His first few years were a financial struggle, and in the midst of that came some highly unsettling news: Although he had been advised that he didn't have to charge sales tax on his design services, the state had other ideas. A several-years-long battle ensued, and David ultimately had to pay the back sales tax the state said he owed. "This was money I had never collected from clients, and it wasn't as if I could go back to them and say, 'Hey, now you owe me this.' I had to bite the bullet and pay it myself." He says he's doubly vigilant now about potential tax issues. "It was really tough to eat that money at that time in my business."

Despite those lean years, David would never change his decision to become a freelancer. "Someone told me, 'You need to decide if you're going to do this forever or just for a little while, because after you're out of the market for awhile, you become a rogue. It's harder for you to go back and it's harder for them to take you back.' After what I endured, I'm definitely committed to this way of life. I've never been tempted to go back. Sometimes freelancing is fun and sometimes it's sheer hell. But I've always known I was in it for the long haul, because I have a passion and a love for what I do. If you don't have that, you'll never make it."

You must also pay sales tax in every state where you sell your products (assuming those states have sales taxes). Locate the state's government Web site to find information there about paying sales taxes.

Here's how sales and use taxes usually work:

1. **You sell your customer a product for a price.**

2. **You compute a percentage of that price as sales tax, add it to the sales price, and collect it from the customer.**

3. **You set aside the sales tax to be sent to the state at a specified time.**

4. **You send the state a tax report and a check for the amount of sales tax you've collected.**

Even if you provide a service and not a product, your work may be considered a tangible product. For example, a graphic designer who creates a logo for a company may not actually give the company a printed logo, but merely e-mails them an electronic file with the logo in it. Yet the logo is still taxable. To be perfectly clear about whether or not your work is taxable, check with your state sales tax agency.

Chapter 18

Securing Insurance

In This Chapter

▶ Protecting your investment

▶ Choosing insurance options

▶ Trusting a professional

Do you like taking risks? (You must, or you wouldn't be working on your own!) Living dangerously is a necessary part of the freelance experience; it may even be the part you like best. But there's a difference between living dangerously and living unsafely. When you're on your own, you're already depending solely on yourself. Why make yourself more vulnerable than you already are? Insurance is a safety precaution that can give you more peace of mind and security. This chapter describes the kinds of insurance to consider purchasing.

Taking an Insurance Inventory

Employees of a corporation have certain insurance coverage that they may take for granted. This insurance creates a safety net to catch them in case health problems or other unforeseen events take them out of commission for some length of time. Not only is the employee protected during such a period; in some ways, the corporation is also protected against a worker being out: It has other employees who can pitch in when someone is unexpectedly gone.

If something happens to you, what's your safety net? And who backs you up? Your most important asset in your business is you. Are you protecting your investment?

In simple terms, insurance categories break down into coverage that can protect you in several ways:

✔ It can protect you against something happening to your health.

✔ It can protect you against something happening to interrupt your income.

✔ It can protect you against something happening to your belongings.

✔ It can protect you against something happening to others who are on your property, who use a product you produce, or even who take your business advice.

As an independent worker, you probably need different types of insurance than you did when you worked for someone else. You have considerations now that didn't affect you as an employee. Just to jog your thinking about what kinds of insurance you may need, do the following:

1. **Make a list of the type and level of coverage you have or had as someone's employee, whether you paid for it or not.**

   Think about the things that your employer provides or provided that you didn't even have to think about or pay for, such as the following:

   • Protection against your equipment being damaged or stolen

   • Protection against accidents on company property

2. **Add notes detailing what would happen if you didn't have any of that coverage.**

3. **Think about how being self-employed changes your needs.**

   Consider the following:

   • What happens if you can't work?

   • What happens if your office burns down or is destroyed some other way?

   • What happens if your equipment is damaged or destroyed?

   • What happens if a client comes onto your property and is injured?

   • What happens if you have an accident while driving for business?

   • What happens if you make a professional mistake that costs a client money?

   • How high are the premiums, and will they increase?

   • Can your insurance be cancelled?

4. **Make a list of all the things that you feel are essential to your personal well-being and that of your company.**

Simplifying Insurance Jargon

Insurance is a pretty complex issue. Policies carry all kinds of legal language and can be hard to decipher even if you know what you're looking for. To simplify things, you look at the five following elements in a policy:

✔ **Coverage:** If something happens, how much compensation will you receive? Every policy has a limit, and you need to know exactly how much you can expect.

✔ **Premium:** How much does the coverage cost you? Most policies allow you to pay in one of several ways — monthly, quarterly, or annually — with a small fee for paying more often than once per year.

✔ **Exclusions:** A policy may exclude certain things from coverage. For example, a policy may cover water damage, but not water damage resulting from wind damage.

✔ **Deductibles and waiting periods:** Policies often require that you pay a certain portion of the first dollars for a claim (such as $500), or that you wait a specified time before receiving benefits. Be sure to check these out.

You can often reduce your premium costs by slightly shifting your coverage from a low deductible to a higher one. For example, if you increase the deductible you're willing to pay from $500 to $1,000, you can probably reduce your premium.

✔ **Cancellation:** Some policies may be cancelled at any time, some may not. Ask your professional to explain what's what. See the "Can your insurance be cancelled?" sidebar, later in this chapter, for more information.

Understanding Insurance Coverage Options

Now that you know what factors you're looking for, you're ready to hear some insurance coverage options.

Health insurance

Most people are familiar with health insurance, which pays for doctor visits, lab tests, surgery, or medication. Health coverage can also include benefits for dental and vision, as well as for long-term care such as that of a nursing home.

Options in healthcare are proliferating all the time, and costs vary dramatically from one type to another. Ask your agent to tell you about choices that include:

✔ **HMO (health maintenance organization):** An HMO is a group plan that dictates what physicians, hospitals, labs — generally what healthcare providers — you can see in order for the services to be paid for by the HMO. In an HMO, you may have a *co-pay,* short for co-payment, which means that the most you pay is a small amount (such as $20) no matter what treatment you receive.

✔ **PPO (preferred provider organization):** In a PPO, the plan usually offers you a choice of coverage levels, but the plan will pay more for a covered expense if you choose a healthcare provider who is in their approved list than if the provider is not. A PPO also requires a co-pay, and usually has a deductible.

✔ **Private insurance:** Private insurance gives you complete control over who you choose to provide your medical service. You pay a *deductible amount* (the first specified number of dollars each year). After you meet your deductible amount, there is a stop loss feature. This feature specifies that for covered expenses, you and the insurance company will each pay a percentage (usually something like you pay 20 percent and they pay 80 percent). Over a certain amount, they will pay 100 percent. These private plans are also called *indemnity plans*.

In both an HMO and a PPO, the plan providers agree to charge a certain amount for covered services. In an indemnity plan, the plan reimburses physicians for a percentage of the covered services.

Medical Savings Accounts

Medical savings accounts (MSAs) are the new rage among some freelancers because they offer tax advantages. MSAs are similar to putting money in a savings account, but they have two big advantages: the money you set aside is tax deferred, and all your earnings on it are also tax deferred, as long as you use it to pay medical expenses.

To set up an MSA, check with your insurance company to make sure it offers MSAs. If so, sign up for a high deductible health plan (HDHP). An HDHP is a requirement for an MSA. To be considered an HDHP, your plan must have a minimum deductible, which is tied to the Consumer Price Index and may change each year. After you're enrolled in the health plan, you can establish an MSA at your bank, investment broker, or even with your insurance company.

You can set aside up to an amount equal to 65 percent of your premiums if you're just covering yourself, or 75 percent, if you're also covering your family.

Another convenience of an MSA: You have money already set aside to pay medical expenses when they occur. And as long as you stay healthy and don't use the money, it can be rolled over to the next year.

One warning: If you make withdrawals for anything other than medical expenses, you will pay tax on the amount you withdraw, plus a penalty.

Getting insurance when you've had a serious illness

Not everyone is fortunate enough to be healthy all the time. People who have had previous or ongoing serious health problems can have a tough time getting coverage. In fact, this issue alone keeps some people working in corporations because they fear losing their healthcare coverage if they leave.

Can you get health insurance if you've had a serious illness? The answer is usually, "Yes," although it may be challenging to find it. Here are some avenues to explore:

✔ **Your current employer:** If you're employed now, check into how you can convert your current insurance into an individual plan. The *portability* law now says that it's mandatory for insurance carriers to allow you to take your insurance with you when you leave. The costs can be quite high.

✔ **Spousal coverage:** If your spouse's company has a company-sponsored plan, you could receive coverage under it.

✔ **State plans:** Some states have plans designed for those who have a hard time qualifying for other types of health insurance. Contact your state insurance commission to find out what may be available.

✔ **Associations:** Professional associations offer group plans that may make it easier for you to get coverage without qualifying.

✔ **Independent brokers:** Speak to an independent broker about plans for high-risk individuals.

Be sure to investigate provisions for *pre-existing conditions* (health problems you've had before joining the plan) that could limit your ability to be covered for a particular health problem for some period of time.

Automobile insurance

Auto coverage for a business owner is usually significantly more expensive than for an individual, because a business owner is expected to have more to lose if an accident occurs. (That's because business owners are perceived as having business assets such as equipment, or to have accumulated wealth in the company, as well as being more heavily insured than an individual. What you have to lose is not only what you own, but also what you use to generate your income, and your reputation, a very valuable asset indeed.) Of course, *you* know you don't have deep pockets, but if you've done a good job of creating a successful image, others will think you do!

Protection can be money-saving

Did you know that you can deduct your premiums for certain types of insurance? As a business owner, you are entitled to certain types of write-offs including:

✔ Fire, theft, flood

✔ Malpractice or professional liability insurance

✔ Business interruption and overhead insurance

✔ Liability insurance

✔ Auto or other vehicles (but check this out because there are limitations)

✔ A majority of the cost of medical insurance for yourself and your family, as well as qualified long-term care insurance

If you have employees, you can also deduct certain types of insurance for them, including:

✔ Workers' compensation insurance

✔ Life insurance as long as you're not the beneficiary

✔ Group hospitalization and medical insurance

You can't deduct premiums for lost earnings, insurance to secure a loan, or self-insurance funds.

For more information about deducting insurance, check out IRS Publication 535.

You may have three options of ways to arrange automobile insurance:

✔ **A business policy:** If you're in a business like lawn servicing, your vehicle may be an integral part of your business. In that case, you would need a business policy.

✔ **A personal policy with a corporate endorsement:** This coverage can be written for people who use their personal car for business.

✔ **Hired and non-owned:** This is a special policy that protects you if you have an employee who drives his or her personal vehicle on company business.

✔ **A personal policy:** Some individual-owned businesses don't require driving for business, in which case your personal policy will be sufficient.

Ask your agent what kind of auto coverage you have when you're driving a rental car. Rental car companies always ask if you want insurance coverage such as collision and liability, and you may need it if your own auto coverage doesn't extend to your driving another vehicle.

Life insurance

Although needing life insurance isn't a situation unique to self-employed persons, some factors have particular interest for a freelancer. If you're a single parent, or contribute a significant portion of your family's income, your death could mean not only an emotional loss, but also a financial disaster.

- ✔ **Term:** Term life is a policy that you pay premiums for and it pays only when you die. As you get older, signing up for this type of insurance gets more expensive. When you first buy a term life policy you can lock into a fixed premium for a set time, such as 10, 20 or 30 years. In the beginning, these premiums might be higher than for a non-fixed rate policy, but in the long run the cost should catch up. Ultimately, you would pay less than if you were on a lower, but escalating plan.

- ✔ **Permanent:** Permanent life builds up value, and you can borrow money against a policy as it gains cash value. Throughout the life of the policy you can cash it in and receive whatever cash value you've built up. This can be a way for freelancers to invest, and also to be able to borrow money and pay it back.

Under the permanent life banner there are three categories of insurance:

- • **Whole life:** This is a risk-free insurance, and everything stays the same. Premiums are fixed, and cash value is fixed. Because it's such a sure thing, returns tend to be quite small. Most investment counselors advise against this because of the low return.

- • **Universal life:** This option offers more flexibility, and more risk. On the positive side, you can adjust your death benefits and your premiums, which is an advantage over whole life. If the market changes in a good way, you benefit; if it changes in a bad way, you suffer.

- • **Variable life:** This option offers the greatest flexibility and allows you to select more investment options with potentially higher returns. Premiums are also variable, so you can't be certain what you will have to pay to maintain your coverage. The upside and the downside is that buying variable life is like investing in stocks; your return can go up or down.

 You may be able to fund your life insurance through your company (depending on the structure and whether you're in business alone) through something called key-person life. This is a type of policy designed to protect your company against the possibility of the death of someone who is a principal in the company and vital to its operation.

Can your insurance be cancelled?

You've heard horror stories of people having their insurance cancelled and being left without coverage. When would you expect to be cancelled? As an individual, you certainly can't expect the same leverage with an insurance company that a corporation enjoys. When the market changes, or you become a liability because of what they consider excessive claims, you may find yourself without coverage.

In general, life, disability, and health insurance can't be cancelled; however, your coverage can change:

✔ The company can raise rates, which is plenty unpleasant and can make your

coverage unaffordable. The insurance company's hope is that you'll find a cheaper provider and pull out voluntarily. Also, unless your policy stipulates that the premium is fixed, your rates will probably increase significantly as you age.

✔ The company can cancel all the coverage in an entire state, in which case you lose your coverage just like everyone else in that geographic area.

All other types of insurance besides life, health, and disability can be cancelled.

Insurance isn't the only way to protect yourself. There are legal avenues that protect your personal assets even if something unfortunate (like a lawsuit) damages your business. Consult an attorney who specializes in issues such as family limited partnerships and trusts.

Disability insurance

If you're not working, who's working for you? In a corporation, if you can't work, you're typically covered by some type of disability insurance, either short-term or long-term. In your own business, when you're not making money, how will you get paid?

Disability insurance guards against your not being able to work, and it pays benefits on a short- or a long-term basis. Short-term usually means from three to six months, while long-term can be up to five years or more.

This coverage pays you a certain amount each month that you're disabled, so it serves much like a paycheck. You and your agent discuss how much your income is, how much coverage you need, and what the premium for that coverage will be. Don't expect to get coverage for the full amount of your income. Policies provide coverage for a percentage of what you currently make, and they also take into account your salary history. (Insurance companies assume that if you are disabled, your expenses will be lower than if you were working full time.) You may also opt for a lower amount of coverage and have a lower premium. The higher amount you have been making, the higher your payment. Of course, the higher your amount of coverage, the higher your premium cost will be.

If you work from home it may be difficult to get disability insurance; your agent can guide you. You may want to consider getting disability insurance before you leave your job with a company; it could be easier to get while you're employed by someone else.

Property insurance

As a part of your business, you may own office furniture and equipment. How you cover this equipment depends on where your office is:

- ✔ **At home:** In a home office, you may expect your equipment to be covered under your homeowners policy. This may not be the case. Check out the requirements for a separate policy or rider that specifies what your equipment is. Be sure you get *full replacement value* insurance, which covers the cost of buying new equipment to replace what was damaged; otherwise you receive only the current value of the equipment, which may be only a small portion of the cost of buying new equipment.

- ✔ **In a commercial space:** If you rent or lease space, a special renter's policy will cover your furnishings. If you own an office building, look into a different type of policy as well.

Ask an insurance professional (see the "Finding an Insurance Professional" section, later in this chapter) about coverage not only for your property, but also for property your client or visitors may own but that is at your place of business.

When you travel with your notebook computer, personal data system, or other portable equipment, check to be sure it's covered under your policy. These items frequently require a special policy addendum. Considering the rate at which laptops are stolen in airports, you'd be wise to check this out.

One thing insurance can't replace is your computer files. Wouldn't you hate to try to recreate everything you've worked so hard to build? Back up your information or you may find yourself backed into a corner should something happen to your office or to your computer equipment.

Professional-liability insurance

In certain professions, a freelancer can do real (or imagined) damage to a client. Say you're a lawyer, and you give someone bad advice that results in their losing a lawsuit. You may in turn be sued, and you could be liable for the damages. That's an obvious example, but your clients can be harmed in more subtle ways, such as the following:

- ✓ A writer is employed to write a memo about a pension plan. The information proves to be incorrect, and employees lose their retirement money because of it. Those employees could sue the company, but they can also sue the writer.

- ✓ An insurance agent allows an automobile insurance policy to lapse, leaving a client unprotected. The client has an accident, and the insurance doesn't cover the damage.

You can buy insurance against such disasters in the form of *professional-liability insurance*. This is sometimes called *errors-and-omissions insurance*. Coverage for professional mistakes costs a lot, but living without it is a pretty big gamble. Unless you're perfect, you can always make a mistake. It could be a small one that has no substantive affect, or it could be a big one with huge repercussions. If you work in a profession in which people's lives or livelihoods are at risk, you can't afford to live without this type of insurance.

Product-liability insurance

Read the newspapers regularly and you'll see toys, automobiles, and other products that are recalled for flaws, many of which are considered safety issues. When people are hurt because of problems with products, people look for deep pockets. Now that you're in business, those deep pockets could be yours.

Product-liability insurance is your protection against being sued for providing a product that fails to live up to your promises or in some way injures someone.

Business-interruption and extra-expense insurance

What would you do if your office suddenly disappeared in a tornado or a fire? Even if you were physically able to work, you'd still have a difficult time doing business without your files, equipment, and all the things that go along with having an office. *Business-interruption insurance* replaces a portion of the money you may lose if something happens to interrupt your income. This isn't the same as disability insurance, which protects your income if you personally become unable to work.

In the event that your office is destroyed, you may have extra expenses to get it back up and running, or to get your job done while your space is being put back together. For example, you may have to rent space, set up phones, or incur other costs. *Extra-expense insurance* helps you defray that cost.

Even if you're insured, insurance can't protect certain documents. Renting a safe deposit box at your bank can be a good way to protect documents that are irreplaceable. Perhaps your insurance papers belong there!

Controlling Costs of Protection

No question about it: Insurance can be a very expensive proposition for the self-employed person. And unfortunately, in a business arrangement where people need coverage the most, some are tempted to cut back on coverage to reduce costs as they focus on the bottom line.

I have several friends who have gone back to work in corporations solely because they couldn't afford the expense or the hassle of buying their own insurance. The truth is, providing insurance coverage for yourself is no cheap matter. How expensive your coverage is depends on what you're willing to give up.

- ✔ **Control:** Usually the more control you have, the greater the cost. For example, if you choose health insurance that allows you to pick any doctor you like, you pay more than if you join an HMO (health maintenance organization) in which the agency specifies which doctor you may see. The more control you're willing to give up, the more you can reduce your costs.

- ✔ **Coverage:** In some policies, you can choose to have a higher deductible and pay a lower premium. In others, you can select a lower percentage for the company to pay and get a lower premium. All these choices can affect how much you pay.

- ✔ **Choice:** Often, the more choices you have about which doctors to see, where to have tests done, and how to get referrals, the higher the cost.

You may be able to save some money on insurance by signing up for coverage through a professional association that provides group rates. Under an association group, the association purchases insurance like a corporation would, but on behalf of lots of individuals. This allows them to get better rates than a single person can. In this type of situation, costs may be lower, but benefits and choices may also be limited. When you buy as a member of a group, you don't have the same options you would as an individual. Before you sign up for this type of plan, make sure the levels of coverage and benefits meet your needs.

Are you healthy as a horse? You may qualify for reduced-rate life insurance if you're willing to take a physical.

To some degree, your business organization will dictate what types of coverage you can have. Corporations are eligible for some insurance that sole proprietors are not. Describe your company's legal organization to your insurance professional (see the following section) so he or she can match your insurance package to your needs.

Finding an Insurance Professional

After you're fully aware of your needs, you're ready to talk with a professional who can specify what coverage is available and how you can protect yourself and still maintain affordable insurance levels. You can get insurance from three professional sources. The easiest way to find a professional is to ask your current insurance contact if they handle small business coverage, or who they would recommend. Check with your freelance friends to see who they use, and how satisfied they are with their service. If you have friends in corporate benefits departments, they may have recommendations as well. Your local small business association may be able to direct you to resources.

- ✔ **An insurance broker or agent:** These professional insurance salespeople are paid a commission on what they sell by the companies whose products they represent. Agents may be *exclusive,* which means they sell one group of products, or they may be *independent,* which means they represent products of a variety of companies. Independent agents shop the various companies they represent to find you the policy that fits your needs.

- ✔ **A direct writer:** These are companies that sell insurance directly to the consumer, and their products are limited to those that their companies offers. Direct writers often feature lower rates than agents, but they also provide a different type of service. You call a toll-free number or log onto a Web site and work with a service representative, who is likely to be a different person each time you need assistance. Direct writers don't specialize in the personal touch.

- ✔ **Consultants:** A consultant is like an independent agent but has access to even more products and companies. Because a consultant doesn't represent any particular product or company, he or she may make more objective recommendations than someone who has a vested interest in what product you buy. You pay a consultant, whereas the insurance company selling the product pays an agent.

No matter which type of insurance professional you choose, you can sort through the numerous professionals available in the following ways:

- ✔ **Certification:** Agents can earn a number of professional designations that indicate their level of education and expertise. Look for designations such as Chartered Property Casualty Underwriter (CPCU) or Certified Insurance Counselor (CIC).

- ✔ **Specialization:** Agents may specialize in a particular type or types of insurance. Be sure to choose someone who can handle all your needs (health, auto, disability, life, property, and so on) and who has experience dealing with small businesses. Your agent should understand the special needs of your business, and be prepared to offer you products that fit your needs and tell you of issues you may not be aware of.

- ✔ **Personality:** To me, personality does count in an insurance agent. In a corporation, you seldom interact with the people who cover you. As a self-employed person, you should have some direct contact with your agent at least once a year when you review your insurance needs. Find someone you can feel comfortable talking to, sharing your confidential information with, and can enjoy working with. This is too sensitive a subject to be working with someone you don't like and trust. Besides, if you ever actually have to use the insurance, it will be a time of stress and, potentially even crisis. You want someone who can be comforting, who will respond quickly and who will be concerned with you personally as well as professionally.

I don't sell insurance, I sell myself

Jody Pendergrast is a walking advertisement for the insurance business. He's working with some clients whose relatives started doing business with his grandfather 80 years ago.

"When I was in the first grade, someone asked me what I wanted to be when I grew up, and I said, 'an insurance agent.'" Jody started working in the business when he was in college, and planned to go to work for his father. Before that dream could take shape, his father passed away, and Jody was thrust head first into self-employment.

"One of my first clients was the son of one of my grandfather's clients. When the guy walked into

our office, everyone figured he was just a young kid, and I was just a young kid, so they may as well give him to me. I guess they didn't think either of us knew any better! Today, *his* kids are working in his business, and they call me 'Uncle Jody.' You don't find that kind of relationship very often in the corporate world."

"You can sell anybody anything, but I believe you're really selling yourself. If the pipes burst at 3 in the morning, I'll be there to mop up the water."

Jody finds the long hours tough, but wouldn't trade working for himself. He considers it insurance against boredom.

Chapter 19

Investing for the Future

Whether you're starting a freelance business or working hard to keep it running, why on earth would you be thinking about retirement? Because time flies when you're having fun, and the next thing you know, you may be wishing you could spend your golden years in sunny Florida.

At times in your freelance career, you may have extra money sitting in your checking account, and you may decide it's the perfect time to buy a new sailboat or a Ferrari. Sure, you can indulge your dreams to some extent, but you also need a way to plan sensibly for emergencies and for retirement. Even if retirement isn't in your near future, figure out how to put away a portion of your earnings each pay period just in case.

I certainly don't claim to know exactly what kind of investments you should make, but I can give you some steps to take to figure out what you need for your individual goals. This chapter offers you some ways that can help you enjoy your freedom and income stream while setting aside money for expected — and unexpected — developments.

Choosing an Investment Plan That Fits

Life would be so much simpler if you had just one formula for investing. Unfortunately — or fortunately — no one investment plan fits every person because different situations require different approaches. If you have children, you may be investing for their education; if you don't have kids, you may be more interested in saving for a dream home. If you're young, you can afford to take a slower, more conservative approach to investing; if you're approaching retirement, you may have to save aggressively in a shorter period of time. The right plan depends on you and your circumstances.

Ask yourself the following questions to guide your investment decisions:

- ✔ **How much can you invest?** Assess your living needs and determine how much you can afford to set aside.

- ✔ **How much do you need to earn on your investments?** What type of payback do you expect from the money you set aside? Are you using your investment to fund your retirement or save for a vacation home? If retirement is your goal, how much will you need to live each month; how long are you likely to live, and will your investments provide enough money to cover your retirement years? Do you have other sources of income that will contribute to your future? Is this investment a way to set aside money to make your dreams come true?

- ✔ **How long do you have to invest?** When do you plan to use this money: at your retirement far in the future, in a few years when you buy a home or send your kids to college, or sooner than that?

- ✔ **What is your risk tolerance?** Some investments are more certain than others, and, for the most part, investments that are more secure pay lower rates of return and those with higher risk have the potential to pay higher returns. See the "Understanding Investment Jargon" section, later in this chapter, for the lowdown on risk tolerance.

Becoming Informed of Your Investment Possibilities

If you're just now leaving a corporate environment (or did so before you began freelancing), you're probably also leaving a savings or pension plan or other form of investment that you haven't had to think about. But when you're self-employed, you have to give considerable thought to how you want to save and invest your money. A variety of professionals can guide you and help you identify retirement options, but you're still the one who knows what your goals are, and you are responsible for working to achieve them. You have to be your own financial expert, at least to the degree that you can define what you want to accomplish.

Boning up on the options

The recent proliferation of stock and bond variations, individual retirement accounts, and an assortment of other investment opportunities make finding the right investment(s) a tough proposition. So before you invest a dime, do some research through the following sources:

- ✔ **Read up on investments.** Both *Personal Finance For Dummies,* 3rd Edition, and *Investing For Dummies,* 2nd Edition, both by Eric Tyson (Hungry Minds, Inc.) offer a good foundation for understanding your investment options.

- ✔ **Browse the Internet.** On the Internet, you can find investment sites of respected organizations, which also offer explanations and tips about various ways to invest.

- ✔ **Talk to other freelancers.** Ask friends who are self-employed whom they use for investment advice.

- ✔ **Interview investment professionals.** Talk to someone you trust, such as your banker. Ask for resources that can help you become informed.

Only when you've made yourself aware of the issues can you choose a course that you can feel confident and comfortable with.

Hiring hired guns

Where do you find someone who can help you sort through the mire of investment tools? Turn to someone who is specially trained and certified to provide investment counsel.

- ✔ A certified financial planner (CFP) must complete educational requirements and pass an exam administered by (and have work experience designated by) the Certified Financial Planner Board of Standards (CFP Board).

- ✔ An accredited personal financial specialist (APFS) is a CPA (certified public accountant) who has been accredited as a financial planner by the American Institute of Certified Public Accountants (AICPA).

Charlatans unmasked

Unscrupulous, greedy characters bilk unsuspecting investors all the time. Does an investment sound too good to be true? It probably is. I have friends who once invested in a gold mine and instead of a golden egg, it turned out to be a rusty screw. They paid for years.

You can't ever guarantee that your money is safe, no matter whom you've chosen for a counselor, because even respected professionals make mistakes. But you can take precautions to make sure you're giving yourself the best shot at hiring a highly ethical and knowledgeable professional. That's why it's important to look at a person's track record, length of time in the business, and personal and professional references.

Professional organizations, such as the CFP board and AICPA, require their professionals to abide by prescribed practices and ethical standards.

Before you trust someone with your finances, check out their credentials. Interview them and ask the following:

- ✔ What are your qualifications?

- ✔ What type(s) of investments do you handle? Does the person only recommend investments, or do they actually sell products? When you're considering hiring someone, you may want to take this into consideration, because someone who has a vested interest in selling a product may not be the best source for objective recommendations.

- ✔ What is your experience in advising small business owners or self-employed people?

- ✔ How do you charge? Some people are paid a commission on the products they sell; others receive an hourly fee or a percentage of your total investments.

- ✔ Do you physically transfer the money, or do you simply make recommendations for me to follow?

In a situation that's as personal and as important as your finances, you want someone you can trust and feel completely comfortable with. Look at the hard facts, such as their credentials and experience, but also go with your instinct. If you have doubts, move on to your next candidate.

Benefiting from Investments

If investing is complicated, why not just leave your money in a checking account? Unless the checking account earns interest, leaving money in a checking account is like putting your money under your mattress: It would be pretty safe, but certainly wouldn't make you more comfortable. Even if your account does earn interest, the interest rate is usually quite low, which makes checking accounts a less favorable investment than others that earn a higher rate. My friend Renee, who is a CPA and has her masters degree in finance, calls this *lazy money.*

Investments let your money work for you. In addition to contributing to your retirement fund, investments can help you in other ways, such as the following:

- ✔ Stashed money comes in handy if you have sudden business or personal setbacks. (Some investments have penalties for withdrawing them before a certain specified time; be sure to take this into account.)

- ✔ You can put your money to work for you, earning interest on excess cash while you hunt for new business. It's great to have more than one way of increasing your income!

✔ By setting aside a portion of your income in certain investments, you put off paying taxes for awhile. Investment income is often called *deferred income* because it gets taxed later, when your income is likely to be lower and you'll pay a lower tax rate.

✔ Investing can contribute to a more comfortable retirement.

To be eligible for some of these benefits, you must take advantage of investments that are prescribed by the IRS. Investments that offer tax incentives are as follows:

✔ Tax-free money market funds

✔ Tax-free stock or bond mutual funds

✔ Municipal bonds

✔ Treasury bonds

✔ Retirement accounts such as IRAs, SEP-IRAs and SIMPLE plans (if you're eligible and follow the guidelines for investing)

For more information about tax deductions, take a look at *Taxes For Dummies* by Eric Tyson and David J. Silverman (Hungry Minds, Inc.) or surf to the IRS Web site.

Understanding Investment Jargon

Before I tell you about some investment opportunities (see the "Sampling Investment Offerings" section later in this chapter), you need to understand a word or two of investment jargon. Investing has lots of special phrases and words just like any other profession. The following explains some that are important to investors.

✔ **Maturity:** Many investments involve agreements to pay a reward after a certain length of time. *Maturity* is the time when an investment pays its rewards. For example, if you buy a bond and the maturity date is Jan. 31, 2002, that is the date when you can cash in the bond and get the agreed-upon interest income and principle. In some cases, if you withdraw any or all of the money before the maturity date, you're subject to a penalty that can be fairly steep. The reason the institution is paying you interest is because you're giving them the right to use your money for a certain period of time. In a sense, they're paying you rent on your money. If they lose the right to use it, you have to sacrifice a part of the rental fee they're paying you.

✔ **Portfolio:** You may hear investment people talk about your *portfolio*. That means the combined collection of your investments. A *stock portfolio* is the group of stocks that you own.

✔ **Interest:** *Interest* is money that people or companies pay you for the use of your money. Interest is usually based on a percentage of what you've put in. For example, if your account or investment pays 10 percent, you have the money you originally paid in, plus you get another 10 percent of that amount in interest. *Compound interest* is when you earn interest on your interest.

✔ **Dividends:** *Dividends* are a return on your investment resulting from ownership in a corporation (see the "Stocks" section later in this chapter). If the corporation makes money, it may pay out part of the net earnings to the owners or stockholders. Dividends are expressed in dollars and cents. For example, if a stock pays a $1.50 dividend, you're paid $1.50 for every share of stock you own in a particular company.

✔ **Risk tolerance:** Few investments are risk-free, but some are more risky than others. Only you can decide how comfortable you feel with a high- or a low-risk investment. Generally speaking:

- The higher the risk, the higher the potential return (payback) you get.
- The lower the risk, the lower the potential return (payback) you get.

Your desire for a higher or lower level of risk is your *risk tolerance level.* If you prefer a lower, more stable return, or if you can't afford to lose money, you have a *low risk tolerance.* If you prefer to take a risk with the chance of earning a higher return, you have a *high risk tolerance.*

✔ **Diversified:** Some experts say that the wisest approach to investing is to have a *diversified* portfolio. That means you have a combination of low-, medium-, and high-risk investments. Diversified is the opposite of having all your eggs in one basket.

Sampling Investment Offerings

You can find quite a variety of ways to invest your money, some that give special consideration to freelancers. This section describes several investment options, but only introduces these subjects to get your feet wet. Whole books are written on some of these subjects, so be sure to do your own research and get specialized investment advice.

The most important thing to remember about investing is to keep your expectations reasonable. The chances of your getting rich quickly are slim — even people who study the markets diligently can't guarantee high returns.

Quitting while you're ahead

Laura Derrington is a freelance copywriter who loves her job. She also loves the thought of retiring from her job and moving to Colorado, where she can become inspired by mountain breezes and write the Great American Novel. At first, Laura put aside a little money in a mutual fund, mostly for tax advantages; more recently, she has become more serious about saving aggressively for retirement.

"I saved a small amount, and I vowed not to touch it. When I needed to buy a computer or something, I would use my business line of credit to avoid dipping into my retirement fund. But in the last four years I've gotten more aggressive about saving. I sat down with a financial guy and talked about what it would take to quit sooner. With my SEP account, I can put aside more."

What's hard about saving? Plenty. "As a freelancer, you never know exactly how much you're going to make, so it's hard to plan. On the other hand, you have kind of an unlimited income potential. If you're willing to work more, you can save more. In my mind, that means I have more control over when I retire."

And, by the way, she adds, "Send all contributions to Adopt-a-Freelancer . . . !"

For many investments, if you take your money out before the maturity date (see the "Understanding Investment Jargon" section for more information), or if you take it out before you reach a certain age, you're penalized. What if you want to take your money out early? If you do, you have to pay tax on the money you take out plus an IRS ten-percent early withdrawal fee. If you're investing to build a fund for something you want in the near future, consider putting your money in a short-term investment or an investment that gives you flexibility in withdrawing funds. You may want to consider divvying up your investment money: some for short-term needs and some for longer-term considerations like retirement.

Stocks

Stocks are official certificates of ownership in a company. A *share* of stock is literally one piece of the company. When you buy a share of stock, you become a co-owner of that company.

As people buy and sell stock, the value of a share of stock rises and falls throughout each day. No one can really predict what a stock price will be at any given time. People make money by buying stock at one price and selling it at a higher price. Because no one can predict when the stock will rise or fall, however, buying stock involves an element of risk: you take your chances that the stock price will go down after you buy it at a higher price.

You can buy stock and sell in a couple of different ways:

- ✔ **Through a broker:** A *broker* buys and sells stock and makes a commission on the purchase or sale. A broker also gives you advice about what to buy and sell.

- ✔ **Through a discount brokerage house:** Because a *discount brokerage house* doesn't recommend investments the way a broker does, you have to know what you want to buy and sell, and they merely handle the transaction for a fee, which is cheaper than the commission.

You may choose to deal with someone in person or on the phone, or you can opt for the convenience of using an Internet brokerage house where you can trade online.

Stocks offer the benefit of easy access to your money, because you can sell them at any time; however, when you decide to sell quickly, you have to take the current price. That price may be lower than the price you'd like to sell them for. Keep in mind that you must pay tax on any money you earn from your stocks. You may hear the term *paper profit*. That refers to money you've made but that hasn't been collected.

Mutual funds

Okay, so you're not rich and famous. Even if you have only a small amount of money to invest, you can still afford to have a variety of investments by becoming a member of a mutual fund. *Mutual funds* pool the resources of many individual investors to buy stocks, bonds, and other investment instruments.

A *fund manager* makes decisions about how to invest the money and handles all the buying, selling, and administration for a fee. The benefit of a mutual fund is that you can put in a small amount of money and still participate in a diversified portfolio (see the "Understanding Investment Jargon" section). Your fees are lower through this type of investment than if you buy and sell stocks or bonds yourself.

Certain types of mutual fund managers follow a policy of investing in higher risk investments; others are known for choosing lower risk investments. By selecting a fund that mirrors your risk tolerance (see the "Understanding Investment Jargon" section), you increase your chances of getting the type of return you want. People who prefer a lower-risk investment consider mutual funds a fairly safe way to invest.

Index funds

A *stock index* is an organization that lists the price and performance of a host of stocks. The New York Stock Exchange (NYSE) and NASDAQ are both examples of a stock index.

An *index fund* is an investment that mirrors the stocks on a stock index. For example, familiar companies like IBM and American Airlines are listed on the NYSE, along with lesser known companies. When you buy a share of the NYSE index, you're buying a combination of tiny pieces of all those stocks instead of buying individual shares of each individual company.

Buying index funds has become popular in the last few years, because it gives people a way to spread their risk across a large group of stocks that represent various industries. That way, if one industry isn't doing too well, another may be doing better.

Because they are comprised of stocks, index funds are as unpredictable as stocks are (see the preceding section). You never know whether the value will rise or fall or whether you'll have the chance to sell your shares at a higher price than you paid.

Bonds

A *bond* is like a loan that you make to a group, such as a company or a government. The bond itself is a promissory note issued by the group that wants to raise money. For example, you may have heard of a local government issuing municipal bonds, with the money earmarked for school development. People buy the bonds, and the group uses the money for what it wants and then pays back the money at a promised time. The people who loaned the money are paid a fee.

Bonds have a *maturity date,* which means that they are worth the promised amount at the time of maturity. If you withdraw your money before that time, there is a penalty.

Savings bonds

The U. S. Department of Treasury issues *savings bonds* in small denominations, which makes them easy for an individual investor to purchase. Savings bonds are considered a low-risk, low-return investment.

Savings bonds have a *maturity date,* which means they aren't worth as much if you withdraw them before the specified time.

Certificates of deposit

Certificates of deposit (CDs) are receipts for money you put in the bank, and they pay a guaranteed, set interest rate for some period of time — six months, twelve months, five years, and so on — as long as you don't withdraw any money from it during that period. CDs are sold in increments such as $250, $1,000, $10,000, and so on. *Jumbo CDs* are for $100,000 or more.

After you buy a CD, you can't put any more in that particular CD, and you can't take any out until it matures. (You can actually withdraw the money, but you'll pay a stiff penalty — sometimes you have to give up all the interest earned up to that point.)

A CD is about as close to a savings account as you can get, except that a savings account doesn't mature at any given time. (See the "Understanding Investment Jargon" section for information on maturity.) When a CD account matures, that means it has run out, and you have to renew it: Put it back into the same fund or reinvest it in something else.

Money market accounts

A money market account is an account that pays interest and usually allows you limited check-writing privileges. It typically pays lower interest than other types of investments, but offers greater access to your money without penalties. Investment experts tend to recommend money market accounts only as short-term investments; a place to put money when you need easy access to it or when you're looking for another place to invest it.

Life insurance

When people speak of life insurance, they tend to only talk about it as a way to guard against financial problems for their survivors. Some life insurance can actually be an investment (although not generally considered a wise one because of the low return). You can find several kinds of life insurance:

- ✔ **Term:** Term life is a policy that you pay on a set payment schedule for a length of time (such as one year), and then the policy renews only if you agree to pay for the next period. The premium may change at renewal time. This type of policy never has any cash value, and the only time anyone collects money on this policy is when you die. It is considered a *protection policy,* meaning that it protects your family from the loss of your income and the expense of your funeral.

- ✔ **Permanent (cash value):** Permanent life insurance gains value over the years, so that you can cash in the policy at some point in the future and get back what you've paid, plus dividends or interest. After you have put in a certain amount, the cash value of the policy may even be sufficient to pay for the premium; thus, it can pay for itself. Permanent life is considered an investment and, in fact, the premiums you pay are invested in a financial vehicle; their payouts are related to the vehicle's performance. In some cases, you can select the degree of risk you prefer. You can find several types of permanent life insurance: ordinary (or whole), universal, and variable.

Just as with most investments, the cost and potential payback in a life insurance product varies with the degree of risk involved. Consider the following factors when looking at life insurance policies:

✔ Your reasons for buying it: as protection or as an investment

✔ The cost of the premium

✔ Whether the premium can change

✔ Whether the policy can be cancelled

✔ What and when the potential payout is

✔ Whether you can borrow against it or use it for things such as paying for your child's college education

✔ Whether you'll have a guaranteed minimum death benefit

✔ Whether you control how premiums are invested

See Chapter 18 for the lowdown on types of insurance you want to consider as a freelancer.

Planning for Retirement

In addition to setting aside money for emergencies and shorter-term financial goals, be sure to consider how you will support yourself when you retire.

SEP: The simplified employee pension plan

Here are some letters you can live by: *SEP,* which is short for *simplified employee pension plan.* This type of investment plan is designed exclusively for self-employed people, and it offers two advantages:

✔ Long-term, it builds money for your retirement.

✔ Short-term, it reduces your taxable income. You don't pay tax on the money you invest until you withdraw the money.

The main advantage of a SEP account is that it is inexpensive and easy to set up and maintain — establish a SEP account just by going to your bank, investment institution, or an online brokerage house. Because you want to get the highest interest rate possible, however, shop around. You can contribute up to 15 percent of your compensation each year to the SEP, with a maximum contribution of $30,000.

If you have employees, you will have to set up a SEP account for them, too, and follow the same contribution rules.

Keogh plan

A *Keogh* (pronounced KEE-oh) plan is another type of retirement program that allows self-employed people to set aside a certain percentage of their income each year. Neither the money itself nor the interest it earns is taxable until you withdraw it at retirement.

Notice the following differences between a Keogh and a SEP account:

- ✔ A Keogh allows you to contribute a higher percentage than a SEP — up to 25 percent of compensation, with a $30,000 maximum contribution.
- ✔ A Keogh requires more reporting to the IRS than does a SEP.

You can invest in two types of Keogh plans:

- ✔ **Profit sharing:** You decide what percentage of your income you contribute each year.
- ✔ **Money purchase:** You make a contribution that's the same percentage of your income every year.

If you set up a Keogh plan, you have to make contributions for your employees, as well.

Traditional individual retirement accounts (IRA)

A traditional *individual retirement account (IRA)* is like a SEP or a Keogh in that it lets you put your money into savings before you pay taxes on it. If you (and/or your spouse) aren't eligible for another type of company plan, you can contribute up to $2,000 (each) of your income before taxes to an IRA. This essentially reduces the income you pay tax on by $2,000 each. Unlike a Keogh or a SEP, an IRA doesn't require a setup fee.

With traditional IRAs, you aren't taxed on the income you put into the IRA until you take the money out of the account at retirement age, which is 59½ years or older. Contributions to an IRA are tax deductible as long as your income is less than an amount specified each year by the IRS.

Individual retirement accounts must be held at an approved institution: a federally insured bank or credit union, stock brokerage, insurance company, and so on.

Roth IRAs

A Roth IRA is a special type of IRA that doesn't offer tax incentives in the year you contribute; instead, you benefit when you withdraw the money, as long as you are 59½ and have had the account for at least five years. Meet those conditions, and all the investment income you've earned is tax-free at retirement.

The maximum amount you can contribute to a Roth IRA is $2,000 a year, as long as you don't have income above $95,000 if you're single, or $150,000 if you're married and file a joint return. As your income goes up, the amount you can contribute to a Roth IRA goes down.

The other advantage of a Roth IRA is that it's easier to take your money out; you can make qualified withdrawals without paying a penalty. In some cases, you can roll over money from another IRA to a Roth account. Check with your advisor to see if you're eligible and if this makes sense for you.

Part V
The Part of Tens

The 5th Wave   By Rich Tennant

"You know, I don't mind hiring freelancers, but I do resent it when their work comes in smelling like suntan lotion and guacamole."

In this part . . .

You're going to be a huge success, right? This part delivers a few well-chosen tips for handling the pressure of being on top, maintaining your sanity, keeping your family life running smoothly, and finding out the real secrets to keeping clients happy.

Chapter 20

Ten Ways to Handle Stress and Prevent Burnout

*B*eing your own boss has many advantages, but it can also be a somewhat stress-filled way to live. Unfortunately, some of the same qualities that make freelancers good at what they do also create stress:

✔ **Catastrophizing:** To a freelancer, the fact that business is slow this week logically leads to the thought that, "I'll never have any business again as long as I live." Rather than take advantage of the opportunity to relax, the idle freelancer starts figuring out where to send a résumé and what to sell to make the mortgage payment.

✔ **Action orientation:** Taking control and doing something is another beneficial personality trait, except that there are times when inaction is perfectly appropriate. A short lull in a project doesn't require that you bug clients ten times a day to get them moving. Of course, a freelancer knows that sooner or later, the avalanche is going to come down the mountain, and sitting around waiting for it can make you a bit testy. Besides, to a freelancer, a moment of inactivity is a moment not billed. Riding that fence and trying to decide when to push and when to leave well enough alone can be a constant internal battle.

✔ **Perfectionist thinking:** This personality flaw is right next to the don't-know-when-to-quit gene on every freelancer's DNA strand. Of course, dedication, perfectionism, and high standards may make you a great freelancer, but they can also make you a bit . . . well, driven.

Combine these natural tendencies with constant deadlines, demanding clients, a bad hair day, and a cat that needs to go to the vet, and you can see that stress is always ready to knock at the door. With the full burden of your livelihood on your shoulders, you may have to remind yourself that everything will be all right, even if you do experience a bit of discomfort (or sheer panic) from time to time.

Ideally, being a successful freelancer means doing what you love and getting paid for it. Having a nervous breakdown shouldn't be part of the equation. To get the jump on stress, build the ten (er, really only seven) healthy habits in this chapter into your work style.

Tell Yourself You're Only Human

Your clients may believe you can leap tall buildings in a single bound, but you're really only human. Do the best you can and understand that you can't control many of the things you'd like to. Freelancers who constantly push themselves beyond human limits burn out. They become resentful of clients and are prone to make mistakes and have errors in judgment. Give yourself a break. Allow yourself to be human and, when things don't work out perfectly, accept that as a routine part of life and business. Treat yourself with as much kindness and understanding as you show your best friend, and then realize that you are your own best friend!

When the Pace Picks Up, Slow Down

Have you ever watched someone zoom past you in traffic, only to end up just ahead of you at a red light? In freelancing, speed kills. When you feel frantic, you need your wits about you more than ever. The more frantic you become, the more likely you are to make mistakes, which in turn makes matters worse. The faster the work pace, the more methodical you must be to ensure that you're thinking straight, making good decisions, and maintaining the quality level your clients expect.

The story of the tortoise and the hare applies: Slow and steady wins the race.

Take a Moment

When you don't feel you have a minute to spare, take a moment to collect yourself. Take a few deep breaths. When you confront a problem that has you stumped, don't think about it. Read the comics. Surf the Net for a fun site. Call a friend. Clear your mind and then go back to your situation. Often, your best decisions will follow a mental break.

Manage by Walking Around

Management by walking around is a corporate term for being visible with employees. In the freelance world, managing by walking around means literally getting out of your office and taking a walk. A brisk walk helps you clear your mind, and exercise reduces mental and physical tension. Pick a park nearby and make a habit of walking there. Or just take a stroll around the block. Fresh air and exercise are great prescriptions for mental blocks or stressful moments.

Stretch Yourself

If your work requires you to sit or stare at a computer for a long time, you can suffer from several maladies.

When you watch a computer screen for a long time, you tend to not blink your eyes. Your eyes need moisture. Every so often, take a visual break and rest your eyes.

Sitting for long periods can get your body parts in a knot. That's especially true when you're working on a tight deadline or on a project that's stressful. At least once every hour, take a minute to get your body moving. Stretch your neck and shoulders. Stand up, bend over, or lie on the floor and do back exercises (your physician can recommend some that will help strengthen your back and abdominal muscles).

Do Something Fun

What's the first thing you abandon when your schedule gets tight? If you're like me, it's your personal time. Because your schedule is within your control, block out a couple of hours to do something you enjoy, either away from your home or away from your office:

- ✔ Work a crossword or jigsaw puzzle.
- ✔ Take the kids bowling.
- ✔ Eat lunch with your spouse or a friend.
- ✔ Go to a matinee.
- ✔ Visit the zoo.
- ✔ Do some woodworking.
- ✔ Cook a fantastic meal.

The whole point of freelancing is to better control your time. Don't let yours slip away without finding the fun in freelancing.

Be Your Own Cheerleader

In your time as a freelancer, you've undoubtedly accomplished some pretty amazing things, met some fantastic people, and completed some great work. (Just starting your own business is quite a feat!) When you feel stressed, remind yourself of how far you've come and think of the things you enjoy about being your own boss. Keep a file of thank-you letters and compliments, as well as a list of the projects you feel most proud of. Make a list of the people you enjoy working with. Review your client list to see how many people have hired you . . . and how many have hired you more than once. Line up all the positive things you've experienced in your freelance career and pat yourself on the back. Everything you see before you, you've created! What a winner you are!

Chapter 21

Ten Tips for Balancing Your Work and Personal Life

In This Chapter

▶ Understanding the dangers of losing your perspective

▶ Keeping your life on an even keel

Starting a new business takes time and energy, and in the beginning, most freelancers work more than 40 hours a week. The fear of not having enough business makes new freelancers take every job that comes along. That's fine for a while, but when your start-up schedule stretches into years, you can become unbalanced in more ways than one.

To stay sane; be an interesting person; and remain a good spouse, parent, friend, and freelancer, you need a personal life. But how do you get one? This chapter offers ten (er, six) bits of practical advice for remaining balanced.

Trust the Process

Freelancing is a feast or famine way of life. Inevitably, when your business is the busiest, new clients will beat down your door, old clients you've forgotten will come calling, and regular clients will need 12 new projects done overnight. Learn to expect this.

I can remember only two truly slow times in my freelancing career, and they both ended just as quickly as they began. Naturally, when I recognized that business was slow, I began to worry that I would never eat again. I scurried around and tried to drum up some business. And then the dam broke, and I was swamped again. Crisis averted.

As long as you're doing quality work, and you're continuing to sell yourself to potential clients (see Chapters 10 and 11), work will come. If you can keep this in mind, you'll be less likely to overwork because you're not sure where your next meal is coming from. It will come. Don't just expect it, trust it. This process is truly more predictable than rain.

Recognize Your Limits

Everyone has biological and emotional situations in which we're at our best. When you stretch yourself past your limits, you go into a slump. Your quality suffers and your personal well-being decreases.

For example, I work well in intense situations that last two to three months. I like to immerse myself in a project, give it my undivided attention, build to a peak, and then be finished with it. During the project, I feel energized, and I can sleep six hours a night and get up feeling rested. After a few months, however, I need to rest, mentally and physically. Projects that last longer than two or three months don't suit my chemistry. They begin to bore and drain me. What I've learned the hard way is that to be at my best I have to choose projects that fit my pattern.

I can't always choose projects that fit my ideal psychic and physical profile (I do have to make money). In that case, my alternative is to recognize the extra strain and do something to offset it: Take a weekend vacation, read great escape books, take breaks midday to do something fun, or eat lunch with friends twice a week.

You have a pattern that brings out the best in you. Find ways to recognize it and honor it.

Post Your Goals

If you're like most freelancers, you chose to go out on your own so you'd have more freedom, greater flexibility, more control over what you do, and so on. As time goes on, you may stray from that path. To stay on course, write down your goals and keep them close at hand.

I was ten years into my freelancing career before I realized that my work controlled me rather than the other way around. It has taken me another five years to take action on the knowledge. I've written down my life goals and keep them beside my computer at all times. Granted, I don't always look at my list (I'm sure it's here somewhere . . .), but from time to time I glance at it and remember why I started freelancing to begin with. Your job is supposed to *complement* your life, not *be* your life. Your number-one goal should be to make a list of your goals.

Close the Door

Home offices are insidious creatures. They can start as 12' x 12' rooms and end up being three-bedroom, two-bath houses. Eventually, your den, kitchen, and bedroom can morph into one big office, instead of the home it's supposed to be.

If you're not careful, when you can't sleep, you'll work. When you're supposed to be eating dinner, you'll work. Instead of watching *Seinfeld* reruns, reading Stephen King novels, or snuggling up with your sweetie, you'll work. You must learn to close the door, both mentally and physically.

The following are some suggestions for keeping your work at work.

- ✔ Don't check e-mail or voice mail messages in your off-time.
- ✔ Don't go into your office just to take care of one little thing. You'll end up being there for hours.
- ✔ When it's time to quit, quit. Turn off the phone, and stay out of the office.

Make a Date with Yourself

Schedule time every week for yourself. Write it on your calendar or you'll constantly be waiting until you get a break to do anything for yourself. There are no breaks unless you make them.

Honor your appointments with yourself just as you would with your clients. You are as important as they are, in fact, more so. Julia Cameron, author of *The Artist's Way,* describes the *artist's date,* a time when creative people replenish their creative energy by going to museums, parks, or other inspiring places. Whether you're a photographer or a market researcher, you need a time to recharge each week.

Get a Hobby

Even if you've never liked crocheting or cross-country skiing; now's the time to find a relaxing activity that you can truly love. You need a hobby that's so enjoyable that when you have to choose between it and work, you'll pick it.

The best incentive I've ever had for not working too much was my grandchildren. In a way, they're my hobby. Through my years as a freelancer, I've made plans for a movie and broken them for work. I've said I would go to dinner with a friend and backed out because of work. I've cancelled trips out of town, let my hair get shaggy, and forgotten birthdays because of work. But when it comes to my grandchildren, they come first. They're fun, and I don't let work stand in the way of my enjoying them.

You may find that something as simple as gardening helps you unwind, or you may have to become engaged in something that requires ongoing participation, such as a team sport. Whatever it takes — by making a commitment to others or just to yourself — get involved in something that transports you to a world outside of work.

Chapter 22

Ten Things Clients Want Most from You

*W*hen a client calls you and says, "I'm looking for . . . ," listen between the lines. Freelancers' expertise may vary, but clients' needs don't. Whether you're an accountant, interior designer, or massage therapist, clients want the same things. And they're not necessarily what you expect. A client may say he's looking for someone to evaluate his departmental process or to plan a media campaign. Don't believe it. You may think people are buying your expertise, but that's rarely the case. Read this short chapter to find out their secret desires.

What They Say They Want

The following is a list of what clients say when they call you to do a project:

- ✔ "I need you to create a (fill in the blank)."

- ✔ "I need you to take a look at (fill in the blank) and give me your recommendations."

- ✔ "We're so busy right now that we just don't have time to do this. I need you to be our extra arms and legs."

- ✔ "We're considering doing a (fill in the blank), and I need you to develop a plan."

What They Really Want

Freelancers get work because a client doesn't have the time, expertise, staff, or support to do a job internally. Sometimes, they hire you to do their dirty work or to carry out a project they're not sure will succeed; when it fails, you're the scapegoat.

You have to figure out which one of the following ten motives drives your client, because your role will vary by situation.

"Make me look good"

People want to look good to their peers, their bosses, and their families and friends. They hire you because they think you can help them appear smart and competent. When you offer a recommendation, they are judging two things:

- ✔ The validity and viability of your solution
- ✔ How it will make them look

Sure, they want a successful project, but more than that, they want a safe solution. Don't put your clients in jeopardy by offering high-risk suggestions that put them in danger. Freelancing is all about personal safety, not about company improvement.

"Make me feel special"

Every client wants to believe you like them best. By "romancing" each one; that is, going out of your way to be nice, you create the sense that they're not just a paycheck to you, but that you truly like them.

Like any relationship, client relationships are built on going the extra mile to recognize and please that other person. Pay attention to their personal lives and jot notes that will help you remember key dates such as birthdays, kids' graduations, and anniversaries. Even small things like e-mail notes build a rapport. Ask how their vacation was or check on their grandmother's health. Clip and send a cartoon you think they'd find amusing. Notice when they seem to be feeling down and express your concern. When they're sick, send a small get-well gift.

"Let's have fun"

Everyone likes to work with people who appreciate their sense of humor, share their likes and dislikes, and make their everyday life more fun. Notice what makes your clients laugh and create that type of atmosphere for them. That may include inviting them to attend an art opening, taking a drive in your convertible, playing golf, sharing your comic book collection, or just telling jokes or laughing at theirs.

Very important: Let them be funnier. Let them get the last word. Let them win. You're there to make it fun for them.

"Make my life easy"

People hire freelancers who make their lives easier, not harder. They either don't have the time or the talent to accomplish what they need internally, so they're hiring you to do what they need when they need it. They may already be under intense pressure when they call you and could make unreasonable demands. Realize that they're looking for someone to make their life easier and get started doing that.

Want to make life easier for your clients? Follow these tips:

- ✔ **Give them peace of mind.** Reassure them that you'll handle all the details and that they can relax. Be sure to demonstrate that you have the project well in hand by keeping them informed of progress before they ask for a report.

- ✔ **Provide information in a way that's easy to understand.** If you see that your client uses lots of charts in a presentation, use charts in your presentation. If the client does lots of narrative, use lots of narrative. People generally deliver information in the way they like to receive information, so look for clues and follow their lead.

- ✔ **Anticipate needs.** Don't wait to be told what to do. Figure out what you would need if you were managing the project from the client's perspective and give them what they need before they ask for it.

- ✔ **Do as much as you can for them.** Take the lead. Figure out what their boundaries are and make as many decisions as you can for them without usurping their authority. Most clients are happy when you relieve them of the details.

- ✔ **Be accessible.** Return phone calls, check your e-mail frequently, and leave numbers where you can be reached.

I've had sub-contractors who made my life difficult by bugging me constantly with questions or not keeping me informed. By the time I supervised them, I may as well have done it myself. Be a help, not a hindrance.

"Be my friend"

Everybody needs someone they can trust. People who work in a corporation have to screen what they tell their coworkers, so they especially need an outsider they can talk to. Because you don't have a vested interest in the corporate politics, you can afford to listen to their side, to hear their frustrations, and to let them vent their anger. They want you to be loyal to them, to keep their confidences, be empathetic with their personal and business problems, and care. What they need is not a freelancer, it's a friend.

"Baby-sit my project"

Have you ever worked with someone who asked you to do something, but was never satisfied with what you did? Two possible explanations are as follows:

- ✔ **They will only know the solution when they see it.** Your job is to keep trying until you narrow down possibilities by showing them all the things they don't want.

- ✔ **They already have a clear picture of the solution, but they don't have time to work on it right now.** They hire you so they can feel that someone is doing something about it, and they can quit thinking about it temporarily. Your job is to baby-sit the project until the client has time to do it.

You may have difficulty spinning your wheels and not accomplishing what you believe needs to be done, but remember that your job is to satisfy the client. If they're looking for a baby-sitter, you supply the pacifier.

"Be my audience"

Inside the corporate family (or perhaps in any family), Joe gets challenged. Mary has to prove her ideas. Kathy must defend her position with logic and results. With you, they can always be right.

Talking to a freelancer gives the client a chance to be right all the time. Of course, they aren't right all the time, but you can help them think they are. As you steer clients away from bad ideas and toward your winning solutions, give them plenty of ear time. Listen more; talk less. Be supportive and clap at the end.

"Solve my problems"

Clients turn to freelancers to solve problems. They don't always know what solution they want, but they think you may. That's why you're there. When they ask you to do a particular task, and it isn't a feasible solution, don't get hung up on proving it's the wrong thing to do. Suggest something else. Chances are, they're not committed to the path — they just don't know what else to do. When you show them a better way, you'll be a hero.

I've had a lot of employees, both inside and outside the corporate world, and I hate hearing someone say, "We can't do that." When I hear this, I know I'm dealing with someone who has a *can't do attitude.* Don't tell me why we can't accomplish what I want; give me alternatives. If I have to do all the thinking, I may as well do the job myself and save the cost of a freelancer. If we can't do what I've envisioned, I need suggestions about how we can reach a solution, not a description of obstacles.

Clients make unreasonable demands; they can't help it. Your job is not to argue with them. It's to help them find a solution.

"Be enthusiastic about my project"

Misery doesn't always love company. We all want to feel excited about our work, and we sure like people who can help us feel that way. Enthusiasm is contagious, and I've seen clients who were burned out on a project renew their excitement when I showed how great I thought it was going to be. The last thing I would want if I were feeling crummy about a job is someone who would drag me down even more by complaining about it.

I've had other situations in which a client was already fired up about a project that was somewhat old hat for me. When you've been in business for a long time, you've done a lot of the same things over and over again. Still, when a client is creating a presentation, or creating a workshop, it's a big deal to her. She wants someone who will be just as excited as she is.

"Perform a miracle"

I've had freelance friends who threatened to print business cards with descriptive titles like, "Miracle Worker" and "Magician." It never fails: The client waits until the last minute to start a project and expects you to accomplish the impossible in record time. Then when you say, "What's the budget?" they look at you sheepishly and say, "Well, we don't really have one."

Performing miracles is fun, because people are generally grateful and you can enjoy your moment of glory as a big hero. As you gain knowledge of your trade, you'll get better and better at doing impossible things: You'll find ways to cut timing corners, reduce spending, and cajole other people into helping you do the impossible. Doing magic builds client loyalty better than anything I can think of. Of course, by doing that, you just encourage them to call you at the last minute or to give you skimpy budgets. You'll just reinforce their behavior and create expectations that you will always be able to pull the rabbit out of the hat. The vicious cycle is that then they end up looking to you for emergency rabbits, and wanting to pay $1.98 for them.

Index

Notes

FOR DUMMIES
BOOK REGISTRATION

We want to hear from you!

Visit **dummies.com** to register this book and tell us how you liked it!

✔ Get entered in our monthly prize giveaway.

✔ Give us feedback about this book — tell us what you like best, what you like least, or maybe what you'd like to ask the author and us to change!

✔ Let us know any other *For Dummies* topics that interest you.

Your feedback helps us determine what books to publish, tells us what coverage to add as we revise our books, and lets us know whether we're meeting your needs as a *For Dummies* reader. You're our most valuable resource, and what you have to say is important to us!

Not on the Web yet? It's easy to get started with *Dummies 101: The Internet For Windows 98* or *The Internet For Dummies* at local retailers everywhere.

Or let us know what you think by sending us a letter at the following address:

For Dummies Book Registration
Dummies Press
10475 Crosspoint Blvd.
Indianapolis, IN 46256

BESTSELLING
BOOK SERIES

LaVergne, TN USA
17 February 2010
173413LV00003B/25/P